Healthy Gut, Healthy Horse

Healthy Gut, Healthy Horse

Carol Hughes and Geertje French

KENILWORTH PRESS

Dedicated to my herd of Welsh Mountain ponies who taught me conservation grazing, low impact and sustainable horse management and to Dr Vera Thoss who taught me organic chemistry and the power of plants.
Carol

For my love, Andrew.
Geertje

Copyright © 2026 Carol Hughes and Geertje French

First published in the UK in 2026 by Kenilworth Press,
an imprint of Quiller Publishing

British Library Cataloguing-in-Publication Data
A catalogue record for this book is available from the British Library.

Paperback ISBN 978 1 910016 58 9
E-book ISBN 978 1 910016 59 6

The right of Carol Hughes and Geertje French to be identified as the authors of this work has been asserted in accordance with the Copyright, Design and Patent Act 1988.

The information in this book is true and complete to the best of our knowledge. All recommendations are made without any guarantee on the part of the Publisher, who also disclaims any liability incurred in connection with the use of this data or specific details.

All rights reserved. No part of this book may be reproduced or transmitted in any form or by any means, electronic or mechanical including photocopying, recording or by any information storage and retrieval system, without permission from the Publisher in writing.

Book design by Becky Bowyer

Appointed GPSR EU Representative: Easy Access System Europe Oü, 16879218
Address: Mustamäe tee 50, 10621, Tallinn, Estonia
Contact Details: gpsr.requests@easproject.com, +358 40 500 3575

Printed in China

Kenilworth Press
An imprint of Quiller Publishing Ltd
The Hill, Merrywalks, Stroud GL5 4EP
Tel: 01453 847800
Email: info@quillerbooks.com
Website: www.quillerpublishing.com

Contents

Preface 15

Introduction 17

1. The Status of the Horse in a Controlled Environment 21
2. The Diet of the Horse in a Modern World 23
3. The Intestinal Tract – Organs – Vital Systems of the Horse 27
   ### The foregut 27
       The mouth 27
       The teeth 27
       The gums 29
       The salivary glands 29
       The tongue 30
       The throat (pharynx) and epiglottis 30
       The oesophagus 30
       The stomach 30
       The small intestine 32
   ### The hindgut 33
       The large intestine 33
       The hindgut fermentation process 33
       Hindgut bacteria 35
   ### The respiratory system 36
       Basic anatomy and function of the airway system 36
   ### The liver 36
       Liver disease 37
   ### The pancreas 38
   ### Blood 38
       Functions of the blood 39
       Blood disorders 39
4. The Brain and Central Nervous System – Gut Bacteria 41
   ### The spinal cord 41
   ### How the horse uses his brain 41

Abstract on genomic sequencing	42
The gut-brain axis	42
The microbe-gut-brain axis	42
Triglyceride – the leptin transporter to the brain	43
Leptin	43
Gut bacteria	44
Inflammation starts in the gut	44
Interaction of gut bacteria and parasites	45
Helminths	46

5. Prescription Drugs, Other Medications and Their Effects on the Gut — 49

Danilon/bute	49
Tryptophan	49
Antibiotics	50
Omeprazole	50
Cyanobacteria	51
A note on other natural compounds for medicinal use on horses	52
Natural medications – the other side of the coin	54

6. Feeding the Horse – How to Prepare Your Own Feeds — 55

How horses digest different types of food	55
Common foodstuffs for horses	56
Cereals	56
Barley	56
Oats	56
Maize	57
Cereals summary	57
Protein sources	57
Linseed	58
Soya beans	58
Alternative sources of protein considered for horse feed	59
Bulk feeds	59
Sugar beet pulp	59
Chaff	60
Bran	60
Compound feeds	60
Preparing your own feeds	61
Preparing linseed	61

Contents

- Preparing raw barley — 61
- Extra calories — 61
- Hay tea and herbal tea — 62
- Fresh foods — 62
  - Nutritious foods that are safe — 62
    - First of the superfoods — 63
    - Other beneficial wild plants — 63
- Foods to avoid feeding your horse — 64
  - Onions — 64
  - Bread — 64
  - Milk and yoghurt — 64
  - Potatoes, tomatoes and aubergines — 65
  - Avocados — 65
  - Lawn clippings — 65
- What to look for in manufactured feeds — 65
  - Issues of concern — 65
    - Testing of genetically modified foodstuffs — 65
    - Glyphosate contaminants — 66

7. The Importance of Vital Vitamins, Minerals and Trace Elements — 67

- Fat-soluble vitamins — 67
  - Vitamin A – retinol — 67
  - Vitamin D – calciferol — 67
  - Vitamin E – tocopherol — 67
  - Vitamin K – menaquinone — 68
- Water-soluble vitamins — 68
  - B1 – thiamine — 68
  - B2 – lactoflavin/riboflavin — 68
  - B3 – niacinamide/nicotinic acid/niacin — 68
  - B5 – pantothenic acid — 69
  - B6 – pyridoxine — 69
  - B12 – cyanocobalamin — 69
  - Choline — 69
  - Folic acid – folacin — 69
  - Biotin — 69
  - Vitamin C – ascorbic acid — 70
- Minerals for health and growth — 70
  - Macro-minerals — 70

Phosphorus (P)	70
Calcium (Ca)	70
Potassium (K)	70
Sodium (Na)	71
Chlorine (Cl)	71
Magnesium (Mg)	71
Sulphur (S)	72
Trace minerals – micro-nutrients	72
Iodine (I)	72
Selenium (Se)	72
Molybdenum (MO)	72
Cobalt (Co)	72
Copper (Cu)	72
Manganese (Mn)	73
Zinc (Zn)	73
Iron (Fe)	73
Silica (SiO$_2$)	74
8. The Microbiomes of Wild Plants	**75**
Phytochemicals	75
Phytochemical balancers	76
Diversity scoring	77
Low diversity	77
Medium diversity	77
High diversity	77
Food intake for survival	78
Wild foraging	78
Five facts about natural grazing by native and feral horses	79
Plants and herbs	79
Acorns	79
Lady's mantle (Alchemilla)	80
Bilberry (Vaccinium myrtillus)	81
Bindweed (Convolvulus)	82
Blackberry tips and old leaves (Rubus)	82
Bog plant – sweet flag (Acorus calamus)	83
Cleavers (Galium aparine)	83
Chickweed (Stellaria media)	84
Quinoa (Chenopodium quinoa)	85
Comfrey (Symphytum officinale)	85
Cow parsley (Anthriscus sylvestris)	86
Dandelions (Taraxacum officinale)	86
Beech (Fagus sylvatica)	87

Contents

Wild garlic (Allium sativum)	87
Ginger (Zingiber officionale)	88
Great burnet (Sanquisorba officinalis)	88
Hazel (Corylus avellana)	89
Ivy (Hedera)	89
Horsetail (Equisetum)	90
Honeysuckle (Lonicera)	90
Holly (Ilex)	91
Common rush (Juncus effusus)	92
Knapweed (Centaurea nigra)	92
Leeks (Allium ampeloprasum)	92
Nettles (Urtica dioica)	93
Oak (Quercus)	93
Peppermint (Mentha piperita) and oregano (Origanum vulgare)	94
Rosemary (Salvia rosmarinus)	95
Wild spinach (Chenopodium album)	95
Pine needles (Lophodermella concolor)	96
Pussy willow (Salix aegyptiaca)	97
Purple orchid (Orchis mascula)	97
Purple willow (Salix purpurea)	98
Willow (Salix)	98
White clover (Trifolium repens)	98
Toxic plants to eradicate	**99**
Ragwort (Senecio jacobaea)	99
Foxglove (Digitalis)	100
Sycamore family (Aces pseudoplatanus)	100
Deadly nightshade (Atropa belladonna)	101

9. Pastures – Paddocks, Meadows and a Walk Through the Seasons — 103

The link between water and soil	**103**
Drinking water	**104**
Water provision	105
Sick and healthy soil	**106**
Growing your own	**107**
Composition and different types of soil	107
Basic composition	107
Soil types	108
Management considerations	108
Sow some wild oats – oat grass	110
Control and management	111

General weed control — 111
Dealing with agrichemicals — 112
    Action you can take — 112
Interaction between stress and the biome — 112
Plants that kill parasites and strengthen resistance to infestation — 113
    How to grow them — 113
Organic grassland — 113
How safe is your grass? — 114
    Haylage — 115
    Mineral imbalance in hay or pasture — 116
    Paddock management for obese/EMS/laminitic horses — 117
    Unique metabolism of Spanish breeds of horses — 118
Medicinal meadows — 119
    Phytomedication — 120
    Best plants to grow and supply for inflammatory diseases and ailments — 120

Grazing habits — 121

Free-foraging horses — 121
The natural digestive process and seasonal influences — 121
    Seasonal disturbance by horseflies — 122
Damage to pastures caused by grazing horses — 122
    Horses eating soil — 123

A walk through the seasons — 123

Spring tonic — 123
Autumn – leaves and scent — 123
    Autumn foraging — 124
    Autumnal benefits of seed heads — 124
    Bracken in autumn — 124
Winter natural nutrition – the potential to help horses with Cushing's — 125
    Winter diet of wild horses — 125
    The best wild antioxidants to feed horses in February — 126

10. Feed-related Diseases and Feed-related Behaviour — 127

Obesity — 127

Assessing obesity — 127
    Obesity crest scores — 129
    Equine Henneke Body Condition Score — 129
Overview of some issues related to obesity — 131
Starting to confront the problem — 131

Contents

Comparison of ecdysterones to metformin	133
The AKT pathway	133
Antioxidant activity	134
Overweight ponies	134
Survival metabolism – 'good doers' thrive on surviving	135
Natural nutrition to help reduce weight	137
GLP-1 pay-it-forward mechanism	137
Hedges for overweight or EMS/IR horses	138
Insulin-resistant metabolic syndrome (IRMS)	138
Insulin resistant 2	139
Colic	140
The role of the equine gut microbiome in colic episodes	140
Studies and findings	141
Possible precursors to colic	142
Onset of colic	143
Factors that may cause colic and how to work on prevention	143
***Clostridium* colitis**	144
Enteritis	144
Polysaccharide storage myopathy (PSSM)	145
Laminitis	145
Visual signs of a pro-inflammatory state preceding laminitis	145
Timeline of laminitis – onset	146
Starch/grain overload laminitis	146
Fructan overload laminitis	146
Toxaemia/systemic laminitis	146
Endocrinopathic laminitis	146
Mechanical onset laminitis	146
Genetic laminitis	146
Laminitis and 'cresty' neck	147
Countdown to catastrophe	147
Treatment	148
Polyphenols and endocrinopathic laminitis	148
Laminitis turnout time	149
Five reasons why a horse needs a daily supply of polyphenols	150
Three feeding suggestions for horses prone to laminitis and/or EMS	150
Changes in the nerves of the laminitic horse	151
Ulcer syndromes – EGUS and SEGUS	151
How to start treatment	153

Managing the cause	153
The standard solution – treating the ulcers	154
Recent discoveries	154
New studies on ulcer treatment with natural compounds	156
Scientific studies of Maytenus ilicifolia	156
Comparison of Maytenus ilicifolia with other drugs used for treating ulcers	157
The evidence for bacterial infections as a cause of EGUS in horses	157

Head-shaking — 158

Developing a microbiome profile for head-shaking horses	158
Plants to help alleviate head-shaking	160

Myofascial and fibromyalgia pain — 160

Symptoms of fibromyalgia in horses	160
The role of the gut bacteria in fibromyalgia and myofascial pain	161
The gut profile of horses with chronic pain/fibromyalgia/myofascial pain	161
Long-term changes	161

White line disease — 162

Cushing's disease — 162

Onset	164
Symptoms	164
Summary of symptoms of advanced Cushing's	165
A broad picture of likely progression	166
Warning signs	167
Scientific research and testing	167
The basal ACTH test	167
Making sense of seasonal variations of ACTH	168
Insulin dysregulation test	168
Testing for insulin resistance	169
Insulin test findings: the importance of accuracy	170
Nitric oxide deficiency	170
Red blood cell levels	172
Treating and managing the condition	172
Pergolide	172
Pergolide and competitions	173
Vitex agnus-castus (chaste tree)	173
Diet-based ways to prevent or control Cushing's	174
List of beneficial plants in order of the adipocyte life-cycle	175

Equine metabolic syndrome (EMS) — 176

Contents

Adipose tissue in horses with EMS	177
How to bring about reduction in adipose tissue	177
Anorexia	178
Leaky gut	179
Five ways of avoiding leaky gut	179
How plant chemicals manage inflammation	179
Leaky gut in older horses	180
Degenerative diseases	181
Scent and gastric diseases	181
Big head	182
Aspergillus-associated asthma	182
Aspergillus in the microbiome and its role in health	182
Aspergillus in soil	183
Aspergillus in food	183
The role of probiotics	183
Symptoms of *Aspergillus* infection	183
Dietary interventions (antifungal foods)	184
How the EquiBiome Test can help	184
Diet and feed-related behaviour	184
Pain-related behaviour	185
Ulcers	185
Colic	185
Other types of unnatural behaviour	185
An issue with calmness in horses	185
Guarding food resource	186
Feed time behaviour	186
Depression and 'shut down'	187
Stereotypical behaviours	187
Possible link between selenium and cribbing in horses	187
The need for awareness and understanding	189

11. Climate Change, Pollution and Their Effect on Horses and Their Environment — 193

Climate change	193
Considerations on climate change	195
Industry-produced pollutants	195
Heavy industry	195
Heavy road traffic and airports	195
Industrial farming	196
Pharmaceutical and chemical plants and factories	196
Micro-plastics	196

Noise pollution	196
Effects of environmental pollutants on horses' health	197
Toxic materials in arenas and the stable environment	197
Wood shavings	198
Feed storage	198
Enrichment tools and toys	199
Textiles and other materials	199
Horse cleaning products	199
Yard management summary	199
Field management	200
Medication waste	200
Horses in the wild/free-roaming	200

12. End of Life Care for Your Horse — 201

Circumstances when euthanasia needs to be considered	201
Protocol – process – application of euthanasia	202
Unavoidable practicalities of end-of-life issues for you and your horse	203
Insurance	203
Livery yard policy and protocol	204
Home burial	204
Cremation	205
Further considerations	205
Coming to terms with loss	205

List of Abbreviations	207
About the Authors	208
Acknowledgements	208

Preface

Between us, Carol and I have nearly a century of equine nutrition and welfare experience and, as qualified professionals, we were becoming increasingly concerned about the health and welfare of horses. We realised that the high incidence of ulcers, laminitis, equine metabolic syndrome (EMS) and obesity, to name but a few of the many disorders found in horses, needed to be addressed. The main objective of this book is to give our readers a greater insight and understanding of the dietary and welfare needs of the horse and the most horse-centric way to feed and take care of horses in a modern-day environment. It is the first step toward a more comprehensive consideration of the health of the horse. We explain how and why we must try to re-establish important ties between the horse and his environment.

Another growing problem is that too many horses are being put under a great deal of stress and their anxiety levels have grown exponentially, which in turn has a direct effect on their physical and mental health. Carol, together with her team and in collaboration with other parties, has undertaken several decades of research on the efficacies of phyto (plant) materials and the important role they play in maintaining a healthy microbiome in the gut of the horse, and to ensure that the hindgut can do its important job of fermenting fibre.

Advanced testing, through the application of artificial intelligence, is also fast becoming a very accurate tool, which is being used to determine the health or imbalance of the horse's gastro-intestinal functionality. In the past decade or so, many equine nutrition researchers, of different nationalities, have started to concentrate on what the horse would choose to eat in the wild and the benefits that a more natural diet has on the overall health and well-being of the horse. For instance, horses out in their wild and natural habitat would not choose to eat raw grain, as it is not palatable and quite indigestible in its natural state. There is, of course, a lot of nutritional value in processed grain, when used in combination with a fresh or dried plant-based diet but, as with all food materials, it does need to be of good quality, without genetic modification, and preferably organically grown. Nonetheless, the horse's gastric intestine system functions at its best when at least two-thirds of his diet is composed of high-fibre, low-sugar, plant-based materials. Commercial feed manufacturers are now, by and large, supplying supplements in the form of dried herbal and other fibrous plant material, which offers the customer a greater choice from

Geertje French. *Photo by Charlotte Snowden*

which to make better-informed decisions. In this book you will find comprehensive lists of plants and herbs, their functions in improving gut health and their medicinal properties. The majority of these are accompanied by clear identification illustrations. We have also been able to source some excellent photographic evidence, supplied by the equine dissection specialist Becks Nairn, which gives the reader insight to the damage caused by ulcers and laminitis. Advanced research clearly shows that we need to move away from exposing horses to low-diversity monocultures, which can have a disastrous and negative impact on the health of the horse as they are low in essential nutrients and fibre, but high in starch and fructans, the main cause of laminitis and obesity.

It has also been found that horses are very efficient at self-medicating, as they will choose specific plant materials, which they would at other times ignore, to address specific health issues. We look at all aspects on how to achieve healthy paddocks and meadows, including how to look after the soil and what to grow for diversity to ensure well-balanced and highly nutritious grassland. Further to this, topics such as climate change and pollution are covered in detail.

We also look at how stereotypical behaviours and other unnatural so-called 'vices' and behaviours affect the physical and mental health of the horse and how these behaviours can, at times, be triggered by factors such as isolation, boredom, incompatible field companions, maltreatment and poor diet.

Another subject – one that is rarely discussed – is the end-of-life procedure for horses who, through either their physical ailments or compromised mental health, no longer enjoy a good quality of life. The chapter on this topic shows the reader everything that is involved when the horse has reached the point of no return and how to deal with the emotionally charged decisions the owner needs to make. We hope that this book will become a valuable addition to any equine enthusiast's collection.

Geertje French

Introduction

In 2009 I moved from a property of fifty acres of prime farmland and a prior history of agrichemical use and intense farming to a smallholding in Wales. The new place was twenty-five acres of mixed pasture, moors and ancient woodland and most of the grassland was overgrown with bracken and gorse. At its centre was a large granite outcrop topped by an Iron Age fort, one of the largest in North Wales, called *Caer Carreg y Fran* (Fort of the Ravens). This large rocky outcrop in the middle of the land helped to form what was to become the core or heart of the perfect natural track system that wound its way through. Previously, the ponies had been forced to retire to a small (¼-acre) patch of grassless earth or a concrete yard for ten months of the year as part of their weight management programme: they lived on poor forage and small handfuls of this and that, but always looked on the edge of laminitis, colic and/or obesity. This was stressful and a continuing disappointment and what on earth could we do with the rest of the 49¾ acres? But I was now swapping the plush, flat green fields, fertilised once yearly, with weeds sprayed to oblivion and post and rail fencing, luxury stables with automatic watering, for a wild abandoned hillside at the edge of Eryri. Initially, I was at a bit of a loss!

However, the move to Wales proved to be a complete revelation in terms of what Welsh Mountain ponies like to eat when returned to their homeland and I soon began to realise that, along with the loss of plush grass and other modern amenities, I'd also lost my feelings of constant anxiety over the health of the ponies. It was a complete learning curve as the ponies ate their way through almost every undesirable plant possible, except ragwort – which was reassuring. I learned to look the other way, as young foals were taught by their mothers how to pick and forage their way through the indigestible and the improbable. Moreover, the results were immediate and highly visible in the form of shiny coats, good feet, and weight loss without any effort on my part. In fact the health of the entire herd improved.

I had initially and immediately turned my nose up at the sight of the water supply (both the ponies' and ours), which was from a spring, being filtered through layers of granite on the way down through Eryri. I fretted about contaminants and unfriendly bacteria until I discovered through analysis that it was pure, clean mineral water – another bonus!

Eventually and thankfully, I took the advice of the fifteen ponies in the herd, consigned the

Carol Hughes. *Photo by Paul Hughes*

complicated weight control management rules to the bin and joyfully entered a whole new era of natural horse nutrition and management. Sometime in those first few years of the move, we were introduced to Dr Vera Thoss and Professor Chris Gwenin at the organic chemistry lab at Bangor University, where the trend at that time was extracting active plant compounds with a high (monetary/pharmacological) value from wild plants. The chemicals could then be used in drug discovery (antimicrobial) or scaled up in production for potentially global use. For us it was a marriage made in heaven and for the next ten years and more, we sponsored students and were involved in major projects that meant we could find out just what was in the plants our horses chose to forage and, perhaps more importantly to begin to understand the language (cross-talk) that is spoken between the two. The wild plants contain thousands of plant chemicals and antioxidants, vitamins and minerals that not only underpin every aspect of equine health and vitality, but also work as prebiotics to promote and balance the gut bacteria that are so important to the horse. We analysed every wild plant possible, plus the sugar content of our newly restored horse-friendly meadows, including the plethora of wildflowers from underlying seed banks, as well as a neighbour's meadow further up the mountain, and we compared these findings to grass grown under agricultural conditions. We found that plants and grasses grown together in a community have lower sugar levels and higher minerals than agricultural seed-type pastures. Furthermore, the minerals are a very close match to those recommended by the National Research Council.

In 2014 we were introduced to Professor Jamie Newbold and a team of ruminant/equine microbiologists who were leading the way in microbiome research at Aberystwyth University. Gaining access to the new sequencing technology opened a whole new world and provided a missing part of the jigsaw. That is to say linking the food the horse ingested to the gut itself revealed more complex multiple signalling processes that take place and ultimately control the physical and mental health of the horse.

As modern horse nutrition has evolved it has moved away from the use of single items such as oats, bran, sugar beet, maize and barley, into the realms of highly manufactured formulas. There are, of course, certain benefits to this approach and social media is full of opinions as to the best rations, supplements, vitamin and mineral balancing, plus hay analysis. We seem obsessed – and I speak from personal experience – with micromanaging every aspect of our horses' lives and many horse owners feel pressured to maintain their horses' health by an ever-increasing number of rules, opinions, and diktats. There are many books covering equine nutrition, driven by the increase in students passing through universities and colleges, many of which originated purely as agricultural colleges before adding on an equine section around the 1970s. A proportion of the lecturers had an agricultural science background, where productivity and performance reign and a trend for measuring, calculating and analysing nutrients for horses was born and has continued unabated for the succeeding fifty years. The obsession with formulating the 'perfect' ration for every circumstance has now been endemic for the last couple of decades. However, although formulated rations are currently relied upon in every aspect of equine life (dressage, showjumping, racing, showing etc.), there is now a growing interest in a more natural way of providing nutrition. I have forage-walked the hallowed turf of Newmarket with high-profile racehorse trainers, together with owners of millions of pounds worth of blue-blooded Thoroughbreds. The discussion has not been about the next potential Derby winner housed in the stables behind us, but instead about the plants that can be identified from the richly biodiverse heath and how these might be of benefit to the horses in the trainers' care. I have had the same discussions with Olympic event riders and many hundreds of horse owners alike, all curious to learn more about the phytonutrient content and active compounds held within a snatched bite of a hedgerow herb.

What is missing from so many of the books on nutrition is an explanation of how and why to evaluate and trust the pastures, hedges, hedgerows, heathlands and woods as sources of vitamins, minerals, phytonutrients, plant antioxidants and secondary metabolites that have a vital contribution to make to the health of horses and ponies. As an example, good metabolism involves a language between the soil, the plants, the gastro-intestinal tract, the gut bacteria, the brain and the endocrine system. A shortfall in any one area can have a devastating effect on the other parts and, of particular importance, the gut bacteria. New sequencing technology allows us and invites us to learn more about these important lines of invisible communication. Armed with this knowledge we can hope to address the silent crisis of the many modern 'syndromes' that afflict many of today's horses.

Carol Hughes

Horses are confined from a young age.
Geertje French

1.
The Status of the Horse in a Controlled Environment

One of the greatest horsemen from the past was the Greek general, philosopher, writer and historian, Xenophon (born *c.*430 BC). One topic of Xenophon's close observations and subsequent writings was the hoof of the horse, the foundation on which the horse stood or stumbled. He had already learned from his own father, a great horseman himself, 'that everything about the horse relied on the health and soundness of its feet'. Advising on what to look for when buying a horse, he said: 'Make sure that the hoof is solid, yet light and moves easily and in supple fashion on the pastern. But above all, it must ring good and true on the earth.' Everyone recognises that 'clop' sound of the hoof striking the ground, hollow and resonant, and keeping the horse well-balanced.

Xenophon liked his horses lean, without pads of fat, as he realised that if horses are overweight this not only affects their energy level, but also puts a great deal of strain on their feet, which then affects everything else, from poll to tail. His 2,500-year-old advice was solid then and it is solid still. Many diseases affect the horse's feet, or have a direct effect on the feet. In Xenophon's world everything the horse ate was extracted from plants: roots, leaves, flowers, seeds, fruits, vegetables, herbs and rough forage such as shrubs and tree bark. Grooms and farriers (many of whom doubled up as horse physicians in earlier times) also used natural remedies derived from plants and herbs, and made them into potions and tonics, poultices and other medicines. And, of course, all feed was organic. Xenophon would also have watched the horses grazing and eating from hedges and trees, noting down exactly what they were choosing and what they were ignoring. In his thesis on horsemanship, he takes into account that the horse needs a well-balanced diet to make him healthy and strong.

Another thing that Xenophon taught his horsemen is that much patience, respect and diligence are needed to make the horse motivated and responsive to training. Xenophon abhorred any kind of corporal punishment inflicted on the horse – a practice some keepers used to unleash their pent-up anger and impatient frustration to 'teach the horse a lesson'. Xenophon held with the philosophy that you get much further with a horse, no matter what his character or idiosyncrasies, if you do not bring any personal grievances or frustration into the stable, where the horse, being sentient, will tune into your state of mind.

In his submissions on horse welfare Xenophon very much drew on his own lifelong experience of working with these noble and obliging animals. He realised that horses needed a quiet and stable environment and extended times of respite, away from the work they were required to do under the training and directions of man. He stood for the horses having long stretches of field time, to play, socialise, relax and improve their muscular strength. He felt that, although perhaps some early developers seemed ready for training, two-year-olds and three-year-olds were not mature and not grown enough to ask of them that they undertook exercise and the beginnings of training for combat. He was entirely horse-centric and observed everything closely, with consideration and the well-being of the horse uppermost in his mind.

What we can still draw from Xenophon's great knowledge and wisdom about horses is that we should feed our horses a healthy plant-based diet and that their welfare should be at the top of any horse owner's agenda. One important corollary to this is that we should never ignore sudden changes of behaviour in the horse, but check to discover what the underlying cause might be. In addition to your horse not being under stress, in pain or anxious, he should also not be blamed for the behaviour he displays, although we do need to bear in mind that in some cases horses can become aggressive and reactionary, for whatever reason, instantly turning them into very dangerous animals. Evident behaviour aside, we also need to ensure that the horse does not suffer in silence, when subtle behaviours may, over time, become stereotypical behaviours – we can't ever take anything at face value.

Neurological problems in horses seem to have grown exponentially, and there are many reports of horses 'losing their minds' or being difficult to handle. The complexity of a horse's brain is a new field of research, as it has become increasingly apparent that the brain plays an important role in how the horse reacts to his environment, diet, exercise and social interaction. The behaviour of some horses can seem erratic and, in the mind of people, irrational, yet there is nothing irrational or premeditated about the way a horse expresses himself, as that is not how he manages his instinctive behaviour. We must take into account that the brain of a horse and the brain of a human are two entirely different countries. The horse is a prey animal and has three basic instinctive responses: fight, flight or freeze, which he needs to hone to survive in his natural environment. It might be thought that the domesticated horse has an easy time of it, but we need to realise that such horses can be subjected to all kinds of practices not entirely in keeping with their needs or welfare. And at no other time has the behaviour and diet of horses been so much discussed, researched and put under a microscope. It is necessary to acknowledge that the horse's state of mind can make him do all kinds of things not compatible with human expectation, and that to anthropomorphise the horse is doing him a great disservice.

Another important factor is that horses are often kept in stables for most of their time, when there is little or no pasture available to them. Some owners do give their horses a holiday from stable life by sending them on a summer vacation to rented meadows, where they spend several weeks and sometimes months out in nature. This is a kindness to the horse, as a horse who lives his whole life in stables, only being outside for the occasional hack, or in the arena for a few hours a day, often suffers from boredom. This in turn, can make the horse start to display stereotypical behaviour like box-walking, weaving or cribbing. For such horses it is a good idea to look into enrichment games, which will entertain and occupy them with an element of play and fun.

2.
The Diet of the Horse in a Modern World

When you look at individual food items consumed by the horse, including their method of production, trends and changes in food types, and how this can have either a positive or, indeed, adverse effect on overall health, you will soon find that there is very little regulation as to what exactly is being offered. And when we look at the environment the horse lives in, including the quality and type of pasture and the effects of ingested pollutants and agrichemicals on the gut, it becomes clear that the horse is being exposed to levels of toxicity that not only have a detrimental effect on the physical well-being but also (and even more worryingly) the mental state of the horse. The horse appears to be hypersensitive to water and soil quality, and to the emerging pathogens that are not filtered or cleaned by the current water treatments and the horse is equally sensitive to a reduction or complete loss of benevolent bacteria in the soil through modern management systems. The microbial community within the gut is a master regulator of health, evolving with the horse over many centuries and in recent times being adversely exposed to significant and detrimental use of antimicrobial antibiotics and long-term medications that reduce the total numbers of species, causing a loss of stability. Another issue to take into account is that the waste products of these medications, found in urine and faecal matter, end up on the land, in water sources and on the muck heap, thus polluting the environment with a potentially adverse effect on all areas where the horses leave their waste.

The microbial population not only affects the gut; scientific research is also discovering links between the microbiota and the physiology of the host (the horse). Bacteria, fungi, archaea, viruses and phages live in a strongly symbiotic relationship with the host: it is the gut community that regulates the immune, metabolic and endocrine systems through the gut-brain axis. Disorders within these systems can be directly linked back to imbalances in the microbial community of the gut, through a pathway of intricate and crucial connections. As a herbivore and hindgut fermenter, the horse relies on feed with a high percentage of rough fibre.

Horses in the wild, without human interference, self-select on all plant materials that benefit their health – that is to say, each horse eats what his body tells him it needs, and it is essential that we help them to continue this behaviour as much as is possible. We can do this by offering plenty of organically grown grass and plant/herbage variety to ensure that their gut receives the right balance in macro- and micro-minerals, vitamins, fibre, fats and protein. (Fats, in the form of lipids or fatty acids, are found in vegetable matter such as nuts and seeds, while protein is available from sources such as broccoli, peas, spinach and barley grass, to give some examples.)

Horses seldom eat things that make them ill because usually they instinctively know (or can smell or taste) that they are poisonous. However, it is unwise to rely absolutely on this discretion, so you should ensure that there are no plants in your fields that are known to be unsuitable or toxic

Healthy Gut, Healthy Horse

for horses, which they might, for example, crop accidently alongside the healthy forage.

Grasslands represent one of the world's largest biomes and whilst the relationship and interactions between the ruminant and plant communities has been well researched, the same cannot be said of the horse. The horse is equally reliant on access to the grassland biome but instead is often malnourished by paddocks containing monocultured high-sugar grasses. Food rations fed from a bag are often highly processed, sometimes containing food waste by-products, often previously treated with a whole raft of agrichemicals.

Furthermore, it is almost inevitable that horses and other animals (including humans) will need to find alternative protein sources in the future and it is, therefore, quite likely that, before long, protein for horses will be extracted from dried insects. Think crickets, locusts and ants, as these provide good levels of consumable protein. The danger, as has already been seen in large shipments of dried insects intended for human and other animal consumption, is that they might also carry unwanted bacterial material, an unintended consequence of producing these insects on such a large scale, with insufficient health and safety regulation. Soon, we will have no idea that there is insect protein in all manner of foodstuffs, for both human and animals, and there is an additional point we wish to make here, which is that horses are herbivores and should not be consuming any type of animal protein (unless a foal needs milk protein additions if their dam doesn't produce enough milk). Thus, whilst the idea of horse feed containing insects is something we may see more and more of in the future, we are not entirely sure that is the way to go, when a horse can get plenty of protein

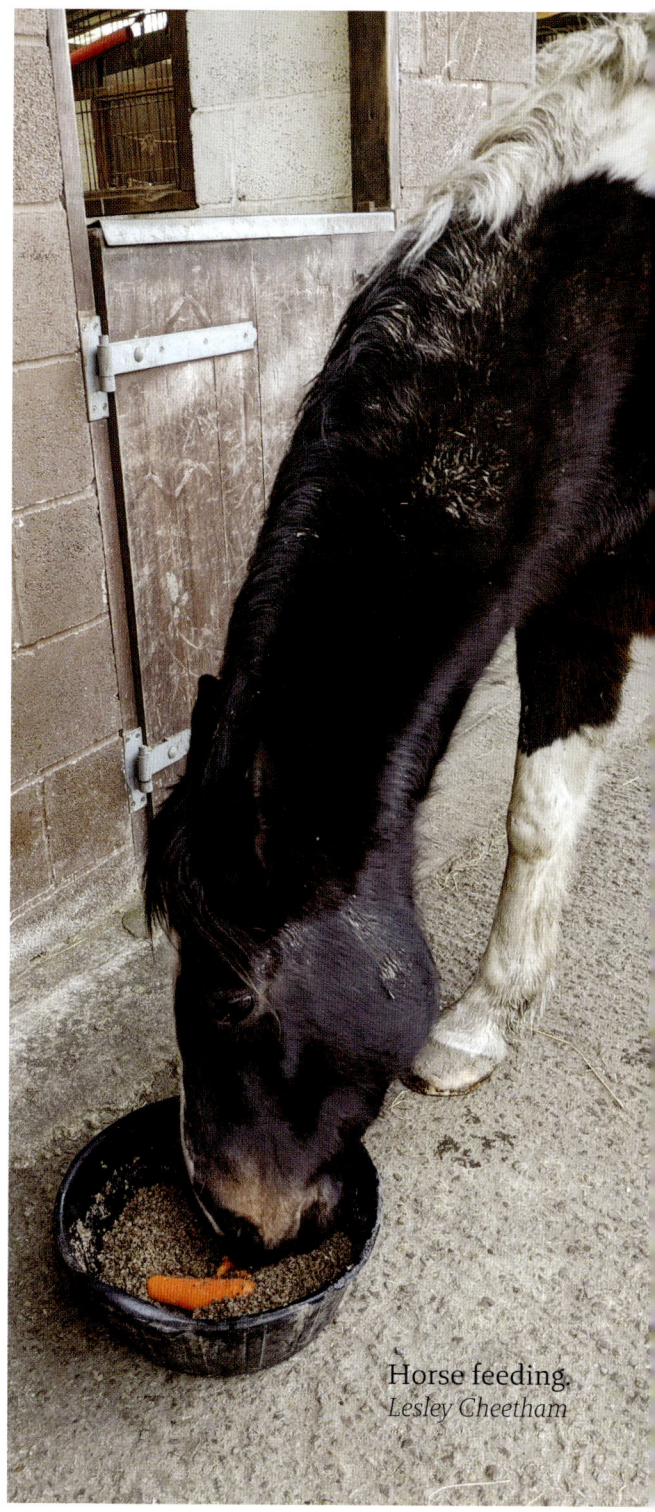

Horse feeding.
Lesley Cheetham

from plant material sources. Nonetheless, we do understand that, for some people, the actual protein source is of less importance than the fact that their horses are stabled most of the time, or the horses are outside but not in meadows where they can graze, and thus they may be lacking in proteins. Given such scenarios, insect protein may become a cheap alternative source and we will no doubt see that the ethical boundaries about horses being herbivores will shift. (The matter of insects as a source of feed for horses is discussed further in Chapter 6.)

Eutrophication (the enrichment of the microbiome by excessive vitamins and nutrients) is common in horses, causing blooms of nutrient-robbing biofilm bacteria. The microbiome of the horse is complex and requires an equally complex diet to maintain the biodiversity within the microbial community. Horses given a diverse meadow grass diet containing a mixture of plant species and including a variety of hedgerow plants, have a more stable and diverse microbiome than those stabled and fed on a processed diet.

Using genomic sequencing it is now possible to identify the shortcomings in a diet and to increase biodiversity using essential phytonutrients. Phytonutrients provide a multitude of benefits to the microbiome and mycobiome and to the host (the horse), since they contain potent antioxidants with anti-inflammatory, anti-ulcerogenic and analgesic effects. The gastro-intestinal microbial ecosystem, known as microbiota, is involved in many physiological processes and plays a crucial role in determining the horse's health. Plants have a similar microbiome to what is already present in the horse's gut, and contain biologically active compounds that modify the host gut bacteria. These chemicals or compounds have low bio-availability and are retained for a long time in the intestines because they are poorly absorbed. Some medicinal plants have hundreds of beneficial compounds that contribute greatly to the overall health of the horse. The capacity of the plant microbiome to communicate with the microbiome of the horse is called 'quorum sensing'. It is an exciting and innovative area of science: it offers tremendous potential to impact gut health and the overall health and well-being of the horse.

3.
The Intestinal Tract – Organs – Vital Systems of the Horse

To understand the highly complex ingenuity of how horses ingest and digest food, we need to look at the intestinal tract and its mechanisms. The function of the digestive tract is to digest and process all foodstuffs. If the intestines are healthy and function well, all nutrients will be absorbed into the bloodstream and support all the vital organs, along with muscle mass, tendons, tissue, the nervous system, bones, coat, tail and mane. If the digestive tract becomes 'blocked' by the wrong kind of feed this can cause disease, hormonal imbalance and neurological problems. Feed- and stress-induced ulcers, known as squamous equine gastric ulcer syndrome (SEGUS) and equine gastric ulcer syndrome (EGUS), along with laminitis, obesity, EMS, inflammation and poor growth can all be direct indicators that the digestive tract is not functioning properly. Besides this, feeds need to have the right balance of minerals (micro- and macro-), vitamins and metallic elements for the horse to enjoy optimum health, both physically and mentally.

The foregut

The mouth

The top lip of the horse is a strong muscle that has been designed to assist in gathering and sorting food. The bottom lip helps gather foodstuffs and is used with the top lip to create a funnel when drinking. Make sure to inspect the horse's lips daily for any signs of damage, and check inside the lips to clean out any pieces of hay or food that can become an irritant. When using any kind of bit, the inspection of the mouth is particularly important to ensure that there is no damage, and you should be aware that feeding the horse whilst he is wearing a bit will compromise his chewing ability. It is therefore better to wait until he is untacked before giving the horse anything to chew on. (A note on the hairs around the horse's muzzle and lips of the horse – these are of great sensory value and it is now unlawful in the UK to shave these off for aesthetic reasons.)

The teeth

The teeth of the horse are diphyodonties and heterodonties, terms that refer to the fact that horses have teeth of different shapes. Up to five different shapes can be found, although not all horse's teeth are identical. The teeth of the foal are oval-shaped; known as the deciduous teeth, they push through soon after birth. They emerge in pairs to a total of twenty-four; over time they are pushed out by the permanent teeth. When they are first coming through, the deciduous teeth are known as 'caps', these usually shed by themselves, but you need to keep a regular eye on them, because if they don't do so they will need to be removed by your equine dentist as they will otherwise interfere with good cropping, biting and chewing actions.

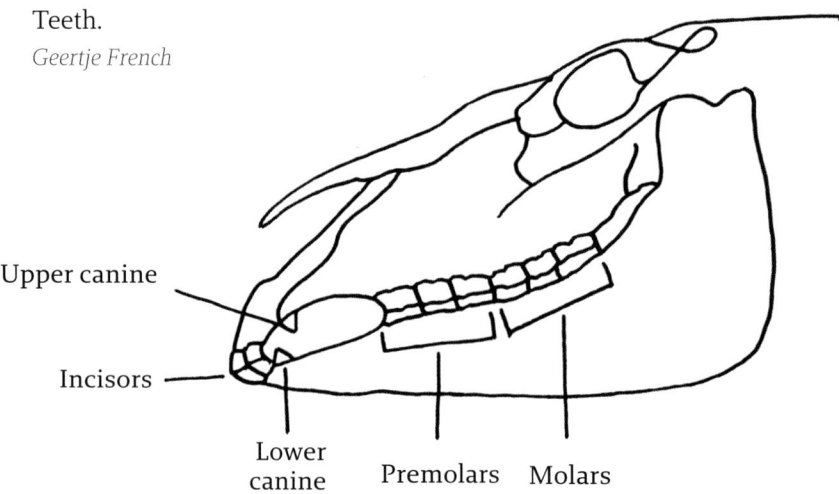

Teeth.
Geertje French

The growth of permanent teeth occurs over a number of years, between the ages of five and six. Once the horse has fully grown, he will have developed between thirty-six and forty-four teeth. The difference in the number of teeth between mares, stallions and geldings is marked by the fact that males tend to develop four extra teeth, known as canine teeth, and these are seen only in about a quarter of mares. When they do occur in mares, there may be only one or two and they are usually not completely erupted and may need to be removed if they cause chewing problems or get infected.

Horses have twelve incisors, to be found at the front of the jaw, used for close cropping and cutting. These teeth are also used when horses bite in aggression, panic or defence. Foals are sometimes 'warned off' with a quick nip when they are too playful. Behind the incisors is the interdental space; no teeth erupt from this part of the gum and it is where the bit sits in the horse's mouth – a convenient space you might say. Behind this space are the cheek teeth, consisting of twelve premolars followed by the back jaw twelve molars. These teeth are used for chewing food before swallowing.

About a third of horses, both male and female, may also present with wolf teeth, also known as vestigial first premolars. These teeth are usually removed as they can become a problem when dentistry work is performed and also for horses wearing a bit.

Wear and tear of horses' teeth mostly depends on the kind of feeds they are offered. Horses in the wild show teeth with much more even wear than those in a domestic environment. This is mainly because horses in the wild predominantly feed on rough forage, including bark from trees. Domesticated horses are often fed 'soft roughage', such as hay, alfalfa and chaff. In horses who are mostly stabled and do not get turnout on pastures where they can crop forage, the teeth will also not show much wear and tear on the incisors. Pellets and pony nut feeds need very little chewing as they are ground into a powder-like substance. However, if horses develop the stereotypical behaviour of cribbing they will, on the other hand, show much more wear on their incisors.

All horses need their teeth inspected regularly by a qualified equine dentist. If teeth become uneven this will inhibit smooth chewing actions and can cause discomfort or pain, to the extent that the horse may stop eating. It is prudent to check your horse's teeth on a daily basis, as pieces of food that become lodged can cause discomfort and infections. Also, some horses grow uneven teeth, which again can cause chewing problems. In young horses some of the teeth may have sharp edges and these will need to be seen to as they will prevent proper chewing and can cut into the soft flesh of the mouth.

When assessing the age of a horse, this is usually done by the shape and star indentations on the surface of the teeth. Your equine dentist will show you what to look out for. Elderly horses' teeth need extra attention, as they can lose their teeth over time. In this event you will need to make adjustments to their diets, in the form of softer feeds and adding extra supplements so they receive the adequate nutrients needed in order to stay healthy. When cutting up foods such as carrots, apples, turnips and other fresh vegetables, be sure not to cut them into slices or cubes, as these can slip between the teeth and cause a choking hazard.

The gums

It may not be immediately obvious but the state and colour of your horse's gums are great indicators as to his health.

- If the gums are a pale pink in colour, it usually implies that the horse has good circulation. The colour may become slightly darker when the horse has done hard exercise.
- When the gums have turned a grey-blueish colour it is time to call your vet, as this may indicate an undiscovered infection, and/or the red blood cell count may be low, which will restrict good oxygen flow – or your horse may be about to go into severe shock.
- Gums that have turned a yellow colour with a brown tinge may be an indication that your horse has liver failure (jaundice); this may also be seen in the white of the eyes.
- Dark red gums denote enlargement of the capillaries and are a danger sign, as this shows that the horse is suffering from severe dehydration or from poisoning, which may happen when they are left to feed on undesirable weeds in the field or are suffering from systemic inflammatory response syndrome (SIRS) – *see* the section on blood.
- Very pale, almost white gums (through contracted capillaries) may show that the horse has a fever, suffers with anaemia or is suffering from blood loss, either internally or externally. If the gums present very pale, do the finger-press test. Press your thumb on the gums for about two seconds then release; the capillaries should refill within two to three seconds. If there is no refill your horse may be going into a state of shock. Check the gums daily to see that there are no issues and to make sure that there are no blisters or cuts.

The salivary glands

These glands are arranged in pairs: sublingual, parotid and mandibular. The glands start to secrete saliva at the moment the horse starts chewing – the horse does not produce saliva spontaneously and continuously as in humans. This is an important point to remember. The main function of good saliva production is to warm and wet the foodstuff, turning it into a bolus before being swallowed. Manufactured hard feed takes very little chewing, so saliva production is minimal, whereas grass, hay and other roughage takes a lot of chewing and the volume of saliva produced is directly proportional to the number of chews. In other words, the more the horse chews, the more saliva is produced.

In addition to being slightly alkaline, saliva contains bicarbonate: this helps to form a lining or buffer in the stomach to deal with natural acid production. Another important component is the enzyme salivary amylase, which helps with the breakdown of starch. If the horse gets enough chewing action, he will produce between 10–12 litres of saliva in a 24-hour period. The chew rate of concentrates is between 800–1,200 chews per kg, whereas the chew rate for roughage will go up to 3,000–3,500 chews per kg. Overall, the horse on a pellet diet will chew in the region of 10,000 times per day while a horse on a good hay and grass diet will chew up to 40,000 times per day. In ponies the chew rate is even more protracted: 3,000–5,000 chew actions for a kg of concentrates and considerably more when they are on hay.[1] And it was found that the development of sharp enamel points is more likely with horses on a concentrate feed. This indicates that horses mostly on concentrates should have their teeth checked more often than horses on a high-fibre roughage and hay diet. All of these findings should also make us realise that horses living on a ration that mainly consists of concentrates do not get the right volume of saliva to help protect their stomach from excessive acid, and the hindgut does not get the amount of fibre required for fermentation.

The tongue

The tongue is a thick muscle that helps with forming the food into a bolus and moves it to the area at the back of the mouth, named the oropharynx. The tongue is susceptible to cuts and grazes, so check it on a regular basis, to ensure that there are no such injuries, or swellings.

The throat (pharynx) and epiglottis

Behind the mouth is a cavity, called the pharynx. The food passes over the trachea (the opening to the windpipe), which is protected by a small piece of cartilage at the base of the tongue, named the epiglottis.

The oesophagus

Along the left-hand side of the neck is the oesophagus, a tube-like structure that enables boluses of food to pass from the pharynx down to the stomach. Running down the back of the trachea, it extends to a length of approximately 1.2–1.5 metres (although depending on the size of the horses it may be longer or shorter). The oesophagus travels through the chest and between the lungs then through the diaphragm (a tough muscle separating the chest from the abdomen). Its function is primarily one of transportation rather than active digestion of food.

The stomach

Compared to the size of the horse, the stomach is relatively small; when empty it is the size of a medium-sized melon. When full the stomach can extend to hold 9–18 litres. There is a small ring valve, named the cardiac sphincter, which allows the food to enter the stomach. Once the food passes, this valve prevents it from being brought back up into the oesophagus: it is important to realise that, because of this strong valve, the horse is not able to vomit, belch or regurgitate food. Only in very rare cases, when the valve has become damaged, will food re-enter the oesophagus. If this happens the food will be brought up again, and this in turn can become a choking hazard for the horse.

The stomach is designed to always have some food in it. It is therefore recommended that you spread out your horse's ration over the day by dividing it into four or even five small meals. Ensure that you give hay that the horse can eat throughout the day and night. When out in the paddock the horse will eat some 70% of the time. Horses do not have the same kind of nocturnal sleeping patterns as humans; they sleep for short periods during both the day and night, so the horse will need to have something he can chew on throughout the night as well as the day. For stabled horses it is essential that they have continuous hay to stave off hunger and boredom.

There are four regions of the stomach, the first being the oesophageal region. As there are no glands in this region the food remains neutral in terms of pH as there are so far no chemical interactions between the food and digestive juices. It is seen as a holding area before the food enters the cardiac region. In the cardiac region there are glands that produce the much-needed mucus that lines the stomach to protect it from hydrochloric acid. Next comes the fundic region, which represents the main body of the stomach. In this part of the stomach three types of cells are found: the body chief cells for the secretion of enzymes, parietal cells (also known as border cells) for the secretion of hydrochloric acid and the neck chief cells for the secretion of mucus. When food reaches the fundic region it is highly acidic. The fourth region of the stomach is the pyloric region, in which the pyloric glands are found. These combine a secretion of mucus and a small number of enzymes that digest proteins.

It takes approximately forty to fifty minutes for most of the food to pass through the stomach, although some foods may take up to two hours. When the food has gone through the first phase of digestion, passing through the different sections of the stomach, where it will have started the acidic process, it continues its digestive progress by leaving the stomach through the pyloric sphincter, which allows entry into the first part of the small intestine.

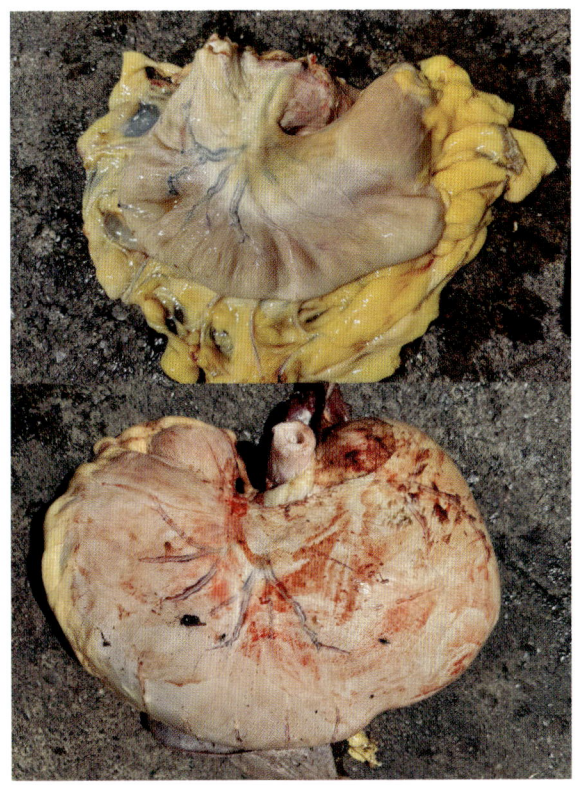

Stomach – The top photo shows an empty stomach with visceral fat nodules. The bottom photo shows a healthy full stomach.
Becks Nairn

When the horse is being fed a diet that is high in carbohydrates (barley, wheat and other high-carbohydrate/starch sources such as oats, maize, rice flour and pulses), his stomach has a job to cope with the sudden arrival of a foodstuff that takes a very long time to digest and, as the starch turns into sugars, combined with proteins, amino acids, alkaline and gastric acid, it should not come as a surprise to find that the combination – a faulty combination for the horse – will cause ulceration in the lining of the stomach.

There is also another mechanism that goes awry when the horse gets most of his rations in grain form, with some added fibrous materials. Research has shown that within the microbiome can be found all the different permeations of gut flora. Through lab analyses one can get up close and personal with the functions of the horse's gut. Domesticated horses rely on our knowledge of nutrition, for us to make the right choices and decisions for them, as they no longer roam the wild and eat what they can find along the way. And what we have discovered is that the health of the stomach in the majority of horses leaves a great deal to be desired. Many gastro-intestinal maladies are a direct result of the wrong type or balance of nutrients, be they macro- or micro-. The horses' stomach is a delicate and complex (eco)system, unlike any other among mammals. Therefore, great care has to be taken to ensure that the horse gets the right chewing time from fibrous nutrition and thus benefit from the carb/starch food we humans choose to feed. It is often said that the feeding of a horse is an art form, and there is certainly something to be said for that.

The small intestine

The small intestine links the stomach and the caecum. It coils itself close to the small colon but is essentially free-moving in the abdomen.

The function of the small intestine is to break down protein, starch and fats, and absorb nutrients. The wall of the gut is made up of two layers of muscles, the circular and longitudinal. These two layers work by contracting in opposite directions (a system termed 'antagonistic contraction') which, despite the name, results in them actually working together to cause the food to be moved into one direction (peristalsis).

The small intestine is divided into three different areas, of which the first is the duodenum. This is an S-shaped bend that measures approximately a metre in length. The duodenum processes foodstuffs with the help of enzymes secreted by the pancreas and liver, which flow into it, and also from bile, which the liver produces as there is no intermediate organ (like the gall bladder in the human digestive system) for separate bile production. The flow of bile is continuous; it facilitates the emulsification of fats and is a contributor to the production of an alkaline reaction of intestinal contents. Its yellow-greenish colour causes colouration in the faeces and urine.

The second part of the small intestine is known as the jejunum, which measures up to twenty metres in length. Once the lipids (fats) are properly digested, they re-assimilate within the epithelial cells of the gut to be turned into triglycerides. Once these triglycerides are bonded with cholesterol and proteins they, and other nutrients such as vitamins, minerals, glucose and amino acids, are absorbed into the bloodstream and distributed by the body's circulatory system.

The third part of the small intestine is known as the ileum. This measures approximately

Gastro-intestinal tract.
Geertje French

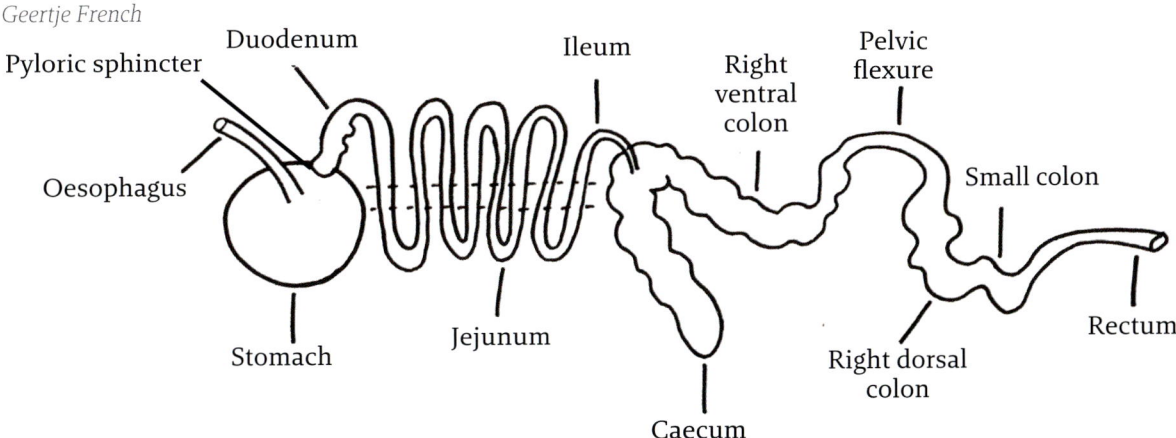

two metres in length. In this final part is the mesentery tissue, which supports the intestines and supplies them with nerves, lymphatics and blood vessels.

These three parts of the small intestine together can support up to 50 litres in volume. To aid absorption of nutrients the lining of the small intestine is covered in tiny hair-like villi, and between these villi there are three different types of glands. Throughout the small intestine the intestinal glands, also known as Crypts of Lieberkühn, secrete enzymes. Also throughout the small intestine are Peyer's patches, where lymphoid tissue comes together to keep bacterial populations under control and for the production of antibodies. The duodenal glands, also known as Brunner's glands are found in the duodenum area of the small intestine and their function is to secrete an alkaline solution.

The hindgut

The large intestine

Adjoining the ileum is the caecum, the first part of the large intestine. The caecum is where the fermentation process of the fibrous foodstuffs takes place. Following along the caecum, we find the right ventral colon, the pelvic flexure, the right dorsal colon, the small colon and finally the rectum.

The hindgut fermentation process

The horse is a hindgut fermenter, which means he is designed to eat fibrous material, fermented in a holding chamber, the caecum, which is home to trillions of bacteria, archaea, protozoa, and fungi working in synergy to break down poor-quality and largely indigestible food material (woody-stalky material, seed heads, etc.) and produce energy. The horse is, of course, also designed to process rapidly degradable starch (grains, the leaves of grass and hay, alfalfa) in the stomach and small intestine.

The fermenting process of fibrous material is slower in yielding energy compared to the rapid release of energy from easily degradable starch. Fermented energy takes time to produce, but this method allows the horse to survive the winters in the wild, when food (especially starch) may be hard to come by. Therefore, he has two existing systems: a 'survival' one to cope with harsh conditions and another designed to consume large amounts of highly degradable starch, especially in the spring, as he emerges thinner from a winter of scarcity and in the summer when he needs the energy for mating, feeding foals, and storing up fat stores for the coming winter.

We both used to, and Carol still does provide the harsh (semi-harsh) winter experience: it was called being 'turned away' or 'being roughed off'. There are but few people who still practice this management system, as for many it isn't feasible, since they stable their horses for most of the time and do not have access to outdoor grazing. We therefore need to look at different solutions to cater for the two differing seasonal nutritional needs of the horse.

We looked at a talented event horse in an international yard that still 'roughs off' their horses (no rugs, no extra feed) through the winter months; it is an unusual situation. We did some tests on the microbiome of nine roughed-off horses and were astonished at how healthy and stable the

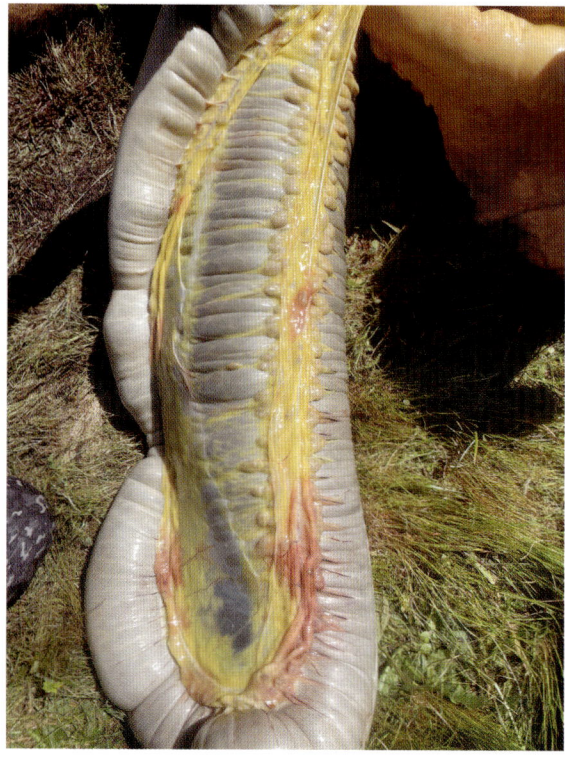

Caecum – This picture shows a full caecum of a four-year-old TB gelding.

Becks Nairn

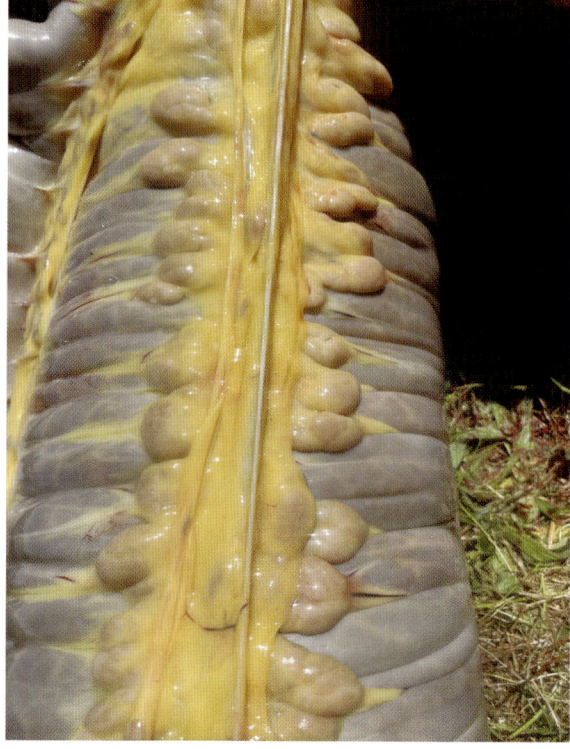

Caecum – The same caecum in close up where inflammation and swollen lymph nodes can clearly be seen.

Becks Nairn

gut population was mid-competition (July), compared to other microbial populations of stabled competing horses not 'roughed off'. With the use of artificial intellegence (AI), we were able to detect patterns of change and in the 'roughed off' group the bacteria linked to immune function and metabolism were higher than in the other group; the horses also had a higher diversity score (Shannon Index). 'Roughing off' will not suit all horses – as an example the horse described above lost too much weight, therefore, his time off in the field has been reduced accordingly.

Getting the balance right for a modern stabled horse can be challenging and metabolic imbalances such as laminitis, obesity, EMS, ulcers, colic and acidosis of the hindgut are very common. The microbes of the gastro-intestinal tract are very sensitive to changes in pH. If the degradable starch levels are higher than the slower release fibrous material, then the lactic acid loving bacteria can outnumber the acid eating members of the gut biota and the horse is then susceptible to low-grade continuous acidosis, leading to the previously mentioned modern metabolic dysfunctions.

The long-term answer is to feed according to work and lifestyle; for most horses this is likely to mean a switch to a diet higher in natural fibre intake.

Hindgut bacteria

The hindgut bacteria control inflammation and energy metabolism; short-chain fatty acids are produced through the interaction of these bacteria with food the horse consumes. Not all short-chain fatty acids are beneficial: some promote inflammation, and some reduce inflammation. Choosing food to suit the needs of the horse is, therefore, so much more than checking the nutrient digestibility and vitamin and minerals content based on NRC (National Research Council) figures. There is also something called 'nutrient interaction', as the absorption of nutrients is also reliant on the health of the horse, and the state of the gastro-intestinal tract; how well he absorbs the nutrients through his system, because it can make the difference between good and poor health.

Butyrate is a short-chain fatty acid, produced in the hindgut. It regulates energy homeostasis by stimulating leptin production in adipocytes as well as provoking intestinal enteroendocrine L cells to secrete glucagonlike peptide-1 (GLP-1). These hormones have the effect of making the horse feel full. Butyrate is produced from bacteria – *Clostridia*, *Eubacteria* and *Roseburia*. It regulates the immune system by reducing the number of inflammatory cytokines and also increases the integrity of the gut wall by increasing the amount of tight junction proteins.

Foods that contain and *increase* the production of butyrate are seed heads, oats, barley, linseed and bran. A food that *reduces* the production of butyrate comes in the form of soya hulls. If you have an obese, EMS, laminitic horse or one prone to gastric ulcers then avoid soya hulls because they reduce butyrate by almost half, the effects of which are:
- A hungrier horse.
- Weak, tight junctions (leaky gut), gastric ulcers.
- A lowered immune system.

The respiratory system

The respiratory system of the horse needs to be in optimum health for the horse to function properly. When the respiratory system fails, for reasons we will discuss here, the horse can no longer function efficiently. And it has been discovered that there is a direct correlation between the health of the respiratory system and the gut biome of the horse.

Basic anatomy and function of the airway system

The horse is an obligate nose breather, meaning that he can only inhale air through his nostrils. The air travels up the nasal passage, into the trachea (consisting of one long tube through the neck), to the bronchi, which consist of a dual tube system, one for each of the lungs. When the horse swallows, the epiglottis covers the trachea to ensure that no food or water enters the windpipe and then opens up again to let air into the trachea. The trachea and bronchi warm and humidify the air as it is inhaled and they benefit from a special mechanism (based on the cilia) that helps to protect the lungs from infection and irritants from polluted air. (Even air that is seemingly clean carries within it all kinds of different external pollutants.) The function of these cilia is to increase the surface area where the filtering is activated to help protect the airways. A coordinated rhythm, which is activated by these tiny fibres, is aided by a thin membrane of mucus, suspended over the cilia, which moves to transport all the contaminants that adhere to it up and out of the airways, from where the mucus is swallowed by the horse.

The main organs of the lower airway system are the lungs, which are involved in gaseous exchange and work in conjunction with the horse's cardiovascular system to pump oxygen throughout the body and brain.

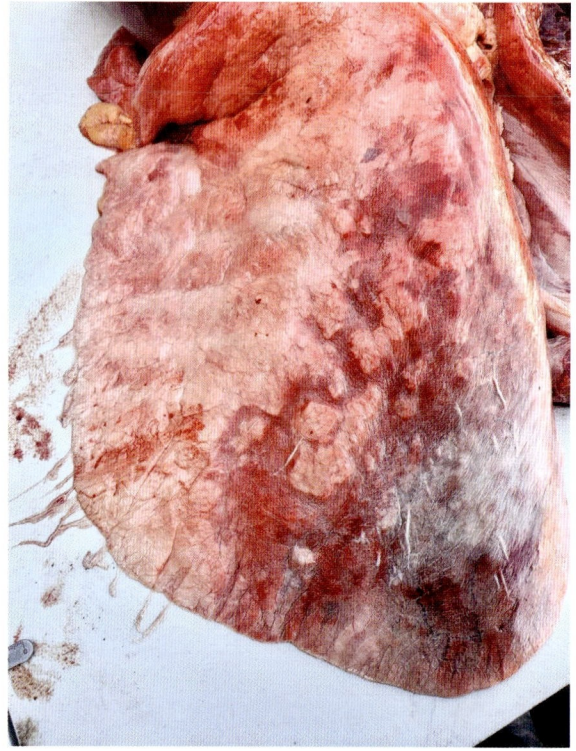

Lungs from a racehorse where chemicals were used to artificially expand the lungs during racing. The horse died of a fatal heart attack.

Becks Nairn

The liver

The liver is an important internal organ and is stituated in front of the stomach and behind the diaphragm. It consists of three lobes and it benefits from a very good blood supply.

Depending on the size of the horse the liver weighs 5–9 kg. It is in the liver that detoxification takes place. In fact the liver can be described as the metabolic centre of the horse as

it has over a hundred functions. Some key functions of the liver are as follows:
- Regulation of body temperature.
- Production of bile salts.
- Breakdown and removal of dead red blood cells.
- Breakdown of excess amino acids.
- Detoxification of pathogens and waste products.
- Cholesterol production and maintenance of lipid levels.
- Storing vitamins such as A, D, B12 and also iron.
- Blood storage.
- Maintainance of blood glucose levels.
- Synthesis of blood plasma proteins such as globulin, fibrinogen and albumin.

The first toxic effects or alterations to the liver begin when this vital organ is exposed to 5ppm (5 parts per million) of glyphosate, which can be found in horse and cattle feeds and the first signs of disruption to the endocrine system (Cushing's or EMS) begin at 0.5 ppm. Permitted glyphosate levels vary in different parts of the world. In the UK they are 400 ppm but in the USA they are even higher than that. European permitted levels are the lowest at 200 ppm. (*See also* Glyphosphate contaminants in Chapter 6.)

As many horse feed constituents nowadays are largely imported it is worth checking where your feed is sourced.

Levels of glyphosate currently allowed in animal foodstuff cultivation in the UK are as follows:
- 400 ppm: for animal feed.
- 310 ppm: for grain.
- 300 ppm: for grass, forage, fodder and hay.
- 120 ppm: for soybean hulls.
- 100 ppm: for soybean forage, corn, cereal forage, fodder and straw.

Levels allowed in human grade foods are lower.

Liver disease

Liver disease in horses is thought to be most often caused by exposure to toxic plants, other toxins or infection. Horses with liver disease may have low blood protein concentrations, especially albumin. We therefore need to consider whether the gut-liver axis could be an underlying and neglected primary cause. An overgrowth of pathogenic bacteria, together with a decrease in the good gut bacteria forming the 'resistome', increases the opportunities for the bad bacteria or bacterial toxins to translocate from the gut into the liver and on through the lymphatic/portal circulation system. Bacteria with translocating potential tend to live (colonise) within the deep layer of the mucus gel of the Crypts of Lieberkühn. The term bacterial translocation was first used in 1979, describing the passage of viable bacteria from the gut through the epithelial mucosa into the lamina propria and then to the mesenteric lymph nodes (MLN), to the liver and other organs. Since then, knowledge of how pathogenic bacteria impact health through this axis has grown rapidly. With 16S rRNA (this stands for gene cycle sequencing used for bacterial identification) real time technology, 'pools' of pathogenic translocating bacteria such as *Bartonella*, *Borrelia* and *Leptospira* have been detected in the guts of bats, squirrels, other wild mammals and cattle, increasing the opportunity for cross-contamination to equines through ingesting grass or other herbage from urine and/ or faeces polluted ground. Clearly it isn't possible to prevent re-contamination from environment pollution, but it is possible to feed the bacteria that form the 'resistome': these bacteria (*Roseburia*, *Eubacteria*) are the guardians along the gut wall, helping to prevent a potential 'break-out'. The best two herbs to help feed the 'resistome' and protect the liver from pathogenic translocation are wild peppermint and wild oregano.

The pancreas

Alongside the duodenum and behind the stomach lies the pancreas. This lobulated gland has two main functions, one being the production of pancreatic juices, which are secreted continually but in greater quantity when food is present in the stomach. This juice contains sodium bicarbonate which is alkaline and helps to reduce the acidity of foodstuffs.

Throughout the pancreas there are small masses of cells named the Islets of Langerhans. These specialist cells produce the hormones glucagon and insulin, which in turn help to maintain blood glucose levels.

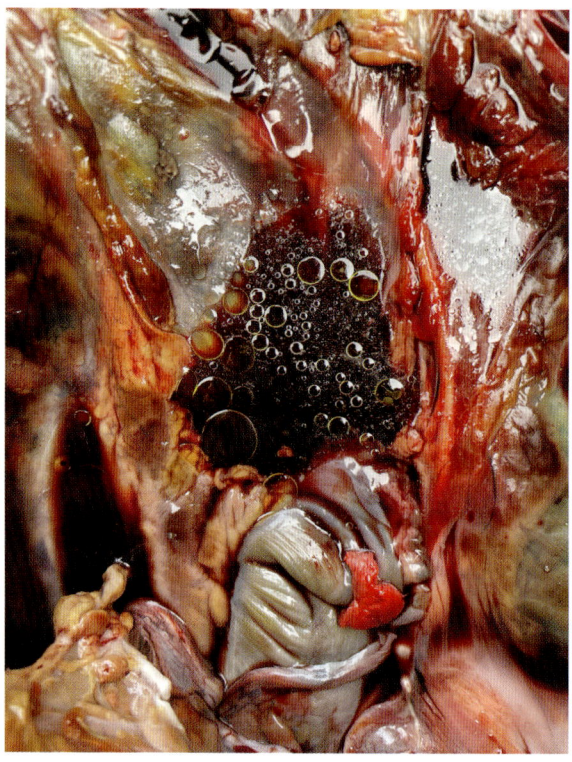

Blood – Three-year-old gelding, showing lipids floating in the plasma.
Becks Nairn

Blood

Blood consists of several cellular elements that all work together to ensure the health and well-being of the horse. These are white blood cells that act to protect the horse from infection, red blood cells that deliver oxygen to the body and brain, and the platelets, which are there to ensure that blood clots when there is a wound. All these are suspended in fluid called plasma. Like humans, horses also have different blood groups, eight in all. These are: A, C, D, K, P, Q, U and T.

The blood cells are predominantly formed in the tissue that is located in bone cavities, known as bone marrow. All red blood cells and platelets are formed within the red bone marrow, as are 60–70% of white blood cells. However, the remaining 30–40% of white blood cells, also known as lymphocytes, begin forming in the red bone marrow and then go on to mature in other parts of the body, such as the thymus, spleen and lymph nodes.

Functions of the blood

Blood is a multi-functional transporter. It transports hormones to different parts of the body. It carries oxygen (oxygenated blood) from the lungs and carbon dioxide to the lungs, to be expelled via exhalation. Blood also takes waste products to the kidneys and liver, where they are broken down and later eliminated from the body through faecal matter and urine. Also, as it is circulating throughout the body, blood carries a number of important nutrients such as fats, minerals, vitamins and sugar to the body's tissues.

Blood disorders

There are a number of blood disorders that horses can suffer from, but by far the most common is septicaemia. This arises when environmental bacteria enter the bloodstream, either by the horse breathing them in or ingesting them. Bacteria can, for example, be found in mouldy foodstuffs such as hay or old hard feeds, or proliferate where vermin have defecated or urinated on feed, but they can also be found in water, or be airborne. Septicaemia can also occur when open wounds are not thoroughly cleaned out and become septic.

    Septicaemia is classified as SIRS. It arises when the white blood cells, which are there to fight infection, are no longer able to cope and the immune system becomes overwhelmed. This will affect all vital organs, tissue and joints and may present by the presence of a high fever, breathlessness, low blood pressure, an increased heart rate and shivering. The horse's behaviour might become erratic as the central nervous system is attacked. He will become inert and have difficulty focusing. If you suspect septicaemia contact your vet immediately.

---

1. Salivary glands
   - Frape, D. (2010). 4th edn, *Equine Nutrition and Feeding*.

4.
The Brain and Central Nervous System – Gut Bacteria

The horse's brain is very small compared to his body size and counts for about 0.1% of the total bodyweight. The brain consists of a fatty sponge-like mass, akin to the texture of bone marrow. There are three sections to the brain namely:
- Brain stem – controls life functions.
- Cerebrum – the centre of conscious decision-making.
- Cerebellum – from here motor control and movement are controlled.

The spinal cord

This emerges from beneath the brain. It is sectioned into three parts which correspond to the vertebral bodies i.e. the spinal bones from neck to tail, in the following order: cervical, lumbar, sacral and caudal (tail) segments. The brain and spinal cord are covered by a thin membrane of specialised tissues – the meninges, and cerebro-spinal fluid serves to protect the brain and spinal cord. The peripheral nervous system is formed by neurons of the cranial and spinal nerves that branch out to the rest of the body. Both the central and peripheral nervous systems contain billions of cells called neurons. These neurons connect with each other to form neurological circuits, which allow information to travel along the body via electrical signals.

How the horse uses his brain

The horse's brain is sometimes known as the 'reptilian' brain; this means that the horse gets triggered readily into the flight, fight or freeze response. As the horse is a prey animal, he needs to respond to these signals quickly for survival. He does, however, have a highly developed cerebral cortex that is responsible for various functions: perception, memory and higher thought processes. The surface of each hemisphere in the horse's cerebrum is made up of this 'grey matter' (the cerebral cortex), which is folded to increase the surface area available within the skull. This contains what are called the 'basal nuclei', which receive information from the cortex and assist in regulation of skeletal movement and other higher motor functions. The frontal lobe within the cortex serves as the 'motor cortex'. It assists the horse to navigate his surroundings, learn how to perform coordinated movements, and to plan action. However, although the cortex covers many functionalities responsible for decision-making, memory and conscious thought, the horse is actually mostly concerned with balance, muscle coordination and general body functions. This is because, as alluded to above, he needs to be alert at all times. In case something comes after him, it is vital that he keeps his mind 'in the moment', being ready at any time to fight or run away. (He will freeze when there is no way out.)

Horses are not capable of manipulation or reasoning, *in the way some people think they are*, when their horse reacts 'aggressively', does not want to get into the trailer, bites, runs away and persists in staying out of their human's reach, or reacts in any way unreasonable to the human mind. By this, we mean that some people become anthropomorphic about what their horse is capable of, and assume that horses can act or react just like humans – for example manipulate someone into doing or not doing something, or behave in a way a human would when faced with a challenge. 'Reasonable' behaviour of this sort is not within their remit as a thought process. If they are pressured into behaving in a certain way, they are not capable of 'reasoning' their way out of something that alarms them. They might react by kicking or running away from someone, which to the involved human, would not be reasonable when that person clearly had no bad intentions. They don't understand why the horse is still protesting when asked to do something which, from their own perspective, seemed harmless.

Another thing the equine brain instinctively concerns itself with is food and water, something the horse is in constant search of. Further to this, when we talk about diet and brain the connection between the horse's stomach and his brain is a field of research that is very much at the forefront of the science of feeding and nutrition. In fact, research suggests that the connection is so strong that the stomach could almost be regarded as the second brain, as indicated in the following text.

Abstract on genomic sequencing

Genomic sequencing and translational metabolomics have allowed us to gain deeper and more meaningful insight into the pathogenesis of metabolic-related syndromes of horses. The data included in this chapter has been gathered from a population of over 2,000 competition horses and racehorses, with freely grazing horses as controls. The aim is to have a greater and more precise understanding of the effects that diet, management and stress have on the health and welfare of the horse.

The gut-brain axis

The gut-brain axis is a signalling or communication system that allows the gut to 'talk' to the brain and vice versa. The two organs do this by way of the immune system, the hormonal and the nervous system.

The microbe-gut-brain axis

More recently the gut bacteria that reside in the gastro-intestinal tract of all mammals have been identified as the major component in the gut-brain communication system. The microbe-gut-brain axis is more extensive than the gut-brain axis and includes immune cells, glands, the gut, the nervous system, hormones, intestinal bacteria and the brain itself. The main purpose of this axis is to maintain homeostasis (balance; a steady state) able to provide the best functioning conditions of the gastro-intestinal tract. When an imbalance in microbe-gut-brain axis occurs an opportunity for disease or discomfort is created. This can be all the gastric discomfort syndromes including colic and colitis, the onset of obesity, EMS and laminitis, and gastric pain. It can also involve other organs of the body, such as the musculoskeletal system.

Triglyceride – the leptin transporter to the brain

Triglyceride is the transporter of leptin into the brain, but it is available only in relatively small amounts in nature and then only alongside more complex lipids.

Triglycerides come from both plants containing complex lipids with few triglycerides, and processed food such as pellets/mixes and extruded grains, which contain few complex lipids but high amounts of triglycerides (high triglycerides are also an indication of EMS). Complex lipids are contained in the seeds and pollen of grass and plants, examples being omega-3 polyunsaturated fatty acids, phospholipids, inositol lipids and second messenger lipids. These are responsible for building healthy membranes, and for central nervous system function. They are also responsible for the transport of leptin across the blood-brain barrier and for building the barriers (rafts) between brain compartments. Triglycerides are purely a source of energy. The adipocyte or fat cells are designed for continuous synthesis and breakdown of triglycerides, but high energy intake, without high exercise, means high circulating levels, which could trigger a negative response from a finely tuned mechanism by causing it to go into overproduction of triglycerides, which in turn may lead to an unhealthy imbalance and make the horse ill with EMS, obesity and other metabolic problems.

Lipids contained in processed oils/foods such as pellets and coarse mixes will produce higher levels of circulating triglycerides than complex lipids from plants. High circulating triglycerides are a symptom of EMS. Beware of including any type of oil as part of the daily ration to any horse who has EMS, is overweight or is doing little or no exercise. Oil is great for short periods but shouldn't be included or seen to be a normal part of the ration for any horse not involved in extreme exercise, needing an extra energy supply. Avoid over-processed and extruded grains, pelleted feed and coarse mixes.

An important message to remember is that all native breeds (except the old and infirm) should be allowed to experience a period of being cold, wet and hungry; they are totally geared to cope with this. This is better for them than a lifetime of metabolic dysfunction, but understandably difficult for the owner to do.

Leptin

Leptin itself is a hormone and signalling chemical that originates and is released from adipose tissue, it starts out as a 'friend' by creating and regulating an energy balance through a wide range of functions. It also adjusts the feeling of hunger and tells the horse to stop eating when full. Its main purpose is to prevent death from starvation through the control of energy when food is sparse. Using gene mapping, it has recently been discovered that, as a consequence of modern diets, the leptin receptor is mutating and it has now taken on a different, more sinister role, although its precise effect will vary between individuals, for reasons related to the following. Because leptin is released from the adipose tissue, more fat deposits equal more leptin. In a well-covered but not fat horse (BMI score of less than 7, 'cresty' neck score of 3 or less) leptin will be working in a normal way, active during meal times, telling the horse to stop eating when the leptin receptors signal to the horse that he is full. The problems start when the horse has access to too many simple carbohydrates (e.g. high-sugar grass, corn syrup sprayed onto many bagged foods) and processed foods, which disrupt the ability of leptin to stop the horse from consuming too much. Unregulated leptin creates 'Hungry Horse Syndrome' in which the horse is permanently hungry and desires to eat continually (we all know a pony/horse like that!). A high-sugar/simple carbohydrate sort of diet triggers a resistance to the action of leptin, causing the horse to gorge on his food and seek to eat more and more high-sugar food to satiate the continuous feeling of emptiness leptin resistance creates. As leptin resistance increases so does insulin resistance, causing spikes of blood sugar levels as the horse is driven to consume more and more sugar without becoming satiated or full.

It's interesting to note that stress and periods of box rest also cause leptin levels to rise. During leptin resistance the hormone starts to act in an uncontrolled fashion and simply starts to 'do its own thing' (self-regulation) and leptin receptors undergo a process of genetic mutation. Evidence suggests that central leptin resistance in horses causes obesity and that obesity-induced leptin resistance injures numerous peripheral tissues, including the liver, pancreas, platelets and the vascular system (laminitis). This metabolic- and inflammatory-mediated damage may result from either resistance to leptin's action in selective tissues such as the vascular system, or excess leptin action from adiposity-associated hyperleptinaemia. In this sense, the term 'leptin resistance' encompasses a complex pathophysiological phenomenon. The leptin pathways include functional interactions with insulin and the innate immune system, such as interleukin-6.

Leptin levels will decrease with exercise and limited or no access to sugar or processed food, so track systems and paradise paddocks come into their own through the long winter months as they prevent the horse from standing for long periods in a box, which causes a natural rise in leptin. (Paradise paddocks contain a great diversity of forage, without feeds that are high in sugars or starch – so a paradise for the horse is that there won't be anything in the paddock that is going to trigger any kind of nutritional dysfunctionality – plus they get the chance to do some free foraging.) For an individual with Hungry Horse Syndrome, if you do have to keep him in the stable for long periods, throw him some willow, blackberry, gorse and hawthorn to pick his way through as these contain antioxidants that help to increase tissue sensitivity, which is a good thing.

Gut bacteria

The microbes in the horse's gut have a profound effect on his well-being. As explained in the *Journal of Internal Veterinary Medicine*, gastro-intestinal problems can start from birth and continue to be a problem throughout life. It has been estimated that gastro-intestinal upsets (dysbiosis) and imbalances affect 65–85% of all horses. Imbalances can manifest in a wide range of symptoms that many horse owners can instantly identify with, the most common being:

o   Changes in temperament.
o   Sore feet.

- o Faecal Water Syndrome.
- o General discomfort.
- o Laminitis.
- o Obesity.
- o Colic.
- o Colitis.

Inflammation starts in the gut

Inflammation of the gut is linked to major health concerns such as laminitis, EMS, colitis, ulcers and colic, as the gut is the place where the 'outside' (grasses, hay, hard feed, water and soil), meets the 'inside' (the gut bacteria). It may be our horses' food and environment that is making our horses sick. If you are struggling to treat the conditions mentioned above using veterinary science, it may be time to try environmental science instead, as all the aspects of gut health reflect the nutrition and environment to which the horse is exposed.

The primary role of the microbiome is to protect the host (horse) from disease; when and if this fails or is compromised then the horse becomes ill – it is that simple. The environment is in crisis now, causing a similar gut crisis. There is plenty of published scientific evidence to show that our environment is sick from the use of pesticides, herbicides, fertilisers and the use of single-species monocrops to provide 'nutrition'. As the decline in the environment has been going on for several decades now, it is realistic to understand that it might take some time to restore a healthy diet/environment and a healthy gastro-intestinal tract for horses. As our equine population database grows, the microbiome of horses with ill health can be defined into two categories:

- o Imbalanced – core; beneficial bacteria present but at the wrong levels.
- o Imbalanced and missing – a portion of the core beneficial bacteria are not present, and the other members are at the wrong levels, i.e. either too high or too low.

Using AI it is now possible to define the patterns and profiles of disease. All of the emerging profiles detected by the machine learning platform of horses with laminitis, EMS, colic, ulcers and colitis have higher than might be reasonably expected levels of antibiotic-resistant bacteria and environmental pathogens, often with an extremely low alpha diversity score. (Alpha diversity is a measure of microbial diversity within a specific faecal sample.) Restoring the diversity of the biome should then become the number one priority.

Interaction of gut bacteria and parasites

There may be an interaction between the gut bacteria and parasites, such as strongyles in horses, as both share the same internal communal area, and this interaction may be the cause of a detrimental health change.

Are there then differences between horses who are naturally resistant to parasite infection and those who are susceptible?

For the first time, this relationship has been studied and was reported in a paper published in March 2018.[1] The study showed that horses resistant to parasite infection had a very different

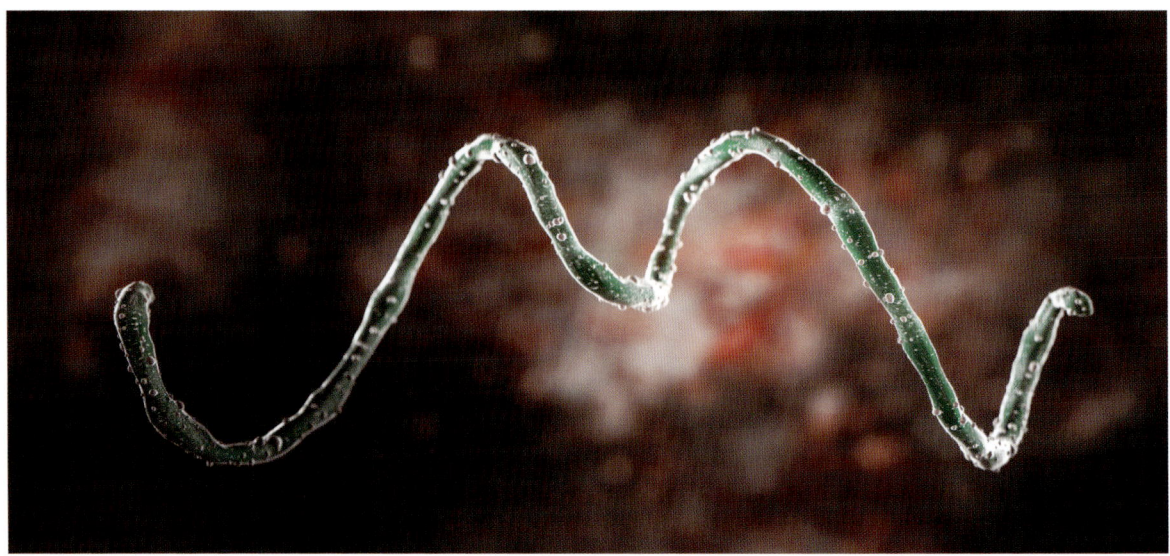

Spirochaete bacteria.
Shutterstock (publication permission)

immunological (immune system) profile from those susceptible to parasite infection, and also a different microbial population.

Following exposure to natural infection, the ten parasite-susceptible ponies had persistent lymphocytosis (an increase in the white blood cells that fight off infections, indicating a change or a challenge to the immune system) with a reduction in *Ruminococcus*, *Clostridium XIV* and *Lachnospiraceae*.

There was also an increase in pathogenic (disease-causing) bacteria *Pseudomonas* and *Campylobacter*, which caused a change in the gut wall mucosal homeostasis and the Immunoglobulin A antibody (IgA) at day 92. The susceptible ponies had a different metabolic profile and reduced immune system response compared to those that were parasite resistant.

Horses with faecal egg counts 0–800 eggs/g, did not exhibit major changes in the gut microbiota. As strongyles are highly prevalent in horses and are resistant to wormers, will this knowledge help you as an owner decide when and whether to use a wormer? Also, if you do choose to worm and the strongyles are resistant, does this mean that your horse's health and metabolism are permanently below par?

Lots of trees and plants contain tannins that work against parasites such as sainfoin, oak, ash, chestnut and heather, and horses will often seek tannins out – in fact sometimes it appears to be a seasonal pursuit.

Helminths

Helminths are the collective name for worm-parasite infestation in the gastro-intestinal tract of the horse. The three main categories are: roundworms (nematodes), tapeworms (cestodes) and flatworm (trematodes). Cyathostomins (small redworms, or small strongyle) are found in the large intestine and mostly affect horses between the age of one to three, although they can be found in all ages. The time from first infection to eggs being found in the faeces is between two to three months, but may take up to two years. When there is a large mass of Cyathostomins present, with the emergence of immature worms from the gut wall, this can affect the horse with weight loss, a dull coat, reduced energy and, in severe cases, colic. Threadworms (Strongyloides westeri or Anguillula) are found in the small intestine of a young foal, usually less than five or six months old. From first infection to eggs being present in the faeces is between one to two weeks. The outward signs are really quite rare, but they may present themselves by the foal developing dermatitis of the limbs and diarrhoea.

Although helminths are regarded as undesirable, there is some evidence that they can make contributions to health, and the following are the top five benefits:

1. Helminths have been shown to exert immunoregulatory effects on their hosts.
2. Removal of the helminth infection removes one aspect of the immunoregulation effect and changes the dynamics of inflammatory responses.
3. Removal of helminths causes a significant inflammatory response.
4. Treating with anthelmintics (wormers) causes an overzealous immune reaction to encysted larvae and may be a factor in the development of acute larval cyathostominosis.
5. Anthelmintic treatment leads to dysbiosis, inflammation and colitis as helminths help to increase alpha diversity in the gut bacteria and getting rid of them causes an increase in inflammation.

---

1. Interaction of gut bacteria and parasites
    - Clark, A., Sallé, G., Ballan, V., Reigner, F., Meynadier, A., Cortet, J., Mach, N. (2018). 'Strongyle Infection and Gut Microbiota: Profiling of Resistant and Susceptible Horses Over a Grazing Season', Frontiers in physiology, *Physiology Journal* 9, 272.

5. Prescription Drugs, Other Medications and Their Effects on the Gut

Danilon/bute

Giving Danilon/bute (phenylbutazone) to horses with laminitis might be the quickest way to ease the pain but, unfortunately, this popular and commonly used drug has no effect on the high levels of circulating inflammatory chemicals causing damage to the sensitive laminae, peaking at 20–48 hours after the onset of lameness. Whilst bute makes sense initially (fast pain relief is essential), there is sadly no resolution to the damage that continues unabated in the feet. The horse will still need extra doses of antioxidants to minimise and mop up the effects of the circulating inflammatory chemicals that bute is unable to change or affect, the symptoms of which are Obel grade 1 laminitis (paddling or lifting one foot then the other, short, stilted gait in trot). Horses with the endocrinopathic type of laminitis will have raised levels of IL-1 IL-1β, IL-6, IL-12p35, COX-2, E-selectin and ICAM-1 in a series of responses to this. Whilst most of these substances are involved in functions of the immune system, COX-2 (Cyclooxygenase-2) increases the enzymes that contribute to inflammation and pain and, whilst the bute will mask the pain, it does not alter the cocktail of deadly chemicals that the laminitic episode has released – these chemicals rapidly causing devastating levels of breakdown. A mixture of five of the strongest plant anti-inflammatories is required to dampen down, buffer and reduce the effects of all the chemicals released, and such anti-inflammatories are usually found in the bark or more woody part of the plant/shrub; the best to use include curcumin, uncaria tomentosa, smilax and Espinheira Santa (more commonly known by its scientific name, Maytenus ilicifolia, which we will generally use through this text). The best way to dose is by finely grinding the dried plant material, mixing 120 g with 20 ml of omega-3 oil and syringing into the ration or over hay three times per day. Freely foraging horses will find enough in wild barberry, blueberry, and white willow.

Tryptophan

Tryptophan is an amino acid, an important building block in the proper function of the nervous system and directly linked through the gut-brain axis. Tryptophan is found in oats, barley, alfalfa and soya, and is an important building block for the horses' nervous system and is the precursor for the synthesis of serotonin in the brain, the synthesisation which regulates moods. Thus it is also known as the 'happy' hormone.

Serotonin acts as a neurotransmitter between nerve cells. It is found in the part of the brain where the horse processes moods of calmness and relaxation. If enough tryptophan is available to produce serotonin it keeps the brain balanced and functioning normally.

Some 90% of the serotonin is employed by the gut. When a horse is stressed and preparing for a flight or fight reaction, the serotonin production increases, causing a 'nervous' gut. The muscles in the gut contract and the horse defecates to get rid of the bulk in his gut, so he is able to react faster when it comes to fighting or running away. However, when stress-related serotonin is used up by the stress factor, there might not be enough tryptophan available to counteract this dysbiosis. The horse will become agitated; possibly aggressive, because the balance within the gut-brain axis and the serotonin needed to keep the horse in a calm and relaxed mood is disturbed. This is why horses are often given tryptophan as a 'calming' supplement. However, a problem arises when the horse has no stress factors to outweigh the balance of synthesised serotonin and enough tryptophan to keep the mood easy and relaxed, and is then given tryptophan as a supplement. This distorts the fragile balance between natural levels to levels that will become a problem rather than an aid.

Research has discovered some interesting 'unintended consequences' in horses given too much tryptophan in an attempt to help them cope in stressful situations. Performance horses who were found to have higher than normal levels of tryptophan tended to be tiring quite soon into the work. It was found that when glucose was used as infusion together with the tryptophan supplement, this would largely negate the side-effect of fatigue and significantly increased the time before energy depletion, without causing the levels of amino acids to change. This happened, despite the fact that tryptophan increases with exercise. The conclusion is that we need to be careful how we use this powerful supplement as it can sedate instead of calm.

Antibiotics

A new study has found that the use of antibiotics alters the profile of the microbiome, causing a loss of diversity and metabolic changes that are long-lasting.[1] The changes appear to be greater in the microbiome of horses having accompanying diarrhoea. Antibiotics cause an increase in Bacteroidetes and Proteobacteria, whilst reducing Firmicutes and Actinobacteria, and thus the dramatic decrease in diversity.

The gut bacteria have a strong effect on the gut metabiome, one of the major changes being in the essential amino acid tryptophan. During antibiotic use tryptophan metabolites are increased in the faeces of horses. This can mean a loss of the metabolite in the gastro-intestinal tract, causing inflammation through the reduction of the gut wall barrier. Other changes include an increase in metabolites that cause a reduction in glycolysis and an increase in lipid metabolism, both of which are linked to colitis.

Omeprazole

Omeprazole is a commonly prescribed drug for gastric ulcers in horses, it is a PPI (proton pump inhibitor), and has until recently been considered a safe drug, but recent information has come to light regarding the detrimental effects to health in long-term use. Omeprazole suppresses the gastric acid that causes gastritis (inflammation of the stomach wall), and also stimulates the production of gastrin, which is a potent growth factor known to cause hyperplasia of the enterochromaffin-like cells adding to the gastritis.

A healthy stomach pH creates an environment where the conversion of ingested nitrates (grass, forage, concentrates, water) to a safe form (n-nitridation) is achieved by the release of ascorbic acid from healthy gastric mucosa. When this is missing, as in the case of long-term use of omeprazole, then the nitrates are converted to substances that are inflammatory and detrimental to the health of the gut wall. Omeprazole also causes the proliferation of some bacteria that also increase the amount of nitrate within the stomach.

If your horse has had long-term treatment with omeprazole, then increasing the amount of dietary plant antioxidants in the diet will help restore the integrity and health of the stomach. All plant antioxidants strongly promote the release of ascorbic acid. Diverse meadow communities are full of plants that are both anti-ulcerogenic and antimicrobial, two of the best being shepherd's purse (*Capsella bursa-pastoris*) and Chickweed (*Stellaria media*). Both are good fresh or dried and can be offered as a daily hedgerow cutting mix for stabled horses.

Cyanobacteria

High concentrations of *Cyanobacteria* can be found in contaminated spirulina or blue/green algae supplements, contamination levels often being over and above the concentration levels approved by the World Health Organization (WHO). Spirulina and blue/green algae are popular supplements for horses, but when scientists tested eighteen of these products, twelve were contaminated in some way.

The presence of *Cyanobacteria* in the hindgut of the horse causes an increase in other opportunistic bacteria; in the case of the horses studied there was a rise in the paludibacter. These proliferate when the hindgut is inflamed and levels are higher in horses with strongyle infection, suggesting that these bacteria thrive and increase during an increase of other pathogens.

The liver must work to process the toxins released by the *Cyanobacteria*, increasing the pressure on internal organs and increasing the chance of developing liver damage or infections.

Diversity within the minor groups of bacteria has been cited as being important for overall health and stability of the hindgut, and of the host. The bacteria, viruses, archaea and fungi contribute to health by acting as a braking system to prevent opportunistic bacteria from mounting a coup.

Tips for feeding:
o If you are feeding spirulina, make sure that it comes from a reputable source, with QC in place.
o Avoid feeding it continuously to give the biome a chance to recover.
o Feed fresh antioxidants alongside or allow the horse to find his own.

A note on other natural compounds for medicinal use on horses

Although the equine market is flooded with alternative remedies for health, they are often used without an in-depth knowledge of the compounds involved and how they best fit in against the framework of medical research of the disease state in question. Therefore, when foods become used as medicine, a word of caution! Some natural compounds can be designated prohibited substances in the world of equestrian sport. The International Federation for Equestrian Sports (FEI) gives warnings about the power of plants that contain compounds with a sedative/anti-inflammatory action that is often stronger than synthetic drugs. The FEI website states that: 'The ingredients and properties of products to be classified as prohibited are valerian, kava kava, passionflower, skullcap, chamomile, vervain, leopard's bane, night shade, capsaicin, comfrey, Devil's claw, hops, laurel, lavender, red poppy and rauwolfia.' Some supplements contain more substances than the ingredients listed and some have been linked to contamination. The FEI provides a warning regarding the use of supplements generally, and that supplement use must be recorded in the horse's FEI Medication Logbook.

Many herbal supplements contained in over-the-counter products contain compounds chemically similar to non-steroidal anti-inflammatory drugs (NSAIDs), or compounds that are on the prohibited or controlled list for competition. Even plants growing in the pasture or hedgerow have the potential to cause a failed test in competition. For example, coumarin is no. 259 on the FEI prohibited substances list and its activity is described as an anticoagulant. The medical dictionary defines coumarin as a 'toxic white crystalline lactone $C_9H_6O_2$ with an odour of new-mown hay found in plants or made synthetically and used especially in perfumery and as the parent compound in various anticoagulant agents (warfarin)'. The synthetic drug warfarin, no. 1003 on the FEI prohibited list, was originally developed from a spoiled clover crop that contained a bacterial metabolite of coumarin over fifty years ago. Whilst the FEI lists prohibitive substances numerically, the British Horseracing Authority (BHA) simply states that the use of any substance affecting blood coagulation is prohibited. *Pharmacognosy* (Trease and Evans), the most respected and accurate source of information about the use of medicinal plants, describes coumarin as being a natural component of plants – around 1,000 have been isolated and coumarin itself has been found in around 150 species of plants, mostly present as trans-O-glucosyloxycinnamic acid. It is only once the plant is cut as a crop (hay, alfalfa, red clover, sweet clover) or damaged (as in the case of hawthorn and horse chestnut during the cutting of a hedge) and dried and gives off the new-mown smell, which intensifies on drying, that coumarin (benzo-alpha pyrone) is formed. The highest content of coumarin is contained in sweet clover, which is grown extensively in America and Canada as a hay and forage crop, and in red clover, which is found in UK swards and sold as a seed mix suitable for equine pasture. Some plants such as sunflowers and soya are actually manipulated or engineered to produce more coumarin as this increases the plant's ability to resist disease.

Whilst plants containing coumarin are on the prohibited list, salicylic acid, described in the FEI list as a non-steroidal anti-inflammatory drug, is on the controlled substance list. The medical dictionary describes salicylic acid as a phenolic acid that is used in making pharmaceuticals and dyes, and as an antiseptic and disinfectant, especially in the treatment of skin. It is also used as an analgesic and antipyretic and in the treatment of rheumatism and is better known to us as aspirin. Aspirin is made from acetyl-salicylic acid and was developed in 1853 from willow bark and meadowsweet, which contain a natural ingredient called salicin – a similar chemical compound with similar attributes to aspirin but possibly without the detrimental gastric side-effects. Both salicin (willow and meadowsweet) and acetyl-salicylic acid (aspirin) break down in the body to form salicylic acid and this is the metabolite found in the urine. At the point when they leave the body in urine, there are no differences between the synthetic and the natural chemicals; they are the same chemical compound. As mentioned above, salicylic acid is on the controlled medication list of the FEI (and is prohibited by the BHA) but now that bute is once more a prohibited substance, meadowsweet has obviously become a very popular choice of additive in anti-inflammatory formulas for horses. This gives rise to some questions:

- Is it accurate to describe salicylic acid as a non-steroidal anti-inflammatory drug as described by the FEI when salicylic acid is the urine metabolite?
- If salicylic acid is on the controlled substance list does this mean that there are threshold limits in urine tests to accommodate the fact that horses grazing may ingest salicin as a common component of native pasture plants and as an additive to many popular feeds and supplements, or does the term 'controlled substance' relate to the prescription and administration of aspirin (Acetylsalicylic acid)?
- Is it acceptable to state on the packaging of formulas containing salicins that they are approved by the FEI, BHA, and any other governing body, or should the label explain that the urine metabolite is on the controlled medication list?
- Do the companies that include willow and meadowsweet add a standardised extract with a quantifiable amount of salicin or, if using the complete herb, do they carry out separate tests using chromatography to determine the likely levels of salicylic acid in the urine metabolites and advise people who are involved in top-level competition about them?
- Meadowsweet is also an anticoagulant well known for its interaction with warfarin. Should meadowsweet now be included on the prohibited list along with coumarin, as the wording from the FEI is that coumarin is prohibited as an anticoagulant along with any other biological substance with a similar action?
- Acetyl-salicylic acid is rapidly metabolised to salicylic acid by plasma and gastric esterases. Salicylate, an active form of aspirin, is widely distributed in the body, metabolised mainly in the liver by conjugation, and excreted in the urine mostly as salicylic acid.

Where does all this leave the end user of a feed or supplement? It is a grey area with many pitfalls for the unwary. Manufacturers used to state on their labels that their supplements are 'approved/allowed' or contain 'no banned ingredients' or are compliant with the rules of the BHA, FEI, British Show Jumping Association (BSJA) and British Equestrian Federation (BEF). Now they provide free 'supplement logs' so that supplements can be recorded, presumably so that an inspection by the governing bodies can highlight the risks of taking supplements that may be regarded as performance enhancers, or so that they can be banned during competition. The rules aren't clear and, as plants contain hundreds of active compounds, it is unlikely that the governing body representative will know what a supplement contains, therefore the end user needs to ask certain things of their supplement manufacturer: Are they trained in ethnopharmaceuticals? Are they able to supply relevant information concerning the ingredients?

In most cases the answer will be no – for example, scientific testing can be hugely expensive, well out of the budget of smaller supplement manufacturers. There are serious consequences of a positive test, but the only way you can be sure about what exactly is in a supplement is through the transparency of the manufacturer you are dealing with and their knowledge of just how the supplements are manufactured. Open and honest dialogue is the key.

Natural medications – the other side of the coin

As we have just seen, there are some natural compounds that could in theory be fed to horses, but might contravene existing competition rules and have unwanted side effects, and some that might be described simply as 'grey areas'. That said, many plants definitely have a potential to be used as medicines, in fact the World Health Organization (WHO) predicts that 70% of all medicines will be made from plants within the next twenty years. One reason for this is that it is predicted that there will be fewer synthetic medicines available because of the cost of development and research and only chronic diseases will eventually be able to carry the costs, so now is a good time to learn more about the natural compounds from plants that can be medicinal without synthesis. In fact the WHO estimates that as many as 80% of the world's more than six billion people already rely primarily on animal- and plant-based medicines. Traditional human populations have a broad natural pharmacopoeia consisting of wild plant and animal species. Ingredients sourced from wild plants and animals are not only used in traditional medicines, but are also increasingly valued as raw materials in the preparation of modern medicines and herbal preparations. One good example is Taxol (made from the yew tree), which is one of the most promising new drugs available for the treatment of breast and ovarian cancer in humans. Its novel mechanism of action has led to the synthesis of several Taxol-like compounds that are used to induce remission in cases of advanced cancers unresponsive to other treatments.

The equine market is far smaller than the human one and, for the financial reasons mentioned earlier, will suffer increasingly from lack of research. Therefore, perhaps it is time to consider different management strategies to promote health in our horses.

Although, as we have seen, the equine market is flooded with alternative remedies for health, they are often used without an in-depth knowledge of the compounds involved and how they best fit in against the framework of medical research of the disease state in question. Plant compounds are best grown as medicinal crops where control of soil and climate are important contributors to effective levels and active compounds.

---

1. Antibiotics
    - Arnold, C., Pilla, R., Chaffin, K., Lidbury, J., Steiner, J., Suchodolski, J., 'Alterations in the fecal microbiome and metabolome of horses with antimicrobial-associated diarrhea compared to antibiotic-treated and non-treated healthy case controls', Animals (Basel). 2021 Jun 17;11(6):1807.

6.
Feeding the Horse – How to Prepare Your Own Feeds

How horses digest different types of food

It is fundamentally important to understand that what you put in will determine what you get out.

Food particle size does make a difference to the health of the microbiome, reinforcing the need to provide horses with fresh green food, which is naturally complex. This is especially important for overall gut health, especially for horses with EMS/laminitis or obesity.

Pelleted hay/grass and chaff are both equally digestible but have a different effect on the gastro-intestinal tract. The main difference between chaff and nuts is that the retention time of the nuts in the caecum and colon is longer, but there is less degradation by the microbial population and a reduction in the selective retention of fibres (to allow for even more microbial degradation). In other words, once in the gut, the pellets go through like a slow soup whilst the chaff is continuously degraded and sorted by the enzymes and microbiota.

Hay that has not yet been cut, or that has been stored for winter feeding (both forms being termed 'standing hay', in the UK and USA respectively) would have an even better effect, as the long particles of hemi-cellulose and cellulose would have been retained and degraded for even longer, providing important nutrition for the microbes.

Pellets produce a lower level of these particles than coarse or straight feed, as in straight micronised oats, barley, corn, soya, etc. These contribute to energy for the horse but are also used to rebuild the gut wall. They are also anti-inflammatory, although some short-chain fatty acids are more desirable than others. Propionate (from grass and grains) will be further degraded by the liver to make glucose, an unwanted end-product for EMS/laminitis prone horses.

Pellets remain in the gut for longer than straight feed, but don't provide the same nutrition to the microbial population – for example, the archaea and fungi require the cell walls of plants for food, but once a pellet has been ground there is no cell wall left. Pellets containing soya and NIS (Nutritionally Improved Straw, which is particularly high in fibre), produce more propionate than is healthy or required and the ingredient list of feeds should be checked for processed grains or ingredients. Nonetheless, good-quality and preferably organic pellets are a great basis for horses and ponies, as long as they are also offered fresh or dried plant nutrition and hay to provide a high percentage of fibre and phytonutrients.

To offer an updated addition to Xenophon's wise observation 'no foot, no horse', in the current environment the new saying should surely be 'no gut, no horse'.

If you want to move away from manufactured feeds, in order to ensure that you know exactly what is in your horse's ration, we provide a breakdown of different types of feed, to enable you to make considered choices.

Common foodstuffs for horses

Cereals

Barley

Barley kernels should be round, plump and shiny and should not be fed whole as they will not be digested but will be passed straight through the intestinal tract, thus adding no value. Barley comes flaked, micronised or cooked. You can also cook your own barley to break up the hard shells and make it more palatable. Owing to its high carbohydrate content barley is a fattening cereal and should not be fed to horses who are obese, laminitic or suffer with other intestinal conditions. Barley is, however, suitable for horses who do need to put on some weight. They are a medium-energy feed. (*See* Preparing your own feeds in Chapter 6 on how to prepare raw barley.)

Raw barley.
Geertje French

Raw oats.
Geertje French

Oats

Good-quality oats have a slightly sweet smell and are pale-yellow in colour. They are plump and need to be free of dust particles. It is important that they are stored in a dust-free and dry environment and away from vermin and insects. If left in a damp environment, moisture will speed up the proliferation of mould spores.

To aid digestion it is necessary for the oats to be bruised or rolled. However, as rolling can decrease the nutritional value, they need be consumed within a few weeks in order to remain fresh. Oats are low in essential amino acids, so do not provide good protein value. On the other hand, they are high in fibre and are kind and gentle on the microbiome. However, they also have a high starch content, which makes them a high-energy feed, so they should only be fed in small quantities and are not for horses who are already 'fizzy'. On the other hand, high-performance horses are fed oats to enhance their energy.

Some horses are allergic to oats and this can manifest on the skin as small nodules, itchiness or other allergic reaction symptoms, which might include shortness of breath and gastro-intestinal discomfort. It should also be noted that horses can become victims of colic when the digestive tract gets impacted with foodstuff and the machinery of the tract comes to a halt because of the obstruction. For this reason oats need to be fed with other feeds; never dry and always micronised or rolled. Steeping oats with some apple pulp and other moisture-filled feeds will ensure that the oats do not clump together in the intestine and cause a colic episode. (This advice applies to all dry bulk feeds such as maize, barley, soya, etc. and all dry food stuffs.) Colic is addressed in detail in Chapter 10.

Maize

Maize should be a good yellow colour: ageing will turn it white. It can either be home-cooked or bought ready-cooked and flaked. As with all cereals it should be stored in a clean, dry place away from direct sunlight, as this will lower its value. Maize is a high-energy foodstuff and is unsuitable for most horses. It is also very low in fibre, so should only ever make up 20–25% of the overall ration for horses in hard work, as it is higher in protein than oats and barley. As is the case with oats, overfeeding of maize can cause an allergic reaction, which will show up as skin nodules. *Be sure not to use genetically modified maize*, as this can affect the microbiome.

Raw corn.
Geertje French

Cereals summary

Although cereals do have a part to play in the horse's ration, they should always be treated with caution because of their low fibre content, high starch and carbohydrate content. Calcium needs phosphorus to be absorbed properly and, as maize and barley both have a low calcium to phosphorus ratio, it is therefore important to ensure that your horse does get a good balance of both calcium and phosphorus. All cereals are low in the essential amino acids lysine and methionine.

Protein sources

Protein is a long-chain amino acid and is an important building block of cellular structures necessary for good muscle development, tissue growth and tissue repair. Protein provides the horse with 'heat' and it is this heat that produces energy. Horses in hard work will need a higher level of protein in their ration, whereas horses in maintenance and light work need less protein – they will get enough protein from hay or haylage and a diverse variety of grasses. When you feed protein it is essential to feed it from different protein sources to ensure a diverse amino acid supply. Feeding excess protein can lead to hyperproteinaemia, which can cause restlessness, thirst and excessive urinating.

Horses receive their protein from plant-derived foodstuffs such as legumes, grass, alfalfa, good-quality hay and haylage, broccoli, linseed and spinach to name but a few. A note of caution regarding feeding old hay; this will be low in protein as ageing will reduce all nutrients. Besides this, it can become dusty and mouldy, which will affect the respiratory system and gut biome. It is also a good idea to wash the hay before feeding to leach out dust.

It may be necessary to feed extra protein to mares who are in foal, lactating mares, and yearlings. This can be done by adding milk proteins in powder form to their ration. However, this is a specific circumstance; in most cases it is better to avoid feeding milk products to horses (*see* Foods to avoid feeding your horse, later in this chapter).

Linseed

Linseed can be purchased as ready-to-use oil, meal or processed as linseed cakes. It may also be found as a constituent of hard feed. It has a high energy value, as it contains protein and oils, so is not suitable for horses who are on no or little exercise. It comes in its raw form as small seeds from the flax plant, and should never be fed in this raw state as the seeds contain the highly toxic substance hydrogen cyanide (formerly known as prussic acid). If you buy the seeds in their raw state they need to be cooked thoroughly. (*See* Preparing your own feeds in Chapter 6.)

Raw linseed.
Geertje French

Soya beans

Soya bean meal is another plant protein source. However, it is important to understand that its chemical analysis is currently incomplete. The horse's system is designed to break down a variety of plant cell walls and has a community of bacteria to complete this task. If a horse were to access a soya bean, in the wild, he would presumably eat the whole bean rather than nibbling off the hard, outer coating before spitting out the endosperm interior to make sure he only ate the 'safe' hull and he probably wouldn't bother with any of it unless there was nothing else to feed on. We are led to understand that soya bean hulls are 'safe' fibre, that they contain no starch and are rapidly digestible, increasing caecal fermentation and microbial biomass production. However, this is not the whole story, as we are currently making decisions on limited studies and limited science. Information of the analysis in relation to the fermentation process of the soya bean is very difficult to find, primarily because the process of analysis is both difficult and expensive. In a definitive study of the in vitro and in vivo fermentation process of soya beans it was found that the whole bean degrades and ferments in a totally different manner from the hull. The horse does not go about choosing to eat husks rather than whole plant items, so his digestive system is made up of the enzymes and microbes to complete the whole task rather than just a selected part of it. The milling process makes a big difference, though we think of soya hulls as 'dust' apparently, for a thorough fermentation process the hulls are not 'dusty' enough. The soya hull should only be one cell wall thick to complete the fermentation process. The fermentation process of soya hulls produces 506 g/kg of glucose, this is over 50% of the total, compared to glucose in the grass at around 9% (from an average of thirteen different species) so we need to be careful when feeding soya hulls to horses prone to obesity and laminitis. Whilst we are used to analysing hay and soaking it to reduce sugar content, and meticulous in paddock management, it is more difficult to manage hidden sugars contained in processed by-products.

Soya meal proteins are usually bought in powder form, but fresh or dried are best. Be sure only to feed products from organically grown soya.

Alternative sources of protein considered for horse feed

We are told there are considerable shortages in sources of protein within the pet food industry, with a need to find alternatives. As mentioned near the start of Chapter 2, recently insects have been identified as the most viable, and there are a growing number of large manufacturers using insect protein in dog food, or who are offering it as the main ingredient. The benefits appear to be substantial and well supported within the industry, with research into insect protein's nutritional benefits showing good results in terms of palatability, digestibility and safety, especially for black soldier fly larvae (BSFL), cricket and mealworm protein. However, as with all factory-farmed intensively reared food items, the mass-rearing of insects poses similar challenges of high densities, a high rate of pathogen transmission, higher susceptibility to pathogens arising from lack of oxygen, high temperatures, and nutrient deficiencies.

Although pathogenic bacteria do not need to be present at source, they may have been introduced by cross-contamination or improper handling when the material is processed or shipped. Among these bacteria, which can seriously compromise the processed insect protein are *Mylobacter, Morganella, Wohlfahtiimonas, Rickettsia, Providencia* and *Candida* species such as *Cyberlindnera sp* and *Trichosporon sp*. It is currently difficult to ascertain what exactly the rules are governing the use of dried insects as a protein source for human and animal consumption. The above-mentioned pathogenic bacteria could form a serious health risk. There still needs to be further research into the safety and efficacity of this material once it has been processed. As mentioned earlier, horses are herbivores, and there is not only the ethical question of feeding horses insect (i.e. animal) proteins, but also research into the effects of doing so, which may be adverse, beneficial or not make any difference – questions that have never really been put to the test since horses don't eat meat. So, there are a number of things to take into account when considering whether to allow feed manufacturers to add insect protein to the horses' diet – and matters of individual choice if they proceed to do so.

Bulk feeds

Sugar beet pulp

There is more to sugar beet pulp than meets the eye. The pulp from the sugar beet is left over when all the sugar has been extracted. Nonetheless, it leaves a highly digestible fibre, high-energy foodstuff, which can be used as a great addition to your horse's ration. And, as the sugar has been extracted, leaving just a minimal residue, it adds only slightly to calorie intake. The pulp also provides a good source of well-balanced calcium and phosphorus. The one thing to look out for in processed commercial beet pulp is that the producer may add molasses – this makes it more palatable, but also more calorific.

Dried sugar beet can be purchased either as cubes, or shredded. It is a safe feed for all horses as it is high in fibre and a good source of energy without being heating, as are some cereals. The small intestine digests the sugar content and the fibre is fermented in the hindgut.

Do not feed sugar beet in its dried form, as this will swell in the digestive tract and become impacted, with a very high risk of causing colic.

As with the pulped form, sugar beet is a great source of a well-balanced calcium: phosphorus ratio, so is useful for feeding along with cereals, that are not. (*See* Preparing your own feeds, later in this chapter.) An additional benefit for the microbiome of the horse is that beet pulp is a good prebiotic. You do, however, need to consider that beet pulp is low in protein and does not contain many vitamins or minerals. The microbial fermentation of beet pulp in the hindgut provides by-products called volatile fatty acids (VFA) which release energy when absorbed. As the slow-release energy produced does not contribute to spikes in either insulin or glucose beet pulp is a safe foodstuff for all horses. Beet pulp provides around 2,000 calories per kg so it becomes a valuable source to add to the ration of horses who are underweight – for example elderly horses who tend to lose weight as they age, because nutrients are not being absorbed as efficiently as when they were younger, could benefit from the addition of beet pulp. However, bear in mind that beet pulp should be used in combination with other foodstuffs as, on its own, it does not provide all the nutrients a horse requires.

Chaff

Chaff is a great mixer, and probably a better choice than bran (*see* below). Nowadays it is made up of oat straw and can be purchased with additives such as limestone flour, vitamins and minerals and other products, including molasses and pony nuts. It is then a great choice to stop greedy horses bolting their feed, as they will take their time to get the best bits out first. Since the oat straw has a high fibre content, the horses also need to take longer chewing their feed. Chaff aids digestion and is suitable for all horses to bulk out their ration and add interest.

Bran

Although bran is a good high-fibre bulk feed, as it is a by-product of wheat, take care when feeding it. This is because bran is high in phosphorus but low in calcium, so not suitable for young horses who need a good balance of both. Too high a level of phosphorus can impair healthy bone growth and cause deformities in youngstock. Nonetheless, bran does have its uses in small quantities: it is a good feed for horses on box rest as it has a low energy value. It can also be used as a laxative, though be careful with quantity! Bran should always be fed dampened down, as dry bran can become a choking hazard.

Compound feeds

Most compound feeds are supplied in cube or pellet form. They are fortified with minerals and vitamins and form the basis of a short ration. It is imperative always to have fresh, clean water available as dried cubes can cause obstructions in the digestive tract and lead to colic or choking. Compound feeds are high in fibre and non-heating. The basic cubes are also suitable for horses on box rest. Different types of cubes for different types of work or breed are discussed below. However, horses do get easily bored with this type of feed as they require little chewing, so are eaten quickly. It is therefore important always to have good-quality hay available alongside compound feeds, both to ensure a good ratio of fibre and to alleviate boredom.

There are some cubes that are specially formulated for specific groups. Stud cubes are designed to add optimum protein value, as well as carefully considered vitamins and minerals to aid fertility in stallions and brood mares and to give foals and youngsters the correct balance of nutrition for good growth and development. Horses in poor condition will also benefit from these types of cubes. To follow on from stud cubes there are other specifically designed feeds to aid in the healthy growth of young horses. There are also cubes available to meet the energy needs of high-performance horses. (These are clearly not suitable for horses on box rest, or just in light work.)

Preparing your own feeds

Although it is not always feasible to prepare home-made feeds for horses stabled on large yards, it may be considered for the smaller or private yard. It will also give you the opportunity to provide your horse with fresh herbage and plant feeds. This will help your horse to develop excellent gut biome for his overall health and well-being, as will be discussed further on in this book.

Preparing linseed

As linseed in its raw state contains the highly poisonous prussic acid it is vital that it is boiled into a thick jelly-like consistency. The liquid produced is referred to as linseed tea and the sticky part as linseed jelly. You can separate the liquid from the jelly and feed them individually. Soak the linseed overnight to soften the small seeds, then strain the seeds and rinse thoroughly to ensure the removal of any remaining prussic acid. Add clean water and bring to a rolling boil for about ten minutes, then simmer with the lid on for another three to four hours. Keep a close eye on it so it doesn't simmer dry; add water when it threatens to become too sticky.

Preparing raw barley

In order to soften the hard outer kernel barley needs to be soaked overnight before it can break down in the boiling process. About 250 g is enough for most horses, spread over the three or four feeds they get per day. However, reduce this when feeding smaller horses or ponies, or add about 50 g for larger horses like big hunters and Shires. Once you have brought it all to the boil, keep stirring to prevent the mass from clumping together. Keep on the boil for about ten minutes and then simmer with a lid on for several hours, stirring every hour so it doesn't stick to the bottom of the pan. Add water if it threatens to simmer dry. Once swollen and rather sticky, leave it to cool.

Extra calories

When feeding something extra, apart from normal daily rations, as a treat or when using food for training, you need to take into account the extra calories you are feeding. You then need to adjust the daily ration to ensure that you don't overfeed as you may set your horse up for putting on too much extra weight. For horses with feed-related disease, such as obesity, EMS, laminitis and gastric ulcers, avoid feeding high-starch or high-sugar treats including fruits such as melon, pears and apples.

Hay tea and herbal tea

Hay teas used to be given to older horses and those who were sick and were unable to eat or refused to do so. By far the best type of hay to use for this is meadow hay with the flowering heads intact, which these days is quite rare to find. Boiling water is poured over the hay, and allowed to steep until cool before being given to the horse. When you do have hay containing herbs and wildflowers and want to give your older or sick horse some herbal tea, use 1 kg of hay, pour on the boiling water, leave for thirty minutes, and then microwave for five minutes (700 W power and frequency 2450 MHz). Through heating in the microwave phenols, inulin and antioxidant levels are raised.[1] In the colder months most horses benefit from a boost to their digestive and immune systems. If you don't have meadow hay to make the tea, try using rosehips; boil the rosehips until soft, then leave to steep for about two hours. You can remove the rosehip parts and mix them with the main ration. Another alternative is dandelion roots; dig up the roots, wash off the earth and let them dry in the sun or a low-set oven – once dried you can grind them up and steep them in boiling water, leave to cool and pour into the ration. Steeped nettle or mint are more fantastic alternatives.

Fresh foods

Nutritious foods that are safe

It is possible to use pharmaceutical drugs and biomedicine together, as plants increase and support health before they target disease. However, plants work in different ways from synthetic medicines: they interact with the body to renew, replenish, protect and strengthen. They have a 'shotgun' effect – blasting many health-promoting chemicals rather than a single bullet dose (as with a synthetic drug) to target disease. No living creature can do without them: as we humans need five plus per day your horse needs at least twenty-five. Horses grazing naturally will have stronger digestive tracts, better immune systems (less arthritis and chronic degenerative diseases), and better wound healing times than horses with no, or little, access to diverse grazing.

In respect of human nutrition, epidemiologists at University College London maintain that the World Health Organization's (WHO's) recommendation of eating five-a-day fruit and vegetables may be inadequate to guarantee optimum health and disease prevention. The recommended amount is now seven per day and at least 400 g total, since plants are packed with important nutrients with antioxidant activity that act as free radical scavengers, ensuring that cells remain healthy and secure. Further to this, the WHO has a list of recommended 'superfoods' to boost health and wellness in humans and as a major preventative against the onset of chronic diseases, many of which originate from an active whole-body inflammatory state.

Degenerative and chronic diseases are on the increase in horses as well as humans but not many horses can access a pomegranate (one of the recommended human superfoods) whilst grazing in the field, or snatch one off a bush whilst out on a hack. So, is it possible to make a comparable superfood list for horses, based on what may be locally available to them, and what they might forage for themselves? If so, looking at average weight equivalence between humans and horses, the equivalent weight of mixed superfoods a horse would require would be around 1.5 kg per day, or around 212 g each if seven superfoods were available, in line with human recommendations. To prevent chronic long-term diseases the horse really needs access to these types of foods every day from a young age.

First of the superfoods

Spinach – Popeye's favourite food – is indeed an amazing superfood for humans and has been analysed with regard to its potential for horses. It is packed with crucial minerals for energy production (potassium and magnesium) and a hefty dose of vitamin A. It is also a powerful source of nitrate, a compound that boosts two proteins key to muscle strength. However, it is actually *too high* in nitrates for horses to eat in large amounts, but the safe wild plant equivalent is Chenopodium album (also known as fat hen and lamb's quarter).

As well as the nutrients described above, Chenopodium contains the following six very well-known and important flavonoid glycosides:

1. Quercetin-3-O-(2', 6'-di-O-α-l-rhamnopyranosyl)-β-d-glucopyranoside.
2. Kaempferol-3-O-(2', 6'-di-O-α-l-rhamnopyranosyl)-β-d-glucopyranoside.
3. Quercetin-3-O-β-d-glucopyranosyl-(1")-β-d-glucopyranoside.
4. Rutin.
5. Quercetin-3-O-β-d-glucopyranoside.
6. Kaempferol-3-O-β-d-glucopyranoside.

Triosides 1 and 2 were identified for the first time in Chenopodium album. Test results suggest that this edible weed should be considered as a nutraceutical food and an alternative source of nutrients and free radical scavenging compounds.

Other beneficial wild plants

The following are some plants that might be given consideration as potential superfoods for horses.

Wild mustard. The whole plant (leaves, seeds and roots) of wild mustard has many beneficial effects in ethnoveterinary medicine, including use as an anthelmintic, antiseptic, antimicrobial, analgesic, anti-inflammatory, immunomodulatory, antipyretic, psychopharmacological, antidiarrheal, and hepatoprotective. A wide variety of unusual phytochemicals have been isolated from this plant, currently being investigated for its strongly anthelmintic properties, especially against Strongylus vulgaris (large strongyles) in horses.

Pomegranate. Pomegranate is one of the fruits with the most antioxidant activity, thanks to polyphenols called ellagitannins and ellagic acid that are great for stimulating circulation and are also strongly antiviral, antimicrobial and antiparasitic. If your horse will eat just one that's fine, but the safer equine alternatives are lingonberries (more commonly known as cowberries). These are widely distributed throughout mainland Scotland, on the Hebridean Islands and in Orkney and Shetland. They grow from near sea level in some sites to an elevation of over 1,000 metres on Ben Lawers in Perthshire. In addition to being a characteristic species in the native pinewoods of the Caledonian Forest, lingonberries also grow in a range of dry and wet heath communities including in North Wales. They are another amazing superfood for horses: the whole plant is consumed with relish and it contains a unique range of the strongest proanthocyanidins, anthocyanidins and anthocyanins possessing analgesic, anti-inflammatory and neuroprotective activities. It will also prevent sugars passing over the gut wall and can soften and reduce 'cresty' necks.

Fennel. Most horses quite like the aniseed flavour of fennel, and you can feed the seeds, tops and bulb. It is particularly beneficial for gaseous or bloating issues.

Melon. This is a great fruit to give as a treat in summer. However, it does have a high sugar content, so is not suitable for horses who are obese, or suffering with inflammatory problems. Remove pips before feeding.

Parsnips. These are another enjoyable addition to the horse's diet; they have a great crunch texture. However, they are high in sugar.

Beets. Fresh beets should be fed cooked and mashed. They have the same nutritional value as beet pulp.

Broccoli. This is a good nutrient-rich vegetable, low in calories and rich in both minerals and vitamins (especially vitamin C). In addition to this it contains a powerful compound called sulforaphane, which exhibits strong anti-cancer and anti-arthritic properties. However, only feed it occasionally as it can upset the stomach. It is best fed cooked and mixed with other foodstuffs.

All fruits and vegetables should be thoroughly washed and checked for freshness. Remove any bruising or rotting parts.

Foods to avoid feeding your horse

Onions

Feeding onions to horses is something that should very definitely be avoided. Although, if eaten in very small quantities, the harm to the horse is likely to be minimal, as a precaution it is far better not to feed them at all. They contain a compound known as N-propyl disulfide; this compound damages red blood cells and can cause anaemia. In fact, another name for onion poisoning is Heinz-body haemolytic anaemia. If you suspect that your horse has eaten onions, the smell of which is detected on the breath, it is vital that you get in touch with your vet, who will advise a detoxification programme.

Bread

Has a doughy texture and the horse's system is not designed to digest a foodstuff with the consistency of bread, which may cause colic and an overproduction of acids. Bread is also very high in starch and sugar.

Milk and yoghurt

Although some people swear by feeding horses yoghurt as a probiotic supplement, any lactose product is not something that is suitable for the horse's gastro-intestinal tract, as this is not designed to cope with these types of products. In some cases, as mentioned earlier, foals or youngstock are fed milk-protein pellets, which are specifically manufactured to be suitable for horses. (Mares' milk is obviously digestible for foals).

Potatoes, tomatoes and aubergines

These all belong to the nightshade family and it is the compound atropine that is highly toxic for the horse. Therefore, horses should not be fed these items. If you find any green leaves belonging to potato plants growing in your pasture or field, remove them completely – you will need to dig them up root and all to avoid further growth.

Avocados

The flesh of the avocado has no adverse effect on the horse, and as an occasional treat they do provide some healthy nutrients and a good type of oil rich in omega-3. However, you need to avoid feeding the skin and stone, as they can cause stomach upsets and bloating.

Lawn clippings

Some people feel that grass is grass, so are happy to feed grass clippings as additional forage to their horse. But as lawn grass holds no beneficial nutrient value for horses and is often cultivated with pesticides, fertilisers and fungicides it should be avoided as a feed. Grass clippings are also prone to rapid mould and spore growth. (In the event that any well-meaning neighbour offers to pass their own clippings onto your fields for your horses, politely decline the offer.)

What to look for in manufactured feeds

There are now a growing number of feed manufacturers who use high-quality organically grown ingredients. These are preferable, as the source of the feed can often be traced to its origins. Another important factor is the freshness of the feed and it should always be used by the expiry date. Old feed will attract moisture and start to form mould spores, which upset the respiratory system and microbiome of the gut. Make sure you feed to the weight and exercise programme of the horse. As manufactured feeds usually contain all the minerals and vitamins a horse requires it is not necessary to add extra supplements. Make sure the compounds are not mixed with barley or oats, as they will add a heating element, and may make your horse unnecessarily fidgety and over-excited.

Issues of concern

Testing of genetically modified foodstuffs

There is an important debate to be had about genetically modified foodstuffs. There have been some concerning results from tests related to this issue in horses. One relevant test is the Next Generation Sequencing (NGS) test and every single one of the horses undergoing this test has shown extremely low levels of good bacteria, especially bifidobacteria, and only one in a hundred has the recommended levels of actinobacteria. Most tests are coming back with high levels of inflammatory and pathogenic bacteria, the actino and bifido bacteria are susceptible to biocides; these bacteria are the guardians of the gut. There are no pro- or prebiotics that are known to increase these bacteria for horses, and the bacteria are not allowed under EU legislation. There is still much work on research to be done on what to feed these bacteria and how to reverse the damage done.

Glyphosate contaminants

Genetically modified and glyphosate-resistant plants are requiring increasing levels of this noxious herbicide. In 2018 the Food Standards Agency claimed there is no adverse reaction in animals to the daily addition of the herbicide glyphosate at 500 ppm, but the effects of these sprays on health are so disturbing that research has been done by many independent bodies and there are indications that the safe level for glyphosate is 800 times lower than the permitted level. There have been appeals to the authorities to reconsider the use of both genetically modified crops and glyphosate.

---

1. Hay and herb tea
    - Petkova, N., Ivanova, L., Filova, G., Ivanov, I., & Denev, P. (2017). 'Antioxidants and carbohydrate content in infusions and microwave extracts from eight medicinal plants', *Journal of Applied Pharmaceutical Science*, 7(10), 055–061.

7.
The Importance of Vital Vitamins, Minerals and Trace Elements

It is vital that horses get the right vitamins and minerals to maintain good health. Vitamins are either fat-soluble and stored in the liver or water-soluble, which are not stored but pass through the gut.

Fat-soluble vitamins

Vitamin A – retinol

This vitamin specifically boosts the immune system, and for foals/young horses it promotes the growth of healthy bones and tissue. It also improves night vision.

Good vitamin A sources are leafy greens, high-quality hay and carrots. However, avoid feeding carrots to horses prone to laminitis, as they are high in sugar. (This vitamin is also found in cod liver oil, although some owners may not want to feed their horse animal-derived supplements.)

Deficiency signs show in the horse in the form of skin disorders, diarrhoea, poor growth, decreased appetite, loss of condition and the horse may become more susceptible to respiratory infections.

You do need to be careful with adding vitamin A as a supplement, since it is stored in the liver, as an excess of this vitamin can cause toxic build-up, however, a good store can see a horse through for several months.

Vitamin D – calciferol

This vitamin is absorbed into the skin by sunlight, as in humans. It is needed for the metabolism of fat and acts as an antioxidant. It is also necessary for the absorption of calcium and phosphorus in the gut. In winter time, when sunlight levels are low, even for outdoor horses, it is advisable to add vitamin D as a supplement. It is found in cod liver oil, but if you are against feeding an animal derivative to your horse you can obtain vitamin D as a powder supplement, which is not derived from cod liver oil.

Not getting enough vitamin D may result in lameness, skeletal defects in foals and young horses specifically and swollen joints. However, as with vitamin A, *too much* of this vitamin can lead to problems – specifically soft tissue ossification, which may lead to pain and immobility on the site of the ossification. It may also raise the blood calcium levels which, in turn, may cause deposition in the blood vessels, joints and heart tissue.

Vitamin E – tocopherol

This is a vitamin with several important functions, but it needs selenium (a mineral which we discuss later in this chapter) in order to be properly absorbed. It aids in the utilisation of oxygen and also in the metabolism of fats which, in turn, improves performance and stamina. This is especially important in horses who work hard such as sports horses, particularly since it also improves muscle development.

Another very important benefit is that it also aids in fertility health. Breeding mares and stallions are given extra vitamin E at the beginning of the breeding season.

Other benefits are that the condition azoturia (tying up) may be relieved with this vitamin and it also reduces nervousness and is often used for racehorses who are high in energy because of their high carbohydrate feed and perhaps naturally quite excitable.

Good sources include linseed oil, alfalfa, green feeds, barley, rye and other grains.

With reference to the opening sentence of this section, it should be noted that deficient intake can result in liver damage if there is not enough selenium present for absorption. Deficiency may also cause degenerative muscle tissue, defects in red blood cells, infertility and low performance.

Vitamin K – menaquinone

This is necessary for the metabolic uptake of cellulose and for blood clotting. The bacteria from green leafy foods produce this vitamin in the large intestine.

Unless your horse has to use anticoagulant drugs, which would interfere with the effectiveness of this vitamin, horses are not usually deficient in it. However, as this vitamin is stored in the liver, caution is advisable if you intend to use it as an extra supplement. Check your bagged feeds to see whether they already contain it.

Water-soluble vitamins

B1 – thiamine

This vitamin regulates metabolism of carbohydrates, fats and, in particular, glucose. It is synthesised in the large intestine by bacteria. Unless your horse eats bracken, which contains a B1 antagonist, there is rarely a deficiency seen. Nonetheless deficiency, if it exists, can lead to loss of condition and impaired growth. Whilst most feeds will have sufficient B1, in cases of deficiency it can be bought as a supplement.

B2 – lactoflavin/riboflavin

This is an important vitamin for heart tissue health and the nervous system, and can help in making the horse quieter and less agitated or restless. It also aids in the metabolism of fats, carbohydrates and protein.

Grass, herbage and dried yeast are good sources and it is synthesised by bacteria in the large intestine. Deficiency will result in poor growth and condition, and will lower the energy levels.

B3 – niacinamide/nicotinic acid/niacin

This vitamin aids metabolism of fats, protein and carbohydrates and promotes healthy skin. Cereals (barley, wheat) provide a good source and it is synthesised by bacteria in the large intestine.

B5 – pantothenic acid

This vitamin is synthesised by bacteria in the large intestine and controls metabolism of fats, carbohydrates and protein. It isn't common for horses to be deficient in this vitamin but, if this occurs, it shows up as poor growth and condition. In such cases, lentils, split peas and whole wheat, broccoli and oats are good sources, and these may be added in small quantities to the feed.

B6 – pyridoxine

This vitamin influences some fifty different enzymes, so it is one of the more important water-soluble vitamins for your horse. It aids metabolism of fats, carbohydrates and protein. It is found in good-quality grass, herbage and green forage. Deficiencies are rare, but will occur when your horse does not get enough grass and dried or fresh herbage, and may then affect growth, skin and blood changes.

B12 – cyanocobalamin

This vitamin aids the metabolism of proteins, fats and carbohydrates. It is specifically necessary for the utilisation of protein which, in turn, promotes healthy growth. It also improves appetite, and helps in the formation of red blood cells. Its role in stimulating appetite is useful for older horses whose appetite may have reduced, and sick horses who may have gone off their food. It can also aid the reproductive process, since B12 is needed to ensure efficient oxygen transport to all organs, including the reproductive organs and tissues. Sometimes pregnant mares may need extra B12 for healthy growth in their foals.

The mineral cobalt, (see later in this chapter), is necessary to aid production of bacteria which synthesises this vitamin in the large intestine. Deficiency, which is not that common, may be reflected in poor coat health, slow growth, and infertility. Anaemia may also occur, although more so in younger rather than mature horses.

Choline

This is a constituent of cartlidge cells (joints). It is also involved in nerve transmission and cell structure maintenance and helps in transportation of fat in the body. It can be synthesised from the amino acid methionine found in plant protein. Deficiency is not common as it can be found in most foodstuffs.

Folic acid – folacin

This vitamin is vital in red blood cell production and necessary in the prevention of anaemia.

It is synthesised in the large intestine from green forage and herbage and good-quality grass. When there is a deficiency, it will be noticed in poor growth, anaemia and inefficient performance.

Biotin

This vitamin is specifically necessary for good hoof health and healthy skin. It also helps to metabolise protein, carbohydrates and fat. When there is not enough biotin in the feed (from sources such as organically grown soya, yeast, maize and green forage), it will show in poor hoof wall health and skin problems.

Vitamin C – ascorbic acid

This vitamin aids in the utilisation of iron, so will help in the recovery from anaemia. It also helps with good energy levels, strengthens the body's defence system against disease and can help to reduce stress and skin problems (and prevent nosebleeds). It is synthesised in the liver from dietary glucose. Deficiency is rare, but will show itself in poor skin health and general poor performance related to stress.

Minerals for health and growth

Macro-minerals

Minerals are chemical elements and are divided into two categories. The first are the macro elements, which are needed in larger quantities. These include phosphorus and calcium (that are utilised correctly when in perfect balance as they work together with vitamin D to aid absorption). Also included are potassium (often encountered in the compound sodium chloride – salt), magnesium and sulphur.

Required in smaller quantities are the trace elements and these include selenium, iodine, copper, zinc, manganese and iron.

Minerals are found in plants depending on the quantity and type of plant and the soil the plants grow in. When soil is mineral-depleted this will be seen in the plants grown in that soil.

Certain trace elements can become toxic to the horse when they receive too high a quantity of them.

Phosphorus (P)

This macro-mineral is especially necessary for good energy production and healthy bone growth; this is of particular importance in foals and youngstock. It is found in good-quality hay, grass and cereals. Deficiency will show in slow growth in youngsters.

Calcium (Ca)

Calcium is essential for good bone and teeth growth, blood coagulation, for the function of muscles and nerves and lactation. Without calcium, muscles would not contract, meaning movement would be impossible.

Limestone flour, alfalfa, sugar beet pulp, good grass and hay and white clover are all good sources of calcium.

See above for the importance of phosphorus and calcium working in tandem.

Potassium (K)

Potassium aids good functionality of muscles and nerves, good heart health, maintains pH levels and helps in osmotic regulation of bodily fluids.

It is found in all good-quality green plant and herbage as well as good hay. Although very high levels of potassium may start to interfere with magnesium absorption this is a rare occurrence, as excess will be passed out through urine.

If a horse becomes deficient it will be seen in decreased appetite and rate of growth.

Sodium (Na)

This mineral is vital for the maintenance of a balanced control of fluids within the body. It is necessary in the formation of bile which, in turn, aids good digestion of carbohydrates and fats. It also helps in maintenance of blood volume and circulation, in contraction and relaxation of muscles, urine formation and cell health, and facilitates nerve impulses. Brood mares who do not get enough salt will have a problem with their milk production.

A good source is to have a salt mineral block for your horse within reach at all times. However, some horses shun this salt source as they don't like the flavour, so it needs adding to their feed by different means. The NRC recommendation for a 500 kg horse, on maintenance and low exercise, is about 30 g added salt to the overall feed, this provides around 11 g of sodium and 18 g of chloride (electrolyte). This should be added to hay or feed in parts over the day, as putting it all in one feed may make the ration unpalatable. Ordinary table salt is not recommended, as it contains anti-caking agents and may be too high in iodine. Good alternatives to the common salt block are Himalayan salt granules or blocks. This salt is pure and the granules contain other minerals, such as magnesium and calcium. Sea salt is another good salt source containing extra mineral elements.

The level of exercise should be an indication of how much salt your horse requires. Hard work makes the horse sweat, so with that, salt is lost. Horses living in a humid or hot climate will also need additional salt. If your horse does not get enough salt, it may cause a condition called pica which, in horses, compels them into actions such as wood chewing or eating soil or faecal droppings. In addition to such actions, pica shows itself in fatigue, a coarse and dull coat and loss of appetite. The horse may also drink less water than required, causing digestion to slow down, and consequent constipation. Another problem is exertional rhabdomyolysis (tying up). This shows itself in muscle stiffness and cramp, and will become evident during exercise and when the horse moves around in the paddock.

Unusual behaviour, whereby the horse is constantly looking for things such as wood to chew, licking stones and rock or eating soil, also indicates that he is seeking salt and other minerals.

While it is essential for horses, too much salt can cause an increased level of heat stress and constantly seeking to drink.

Chlorine (Cl)

This non-metallic element is necessary for body fluid regulation and pH balance as well as being a component in the gastric juices that helps to ensure good digestion of protein. Often found in combination with sodium as salt (*see* above) it is a component of most compound feeds and supplements. As long as a good-quality salt/mineral block is provided and coarse mix or concentrate cubes are fed deficiency is unlikely.

Magnesium (Mg)

This vital mineral aids in the activation of some 300 enzymes. Without magnesium your horse would truly be unhealthy as it is necessary for good energy production on all levels, in nerve and muscle formation, and in assisting with cell metabolism. It also aids in the formation of bone and strong teeth, so is especially needed in growing horses.

In fact, about 65% of magnesium in horses is to be found in the skeleton and teeth and the best sources are foodstuffs such as soya beans, carrots, linseed, pulses, alfalfa and good-quality hay and high-quality grass and herbage. When a horse becomes deficient it may show up as muscle spasms and nervous tension.

Sulphur (S)

Sulphur promotes hoof growth, activates enzymes and is present in insulin. It is found in good-quality pasture and is synthesised from plant proteins (amino acids), When a horse becomes deficient this can be seen in poor hoof growth as well as a dull coat and poor skin condition.

Trace minerals – micro-nutrients

Trace minerals are needed in smaller quantities than macro-minerals.

Iodine (I)

This mineral is important in the formation of the hormone thyroxin, which is necessary for good metabolic rate. It also assists in the reproductive process and encourages growth.

Seaweed and herbs, as well as a good mineral lick, are good sources or it can be bought as a supplement. When a horse becomes deficient it can be noted in poor growth, abnormalities in cell structure, infertility, foal weakness and swelling of the thyroid gland. However, be careful not to overdose with iodine as it can become toxic for the horse.

Selenium (Se)

Selenium acts as an antioxidant and, when used in conjunction with vitamin E, it may help prevent cell damage. It is thought that, in some cases of azoturia, a deficiency of selenium in the diet may be implicated. Deficiency can also weaken a foal and cause joint problems. It is found in linseed, herbage and supplements. High-performance horses are often given selenium as a supplement, but caution is needed as too much selenium can become a toxic element, which in turn can cause hair to fall out and hoof deformities.

Molybdenum (MO)

This trace element can be found in good-quality grass and green forage/herbage. It is an enzyme reactor and deficiencies are rarely seen.

Cobalt (Co)

Cobalt is a component of vitamin B12 and helps prevent anaemia. It is necessary to start bacterial activity for digestion and aids synthesising B-complex and other vitamins. It is found in mineral blocks, green herbage and most other feeds, including compounds. Deficiency will impair B12 absorption which, in turn, can cause poor growth and weight loss in addition to anaemia.

Copper (Cu)

Copper helps in the utilisation of iron and the synthesis of haemoglobin (a red protein responsible for the transport of oxygen in the blood). It is also important for healthy bone growth, cartilage and elastin and aids in the formation of a healthy coat. It is found in good copper-rich soils, so any feeds grown in this type of soil will provide a good quantity, as will feeding linseed. Nevertheless, any deficiency will be noted in poor, uneven pigmentation, including depletion in pigment of the coat, slow growth, poor performance and diarrhoea. Furthermore, when youngstock doesn't receive the right copper balance in their diets it may become a precursor for the development of orthopaedic disease (DOD). If there are high levels of molybdenum in the diet the availability of copper is reduced.

Manganese (Mn)

Manganese is important in the activation of digestive enzymes. It aids a healthy appetite, good cell metabolism, a healthy coat and skin, fertility and good health in the hoof and skeleton. It is found in good-quality hay, herbage, mineral blocks, barley, oats and wheat, or may be added as a supplement. Deficiency will show itself through abnormal skeletal growth, a dull, sparse coat and reproductive problems. It is, however, rare to see a deficiency as it is found in such a variety of foodstuffs.

Zinc (Zn)

Much the same applies to zinc as to manganese and, again, deficiency is not common. However, if it does occur this may lead to poor growth in foals and youngsters and reduced appetite.

Iron (Fe)

Iron is a vital component of haemoglobin, a protein found in red blood cells. Haemoglobin binds to oxygen in the lungs and transports it to muscles and tissues throughout the body, ensuring proper oxygen supply. Good sources of iron are herbs such as comfrey, mineral blocks and most natural foods. If there is a lack of iron it may reduce healthy growth and lead to fatigue. Also a heavy worm infestation, may prevent good iron absorption and exacerbate anaemia.

We have already warned that an *excess* of some essential elements can cause problems. This is also the case with iron, but the underlying issue is quite complex and this, and the avoidance of it, merit more detailed explanation.

Excess iron in the diet will readily trigger the inflammation of the Nf-kB pathway, because the horse has no other way of dealing with an iron overload. The mechanism for activation of Nf-kB by iron and other metals is not clear but it is, and can be, completely nullified by plant phenols both in the horse's gut and in the body tissues. A diet too high in iron generates hydroxyl radical (a free radical) causing cellular damage and is being directly linked to many degenerative diseases. If you are concerned about high iron levels in your hay or in the grass (perennial rye has the highest levels) then this needs to be analysed and you should make sure that the horse also has access to other plant material and allow him to make the right choices from this more diverse forage.

In all probability, if your horse already has access to wild flower meadow plants or is a hedgerow forager, it is likely that his iron levels are already balanced. However, as a matter of good practice, it is better to allow access to some plant antioxidants rather than trying to balance the diet by the addition of other minerals, or stripping the diet completely of iron without really knowing what levels individual horses might require. So, if you want to be assured about balancing the iron in your horse's diet without constant analysis or by adding other minerals, try adding small quantities of the following commonly available plants containing the pro-oxidant, quercetin. Purple loosestrife (Lythrum salicaria), meadowsweet (Filipendula ulmaria), willow herb (Epilobium angustifolium), cloudberry (Rubus chamaemorus), wild raspberry (Rubus idaeus L.), Downy Birch (Betula pubescens), Pine (Pinus sylvestris).

Only a few mg of quercetin are needed, so just nibbles or snatches of pine or the other plants will be sufficient. Meadowsweet is easy to buy as a dried dietary supplement and can be added to the daily diet.

Silica (SiO$_2$)

Silica is the natural oxide of the element silicon (Si); biogenic silica (bSi), also referred to as opaline silica, is one of the most widespread biogenic minerals. Native grasses contain high levels to protect themselves against being eaten by small herbivores. Danthonia decumbent, formerly known as sieglingia decumbent, has the highest levels of silica of any native grass species.

A study of a silicon dietary supplement found that adding bio-absorbable silicon improved performance and reduced injuries in racehorses. Silicon stimulates the production of glucosamine, naturally creating stronger joint function and reducing the need for extra supplementation. Nitrogen fertilisation reduces biogenic silica so grazing the verges and heathland rather than the main pasture for a top-up is recommended. Heath grasses provide an awesome range of nutrients for horses, and can be found in every county of the UK, although they prefer sandy or peaty soils, moorland and heathland, and moist or wet areas.

8.
The Microbiomes of Wild Plants

Plant roots contain large and diverse communities of bacteria; when grown naturally (i.e. in a diverse environment without fertiliser) they have a distinct and unique microbiome profile. As an example, we look at yarrow (Achillea millefolium) used as a medicinal plant for digestive disorders, ulcers, colic, diarrhoea, bloating and constipation. Yarrow contains a spectacular array of secondary active plant metabolites such as flavonoids, phenolic acids, coumarins, terpenoids, monoterpenes, sesquiterpenes, diterpenes, triterpenes and sterols. All of these are recognised for their health-providing, disease-treating properties, and production is stimulated in the soil as follows:

1. Soil bacteria, called *Rhizobiales*, first colonise the plant roots, secreting proteins and metabolites (by-products), helping the plant to acquire nutrients and stimulating it to produce a wide range of polyphenolic secondary plant compounds. The plant uses these chemicals in defence against stress, radiation and predators (being eaten by insects or horses) and by reducing pathogenic bacteria. The bacteria then travel to all parts of the plant above ground where they may be ingested by the horse.
2. The soil phytobiome of yarrow also contains bacteria from the family of Alphaproteo bacteria, which make nitrogen available for the plant, reducing the need for fertilisers.
3. A third group of predominant bacteria in the soil are called bio-control agents. This group produces toxins that are transferred through a powerful nano-weapon system able to kill pathogenic fungi, oomycetes and bacteria that are antagonistic towards the plant. They signal to the host plant to trigger a system called immunity pathway-induced specific resistance, the plant then manufactures higher levels of antimicrobials, which find their way into the gut of your horse and continue to be a benefit.[1]

Phytochemicals

Some plants contain a wide range of vital and potent phytochemicals to help support horses' health. These health-providing plants prefer to grow together in defined communities. Species-rich meadows and roadside verges provide the horse with anti-inflammatories, anthelmintics, anti-ulcerogenic compounds, antimicrobials plus an entire range of vitamins that match the requirements of the NRC.

The upland meadows of the UK offer a rich and diverse, as in 'species-rich', environment, which has been classified as the sweet vernal-grass-wood Cranesbill community (MG 5). These wonderful natural hectares of lush and fertile meadow are now only to be found in the north of England and in grass verges. (However, don't allow horses to forage on verges that are part of busy

or main roads, as they will be tainted through petrol fumes, which will also be in the soil.)
One of the most significant medicinal plants within this community is the great burnet, which we will discuss in further detail later in this chapter.

The second most valuable for horses is the crested dog's-tail/common knapweed found in the lowlands of Britain, once common but becoming increasingly rare. It is found in circumneutral brown soils of loamy to clayey texture with a pH ranging from 5 to 6.2.

Within the MG5 community (a classification of soil quality), the range of herbs that contribute the most to horses' health include ribwort plantain (Plantago lanceolata), black knapweed (Centaurea nigra), common sorrel (Prunella vulgaris), common self-heal (Rumex acetosa), yellow rattle (Rhinanthus minor) and eyebrights (Euphrasia). An important sub-community within this group is predominated by lady's bedstraw (Gallium verum).

Phytochemical balancers

A bagged processed feed and monoculture seed hay diet is unable to provide the full range of antioxidants horses need to stay healthy. It is therefore important that we balance the horse's diet with natural resources.

Antioxidants are phytochemicals. These are often overlooked because the complexity of phytochemical interaction with the body is not all that easy to understand. Nutrients from processed food and hay are easier to analyse for vitamins and minerals –including their impacts on health – and, whilst these provide important sustenance, they lack many of the medicinal properties of phytonutrients.

One important job of phytochemicals is that they help the horse to cope with the over-ingestion of water-soluble carbohydrates (WSC) and starch. A diet too high in either produces unwanted fat pads, 'cresty' necks and also predisposes to other diseases such as laminitis and EMS. It is estimated that over 55% of our horses are obese, and this percentage is forecast to increase. In a natural environment, a horse would have access to many different phytochemicals from a wide range of plants, interacting with the body chemistry in a myriad of different ways to increase health and vitality.

In the colder months a naturally grazing horse would eat large quantities of woody, stemmy material from herbs and shrubs. Although the current thinking is that this may be an inferior type of diet, it might be time for a rethink, as many shrubs contain phytochemicals such as quercetin, luteolin and fisetin which produce lipolysis within the fat cells (adipocytes) releasing energy for use in the winter months. As the adipocytes shrink the release of the inflammatory chemicals responsible for many chronic diseases also falls dramatically. The best plants at this time of year are gorse tips (Ulex Europaeus) and the bark/leaves from blackberries and wild blueberries.

Clostridium has been associated with grass sickness in multiple research papers,[2] and some soil types contain much higher levels than others. *Clostridium* increases in certain conditions such as heavy rain, poor drainage, compacted soil and continuous grazing by horses. Not all *Clostridium* species are pathogenic, although soil continuously grazed by horses contains higher levels of known clostridia pathogens.

Diversity scoring

Diversity scoring is the method whereby you test the microbiome of the horse to find out the types of different bacteria present in the gut.

Low diversity

Approx 20% (calculated from the EquiBiome Database 2023 as indicated below) of all the horses we see are in this group, commonly those with gastric discomfort such as colitis, hindgut ulcers and leaky gut. There is often a history of long-term medication, especially antibiotics. Horses with low diversity often have a missing core member of the microbiome – most commonly the missing bacteria group is associated with metabolism. Horses with low microbiome diversity are likely to have an increase in the bacteria that form biofilms (protective layers). Biofilms can be beneficial in three ways:

1. By providing a protective layer of mucus on the gut wall to deter pathogenic bad bacteria from translocating across the gut wall.
2. By protecting the good gut bacteria from a fall in pH (acidosis).
3. By capturing nutrients and moisture that are beneficial for the good gut bacteria.

Biofilm overgrowth happens when the pH of the gut falls, an event that will reduce the numbers of good gut bacteria and, in the case where the biofilm consists of pathogenic or harmful bacteria, there is the potential for a release of toxins into the bloodstream. Horses with a low gut biodiversity score and high biofilm formation take the longest to rebalance and restore.

Medium diversity

A horse with a medium diversity score is likely (EquiBiome Database 2023) to have an increase in the bacteria associated with inflammation and will often have a lower percentage of bacteria that support the health of the gut wall, than a horse with a higher diversity score, resulting in an increased risk of tight junction failure. Tight junctions are layers of cells that bind to form a barrier. In this case the barrier of tissue that stops unwanted bacteria from entering the bloodstream. When the tight junctions lose their stability and become weakened or damaged this causes a condition called 'leaky gut'. Around 60% of horses are in this group.

    It is easier to increase the diversity score of a horse in this group than for the group who were already filtered out into the high diversity scoring tests, as there exists a core of good gut bacteria that help support health and vitality. Horses with a medium score often have EMS, food sensitivities and faecal water syndrome.

High diversity

The gut microbiome is an ecosystem, and the biodiversity of species and species richness are often used as measures of ecological health. High biodiversity, with many species present and a high variety, is vital for the health of the horse. A Shannon Index Score (or Shannon Wiener Index) is used to quantify the diversity of different plant species in a community, which can be a field or forest. A high score usually means that an ecosystem is healthy and relatively undisturbed by medications, diet and environmental factors, whilst low biodiversity is characteristic of an unhealthy or degraded gastric environment.

Food intake for survival

Driven by the need to survive, and influenced by complex genetic and physiological factors, the desire to eat is one of the strongest of equine instincts (unless sick or over-trained). In cases of food deprivation, powerful hormones stimulate the appetite. Restricting food intake and calories alone can cause the equine metabolism to resist further weight loss; this is particularly true of many native species bred to survive a harsh environment. Equines (especially natives) can resist weight loss by the release of signalling hormones. These hormones, which include cortisol, ghrelin, insulin and leptin, all promote the storage of fat, which is deposited around the organs and also subcutaneously, and increases energy efficiency. At the other end of the scale, in times when food is too calorific or highly processed, there are no hormones that tell the horse to use up energy faster, eat less, or store food less efficiently. Horses that have been blessed with an efficient energy-storing system may have it overloaded by being too sedentary, too warm, or by having access to highly calorific food, and the net result of this is the inevitable creeping increase in weight even when rations are kept to a minimum.

Freely grazing horses are thought to seek out and favour plants not only for nutrient content but also for phytoactive chemical content. Some of these interact with the horse's hormones of metabolism to help maintain a normal appetite and prevent weight gain. Phytochemicals have several different mechanisms for preventing weight gain, one of the most important and well-studied of which is the prevention of the breakdown of fats and carbohydrates in the gastro-intestinal tract, otherwise known as pancreatic lipase inhibition. Hedera (ivy) contains high levels of this potent chemical and is nature's alternative to Orlistat (a drug used to treat obesity) – its effects on metabolism and carbohydrates are so powerful only a mouthful is needed. As plants contain multiple useful chemicals there are other reasons why a horse will choose to eat hedera, the first being to relieve respiratory infection and the second to relieve dysbiosis (imbalance) of the gut bacteria, reducing the bacteria that cause bloating. Eating ivy is more common in the summer months when food is plentiful.

Wild foraging

When your horse snatches a bite of something tasty from a hedgerow, this is what's happening inside the gastro-intestinal tract.

Hedgerows and plants other than grass contain multiple (sometimes hundreds) of phytochemicals used by the plant to keep itself healthy and these chemicals are biologically active with anti-inflammatory, antimicrobial and antioxidant properties. Some of the phytonutrients have small molecules and these pass through the gut wall where they go on to interact on the physiology of the horse wherever they are needed. Some phytochemicals have larger molecules and poor bioavailability (are poorly absorbed). These are retained for long periods of time in the gut, where they modify the gut microbiome community and act as antiparasitics and anthelmintics.

The horse's brain is continuously receiving messages from the gut bacteria in the microbiome alerting the horse to deficits in phytonutrients and setting up a desire for the horse to seek them out – a process called quorum sensing. Horses stabled for long periods and being fed a diet of processed food will have fewer bacteria with a quorum-sensing ability and receive fewer messages alerting them to deficits; this can be remedied by increasing the diversity of the diet.

Five facts about natural grazing by native and feral horses

1. On average, free-grazing feral horses will consume around thirty-three out of one-hundred different plants (a third of what is available in a grazing area). They may not eat the same plants over and again, but may choose plants at different times of the day or even season. With a large area in which to roam they can benefit from all the different phytonutrients available to them. Horses are self-selective when it comes to medicinal plants: when a horse is not ailing, he will not eat certain plants, but when he is unwell he seems to know what to choose to relieve the symptoms. Horses would not have survived and thrived in the wild had they not known instinctively what to eat from what was available to them, again 'quorum' sensing what they need. This might be a bitter herb to settle the stomach, or an antibacterial plant, or a pain killing plant. In winter a high percentage of nutrients come from flowering shrubs such as gorse, and green-leaved shrubs such as purslane.
2. Feral horses eat selectively from available high-nutrient grasses such as paspalum or knot grass (Polygonum aviculare), it grows in watery meadows and on verges. This plant has been identified in mainland Europe and the UK as an invasive species because of its fast spreading and pernicious growth. Spreading rapidly along the surface of the soil, it branches out and, from its rozomes stolons (nodules), it grows what looks like grass. The origin of this plant has been traced to the tropical Americas and Eurasian parts. Wild barley and grasses from the millet family are other plants of a very high nutritive value. Feral horses' diets are most likely to be deficient in protein and energy and less likely to be deficient in minerals and antioxidants.
3. Feral horses do not roam around to seek out highly nutritional grass and plants if they are scarce, but instead will choose to eat lower-value grass and plants in order to maintain a high gut-fill level, leaving it to the efficient gastro-intestinal tract to extract as many nutrients as possible from the food available.
4. Feral horses favour high-quality low-fibre components and then seek to dilute them with large amounts of over-mature leaves and stems. The green shoots contain the most nutrients but the gastro-intestinal tract needs to be maintained full, so the feral horse chooses to top up on high-fibre food with a lower nutrient value until the gut is satiated.
5. The weight of the gastro-intestinal tract content represents 13–20% of live weight and intake is constrained by the need to be agile in order to avoid predators.

Plants and herbs

Acorns

Horses eat acorns, which is a concern to many horse owners but, whilst gorging on acorns isn't recommended, they do have benefits. Horses may find acorns to eat on the edge of their field when there is an oak tree present. A few mouthfuls will not do any harm but, nonetheless, we advise that you remove acorns from the field if there are a lot on the ground. Most horses will not even bother eating them, but as horses are self-selective they may eat some without ill effect. However, if you don't feel comfortable with your horses eating them, remove them all from the field.

Here are a few comparisons to another hull commonly used in horse feed:

1. Soya bean hulls contain more tannins than acorn hulls. If acorns were listed as an ingredient on a bagged horse feed, this would be likely to cause some debate. However, horses do eat acorns and most of us will be aware of the advantages and disadvantages, but we have never heard of any such debate about the tannin content of soya hulls.
2. High levels of gallic acid were found in the urine of horses thought to be poisoned by acorns. However, black soya bean hulls contain three times higher levels of gallic acid than red/brown soya hulls, and twice the levels of acorn hulls.
3. Tannin-rich hulls (like those of soya beans) cause the inactivation of some amino acids (especially cysteine and methionine), so if you are supplementing your horse's feed with soya hulls, you won't be seeing much improvement in foot quality as the supplement won't be working.
4. The good news is that less starch and fewer lipids are digested when the hulls are high in tannins; the downside is an increase in hindgut tannin-resistant bacteria, such as the multi drug-resistant *Enterobacteriaceae*.
5. Tannins are classed as an anti-nutrient because they inhibit trypsin. This is linked to pancreatic health, and is in direct conflict with research promoting the use of soya hulls as a safe replacement for hay.

Lady's mantle (Alchemilla)

All varieties of lady's mantle (Alchemilla) contain more than twenty-five unique and complex chemicals and are deeply rooted in medicine around the world. As its name suggests, this plant was extensively used and highly esteemed by alchemists in traditional medicine. Alchemilla is used as a treatment for so many ailments that, like aloe vera, is termed an adaptogenic. This has a very low toxicity rating (especially a plant extract) to denote the fact that you should not give more than is stated, but it is termed

Alchemilla.
Geertje French

'safe' in herbal medicine monographs. It is held to increase the body's ability to resist the damaging effects of stress and promote or restore normal physiological functioning. It is also used for mild diarrhoea, gastric ulcers and pain, abscesses, as a general anti-inflammatory and to regulate hormones. Recently it has been shown to help regulate insulin and glucose in overweight humans, and it is also used as a diabetes treatment in Arab countries. A daily equine dose is only 200–500 mg so it packs a punch owing to the high levels of complex chemicals. (The leaves contain the highest levels of beneficial phytochemicals.)

The three varieties of Alchemilla: Alchemilla Acutiloba Opis (starry lady's mantle), Alchemilla Monticola Opis (velvet lady's mantle) and Alchemilla Subcrenata Burse (large toothed lady's mantle) mentioned here are all endangered, but can be found growing wild in northern areas of the UK such as Yorkshire, Lancashire, Cumbria and north Wales, especially in old unimproved permanent grassland. It is also likely to be found growing on roadside verges and is sometimes a domesticated plant.

Bilberry (Vaccinium myrtillus)

This plant is also known as blaeberry, whortleberry, whinberry and myrtle berry. If you are fortunate to have an H22 soil grading heath plant community nearby, look out for a favourite equine snack in the form of bilberry (Vaccinium myrtillus) or cloudberry (Rubus chamaemorus). Horses enjoy grazing all parts of this plant. Ours, living on Welsh pasture, eat most of it in the spring when the first new leaves appear, but any plants missed in this session are grazed continuously throughout the year. Full of polyphenols, this plant is great for the gut bacteria, and includes glucosides and galactosides. Arabinosides of delphinidin, cyanidin, petunidin, peonidin and malvidin are included in the anthocyanidin content. It is especially beneficial in the autumn as the leaves turn red, increasing the levels of antioxidants (anthocyanidins) which help to reduce insulin levels and other metabolic dysfunctions relating to EMS, including a reduction in lipid absorption, a decrease in preadipocytes, and prevention of the systemic inflammation that accompanies obesity.

Beech bark.
Geertje French

Birch bark.
Geertje French

Bracken.
Geertje French

Mineral content of the leaves and fruit include the macro elements calcium, phosphorus and magnesium and seven micro elements iron, barium, sodium, manganese, copper, sulphur and zinc.

Bindweed (Convolvulus)

Bindweed is one of 250 species of Convolvulus, common around the globe. Horses seem to prefer the smaller plants often found growing along the ground, rather than the large version (morning glory) that climbs through the hedges and makes its way even up into the trees. All species of Convolvulus contain a higher quantity and quality of the potent calming/sedative alkaloid compounds than Indian snakeroot (Rauwolfia serpentina), a plant used extensively in herbal medicine as a sedative/calming herb. (Here, the active component is reserpine.) Convolvulus also contains ten times higher levels of saponins than is found in soya, oats, garlic, liquorice and ginseng, making this weed something of a superfood. Saponins influence muscle development, metabolism and regulation of several hormones making bindweed an interesting foraging plant for ageing horses and those with pituitary pars intermedia dysfunction (PPID). (This condition, commonly known as Cushing's disease, is discussed in Chapter 10 and referred to by its common name throughout the text.) Bindweed is not suitable for competition horses, as it contains the above-mentioned reserpine and is prohibited under FEI rules beceause of its mild sedative properties. For horses on box rest or restricted grazing, only include very small amounts in your daily hedgerow selection and the rule of thumb is; if they don't need it, they won't eat it. Remember also that the gut bacteria play a part in the selection of food and it takes some time to educate the gut to accept and metabolise some bitter-tasting plants.

In general the horse's gut is used to fairly bland ingredients, as is the palette. Apart from sweet, sappy flavours and other identifiable flavours, including salt (from salt licks and blocks) the gut does not get much chance to experience different, perhaps more spicy or pungent flavours. When new flavours, such as bitter or peppery flavours are introduced, both the palette and the stomach are caught 'off guard'. Also, the gut has to adjust its gastric juice concentrates to accommodate the new chemicals that are introduced.

Blackberry tips and old leaves (Rubus)

Horses love to eat this plant; for some reason the colts and stallions in our herd like it more than the females. The stallions start to concentrate on the old remaining leaves after Christmas and then go on to the young buds that are emerging around the end of February.

If you are clearing any blackberry patches, throw the roots into the field and let them dry in the sun; this helps reduce the saponin content, giving them a better flavour. The roots contain potent antibacterial phenolic compounds that help reduce gut pathogens. Gallic acid (used to make antibiotics), is mainly prevalent in the leaves and roots and, in the leaves, there are high levels of p-coumaric acid, which has multiple health benefits, including an increase in melanin production (good for skin and coat) and chlorogenic acid (needed for glucose regulation).

The young leaf buds and tips contain gastro-protective antioxidants, which lower the pH and protect against the onset of the inflammation that precedes gastric ulcers. Blackberry leaves, flowers and fruit all contain a polyphenol antioxidant called ellagic acid, which protects against the oxidative stress of chronic diseases such as arthritis.

Bog plant – sweet flag (Acorus calamus)

Horses love eating reeds and foraging in bogs and one of the best and most medicinal is the sweet flag or sweet sedge, which is actually a sedge grass or reed rather than a flag iris. Sweet flags (Acorus calamus) grow wild along ponds, canals, and wetlands. The plant has been considered to have huge medicinal properties since biblical times. The flowers are rush brown and the leaves are reed-shaped but wavy. Horses will eat the whole plant which has been found to contain high levels of saponins, alkaloids, tannins, and mucilage. Mucilage is a sticky substance often used in medicine (demulcent) as an agent that forms a soothing film over a mucous membrane, relieving minor pain and inflammation of the membrane. Demulcents are sometimes referred to as muco-protective agents.

Sweet flag/sedge also contains beta-asarone – an antibacterial chemical. In the current pharmaceutical-led research into the screening of plant chemicals to combat the growing problem of antibiotic-resistant bacteria that cause gastro-intestinal inflammation, sweet flag/sedge came out as a serious contender for drug development. Beta-asarone was shown to be active against drug-resistant *Escherichia coli*, MRSA, *Enterococcus* and *Pseudomonas aeruginosa*. The beta-asarone in sweet flag was found to completely knock out *Cryptococcus neoformans*, a type of saprophytic yeast that causes equine Cryptococcosis, a disease with a poor prognosis and symptoms of meningitis. It can also cause pulmonary disease i.e. pneumonia and abdominal granulomas in horses. Equine cryptococcosis is most frequently acquired through airborne transmission i.e. inhalation, and is also thought to be linked to the Australian Redgum tree, a native of Australia also known as Eucalyptus camaldulensis, which may lead to opportunistic infection in immunocompromised animals and people.

Cleavers (Galium aparine)

Cleavers contains multiple important antioxidants to support health but also has a strong action against pathogenic bacteria common to horses. Two of the antibacterial antioxidants are called thymol and carvacrol (which can also be found in oregano and thyme); both are effective against the gram-negative bacteria *Pseudomonas aeruginosa*.

Pseudomonas are part of the natural environment around the stable and soil and also live in the skin, lips and intestines of healthy horses. They will take over and cause an infection if opportunity arises, for example

Cleaver.
Geertje French

around a wound or other injury or if a horse has a primary respiratory virus. *Pseudomonas* can also infect the eye from a small scratch from a haynet hung too high or if sustained whilst hacking through thick woodland or shrubs. It is the bacterium that is responsible for the sweet-smelling greenish/yellow pus.

Pseudomonas is very resistant to antibiotics and steroids, meaning that any horse with a history of long-term use of these will be more vulnerable to infection. The bacterium can be particularly active in horses with a long-term illness, whether hospitalised or stabled with many other horses and, as reported by Veterinary Ophthalmology ('*Pseudomonas* causes ulcerative keratitis') it is highly resistant to commonly used disinfectants, such as gentamycin and tobramycin. *Pseudomonas* is fast-growing and will quickly swarm and produce a biofilm colony, producing toxins and enzymes that are ulcerative in nature and can quickly replicate – in the case of the eye infection sight-threatening damage may be caused in 24–48 hours.

Feeding cleavers herb will help diminish and prevent opportunities open to *Pseudomonas* to cause an infection. There are also other benefits. Traditionally cleavers has been used as a weight-loss plant. The antioxidants thymol and carvacrol both protect against the oxidative stress caused by laminitis and also help to protect against 'leaky gut' syndrome.

Chickweed (Stellaria media)

Chickweed has tiny white flowers and creeps along the ground, and will be quite persistent once it has taken hold. It is resilient to the poaching of horses' hooves, which occurs when horses go up and down the fence line continuously. It grows well throughout the UK in most soils. Its growth should be encouraged around gateways and poached areas. It is a cost-effective method of managing gastric ulcers since it contains multiple beneficial phytoactive compounds to help reduce pain and inflammation and to restore balance to the gastro-intestinal tract. The antioxidants in chickweed also strengthen the wall of the gastro-intestinal tract, significantly preventing the return of gastric ulcers which, following treatment with omeprazole, can be as high as 80%. It is also a very good source of copper and other minerals, vitamins, flavonoids, triterpenoids, Gamma-linolenic-acid, phenols and beta carotene and is also good for respiratory disease such as COPD (chronic obstructive pulmonary disease). It is a great herb for gathering in the summer and freezing, to be fed at 125 g daily, although for severe cases of ulcers three times this daily dose may be needed for around a week or until the horse leaves it in the manger.

Any skin condition, including sweet itch, will benefit from application of an ointment made from chickweed, although if the skin is very broken or inflamed feeding chickweed is the better option. To make an ointment, when the plant is in full flower, gather 500 g and finely chop the whole plant and add to a small just simmering pan of goose fat (available from any major supermarket). Before it has time to set, you will need to pass it through a sieve quickly. Apply just a very small amount once daily; any more than a light application will cause a slight inflammatory effect. It can also be used in this way as a very mild blister for stubborn windgalls or other small puffy joint swellings. (Avoid leaving the container at dog height as any dog will eat it in a flash.)

To make eye drops for persistent sticky or gungy eyes, take a handful of chickweed and make a tea using 300 ml of water; leave to cool and store in the fridge.

Chickweed contains chemicals that influence the IL-1Beta major inflammatory pathways in many diseases such as gastric ulcers, tumours and cancer and it is currently being investigated as being likely to be therapeutically useful for cancer.

Chenopodium quinoa

Commonly known simply as quinoa, this plant is widely grown around the globe and even grows wild in the UK; all sub-species have excellent medicinal properties. Colours can be purple, deep red or muddy orange, brown and yellow. Other wild Chenopodium species to look out for with similar properties are fat hen, pit seed goosefoot, good King Henry and amaranth. Horses can eat the whole plant but show a clear preference for the seeds; these do contain carbohydrates, and the beneficial antioxidant dose can be achieved in a just handful of seeds. Goosefoot and fat hen have much lower carbohydrate content than Chenopodium. The plants are a rich source of phenolic acids, terpenoids, flavonoids and fatty acids, tannins, proteins, alkaloids, sterols and aromatic compounds. The essential oils have several important pharmacological properties: they are antibacterial, antifungal, antioxidant, antiviral, antiparasitic, analgesic and anti-inflammatory. The essential oil contains high levels of rosemarinic acid, also found in rosemary, plus five other potent antioxidant compounds (p-hydroxybenzoic, caffeic, chlorogenic and p-coumaric acid) effective in wound healing and as a remedy against the gastric dysbiosis caused by EMS.

Comfrey (Symphytum officinale)

There are several varieties of comfrey. It can be a tall plant with blue flowers (Caucasian comfrey), or a low-growing plant with white flowers (creeping comfrey) or a hybrid with pale blue flowers, escaped from a garden (Hidcote blue), or a very tall variety (1.5 m) with purple flowers (Russian comfrey, thought to be a cross with rough comfrey and common comfrey). Rough comfrey is now a very rare plant in the UK, although it can be grown from seeds sourced from specialist herb seed companies. If you see this plant, please protect it, don't pick it. The other varieties are extremely common in the UK.

Comfrey is a veritable medicine chest: it contains active anti-inflammatory, analgesic and anti-ulcer compounds – tannins, allantoins, symphytine, echinidine, phytosterols, asparagine, cynoglossine, consolidine and inulin. It also contains vitamins B12, A, C and E. Comfrey was traditionally fed to horses and cattle as forage; the active plant compounds increase if the plant is grazed or cut down. A

Comfrey.
Geertje French

handful of leaves can be fed direct to the horse or made up into a tea (250 ml) as a great pick-me-up tonic, which can be given every day for a month. The roots can be crushed and given daily as a prebiotic.

Cow parsley (Anthriscus sylvestris)

From around the beginning of March you will see the first signs of cow parsley (Anthriscus sylvestris), one of the best functional foods for horses.

Cow parsley contains a whole cocktail of potent plant chemicals, which is the reason why it turns some horses' noses pink and will also produce a skin reaction on your own hands when picked. It is strongly antibacterial and, in Asia, it is classed as an important medicinal plant containing many important active compounds.

For the laminitic it offers protection against the gastro-intestinal onset of laminitis caused by endotoxaemia which, in turn, is caused by the toxin lipopolysaccharide (LPS), which can be found in the cell walls of gram-negative bacteria. Some types of gram-negative bacteria are naturally in the gut flora and don't cause any harm unless the horse is sick for some other reason, which is when these bacteria begin to multiply excessively, eventually leaking through the intestinal wall and into the bloodstream. When these bacteria die, their cell walls rupture, releasing the LPS into the bloodstream and causing endotoxaemia.

Antibiotic-resistant *E. coli*, *Salmonella*, and *Enterobacter* are common gram-negative bacteria that cause endotoxaemia and gastric ulcers. The plant chemicals in cow parsley are effective against these bacteria.

Cow parsley also contains a chemical that prevents the action of topoisomerase11, one of a group of ubiquitous enzymes, found in all living organisms. (Many drugs, including antibiotics, work through a similar action.) It also contains deoxypodophyllotoxin which prevents viral replication and tissue contamination, the same compound also being anti-inflammatory and insecticidal. Furthermore, it contains monoterpenes, which influence and prevent respiratory allergies. Scopoletin is another chemical that has bacteriostatic activity against various species of bacteria, including *Escherichia coli*.

It is difficult to measure precisely the antibacterial efficacy of a wild plant without spending a few million pounds on equine medical research. However, it is possible to read and understand its significance as the plant progresses through the drug development process as a novel human antibiotic. Until that time, you can be secure in the knowledge that, if nothing else, your horse's immune system will be healthier and stronger as a result of adding it to the diet.

Dandelions (Taraxacum officinale)

There are five good reasons why a horse with laminitis might prefer and actively seek out dandelion flowers.

1. The flowers contain more polyphenol compounds than the leaves or roots, helping to reduce blood sugar and aid digestion.
2. The plant is strongly antimicrobial, helping to reduce the lactic acid-producing bacteria in the gut.

3. It provides high levels of flavonoid C-glycosides with a strong antioxidant activity, protecting the liver, being anti-inflammatory and helping to prevent the passage of sugars across the gut wall.
4. It contains luteolin, which helps to strengthen the immune system and immune response.
5. It is high in chrysoeriol, a plant compound that aids blood circulation, and monocaffeyltartaric acid, which helps control blood sugar.

Beech (Fagus sylvatica)

Fagus sylvatica purpurea, the copper beech, is a non-native member of the Fagaceae family; both the copper and the green versions (Fagus sylvatica) are happily foraged by horses. The green version is served as a salad ingredient in parts of Europe and is also considered to be an important fodder item for all animals. The fruits (known as beech mast) are full of oleic and linoleic acid and tocopherols. The leaves contain phenols and polyphenols such as flavonoids, hydroxycinnamic acids, procyanidins and triterpenes. The leaf, therefore, has strong antimicrobial activity and is gastroprotective and especially effective against *Helicobacter pylori*. The main active compound is a flavonol monoglyceride strongly effective against the herpes virus. There are nine known strains of Equine Herpes Virus (EHV) and some horses are silent carriers.

Wild garlic (Allium sativum)

Garlic helps reduce leptin resistance in overweight horses. This can be cultivated or else found in dense woodland during spring and early summer. Our own horses will all eat the flowers with relish whilst only a few will eat both leaves and flowers. The leaves contain higher levels of phytochemicals than the flowers and are therefore more potent, so only small amounts are needed to gain a benefit. Introduce the plant to a horse's diet by letting him graze the hedgerow or, for the stabled horse, by providing a mixture of cut hedgerow plants, with a handful of wild garlic included. Provide it fresh and, whatever hasn't been eaten, throw out at the end of the day.

Dandelion.
Geertje French

Cranesbill.
Geertje French

Chestnut.
Geertje French

Garlic sometimes gets a bad report because it is said to cause haemolytic anaemia, although you would need to feed 700 g of cultivated garlic bulbs for around three weeks to see changes in the haemoglobin associated with disease.

Ginger (Zingiber officionale)

Ginger is a wonderful and highly effective spice, especially as an aid to support the digestive tract for horses who have suffered with colic, and stomach soothing for horses who may get stomach stress when travelling. The antioxidants found in ginger – shogaols, gingerols and paradols – are known to reduce inflammation so are effective for horses with arthritis and rheumatism. Ginger also helps boost blood flow and circulation. You can use it in powder form, but fresh is best. Peel the ginger first, as commercial crops, especially of non-organic ginger, carry fungicides, pesticides and fertilisers in the skin. Chop the ginger finely and steep for about five minutes in boiling water, then leave to cool. This can then be poured over hay, with the bits, or over the ration. It is not recommended for mares in foal or lactating mares as it may make the milk unpalatable for the foals.

Great burnet (Sanquisorba officinalis)

This plant is a perennial and grows to about 1.5 m tall; the flowers are thick oval buds with tightly formed leaves and grow in abundance in fields and meadows. You may also find it in verges –although don't use any fodder forage from busy roads.

Great burnet offers a wide variety of beneficial substances, the overall properties of which are astringent, antiseptic and anti-inflammatory. The medicinal compounds include flavonoids, saponins, ursolic acid, arabinose, vitamin C, essential oils and tannins (the rhizomes contain a high level of tannins, up to 17%). It also contains very high levels of polysaccharides with multiple applications to activate the innate horse's immune system. (Other immuno-drugs including cytokines and antibodies, either organic or synthetic, have been used for this job but with limited success and most have serious side-effects because they only act on single-target pathways, often causing death to cells around the area of disease.)

Great burnet has been used for thousands of years in Western and Chinese herbal medicine. The roots and rhizomes are

Garlic.
Geertje French

Ginger.
Geertje French

best harvested in autumn. Wash and cut them up, leave to dry (either by air or in a very low oven). Once dried, store in an airtight container: they are best used after two or three years of maturing. They can then be ground up into a powder, easy for mixing in rations. The roots taste bitter and sour, two flavours your horse may not be used to, but you can also mix with a little sweet molasses to make the powder more palatable. The leaves and flowers can be air-dried and milled or put into the ration dried, which often reduces the flavour of fresh plants.

Hazel (Corylus avellana)

Hazel may well be the oldest and most ecofriendly horse fencing in the world. Evidence indicates that it has been in use as fencing for over 5,000 years.

Recent scientific analysis of hazel leaves show they contain eight big-hitting antimicrobials active against pathogenic bacteria and fungi such as *Pseudomonas*, *E.coli* and *Candida*.

The leaves are also high in manganese, copper, magnesium, vitamin E and thiamine. The branches and bark contain high levels of saponins and other antioxidants that support gut health, including analgesic compounds that provide pain relief and help repair the gut wall.

Ivy (Hedera)

Ivy (Hedera) is a highly effective natural anti-inflammatory. Diclofenac is a non-steroidal anti-inflammatory drug (NSAID) used to treat arthritis. It reduces swelling caused by inflammation and joint pain, and can be applied topically, and has pain-relieving abilities that are rated at 94.44%, while the same abilities of hedera are rated at 88.89%. Whilst the effectiveness of hedera is a little lower than that of Diclofenac, it is still pretty high and, since the latter can cause side-effects such as stomach upsets, the comparison here shows that using ivy is a better natural option.

A horse with arthritis or other inflammatory condition will choose to eat the fruit and the leaves of hedera and a topical application can also be made to treat joint pain. This is made by shredding the leaves and fruit in water, bringing to the boil and simmeing for three to five minutes;

Hazel.
Geertje French

Hazel bark.
Geertje French

Hawthorn tree.
Geertje French

it should foam slightly as the saponins are released. It should then be strained and stored in an airtight jar once cooled. The mix will feel a bit soapy, which makes application easier. This can be applied daily until the symptoms are relieved: for horses with white hair or markings apply every other day to avoid irritation or blistering.

Only small amounts are needed to improve health and a snatched mouthful is enough to make the difference.

Horsetail (Equisetum)

There are fifteen different species of horsetail; some contain an alkaloid that has been identified as being a toxic constituent and some do not. Overeating horsetail with a high alkaloid content reportedly produces a range of symptoms, predominantly in cattle grazing on infested land with limited access to other food, and it causes scouring in horses. There is one reference to more serious symptoms including thiamine deficiency leading to weakness and 'staggers' in horses, but the link to the reference given draws a blank. In another trial ponies were fed marsh horsetail (Equisetum palustre) for two months at a concentration of 22.6% of the diet with no ill effects, including no drop in thiamine levels at any time. Equisetum-type alkaloids (mainly palustrine and palustridiene) have been detected in only three species of the plant; E. palustre (marsh horsetail), E. bogotense (grows in Colombia) and E. giganteum (grows in Tropical and sub-Tropical America). For E. giganteum, palustridiene was detected at levels around the limit of detection (LoD) (25 μg/kg), whereas in E. palustre and E. bogotense, both alkaloids (palustrine and palustridiene) were detected at much higher levels (20–800 mg/kg).[3]

Honeysuckle (Lonicera)

Honeysuckle grows in the wild, sometimes using a tree to cling to, and amongst the wild rose bushes. Horses eat the leaves, berries and bark at certain times of the year.

There are varieties that are high in fragrance, exceptionally resistant to the cold and seem to stay beautifully healthy and vigorous during the growing season: this could indicate naturally high levels of beneficial phytochemicals such as flavonoids and anthocyanins. Both of these are known to inhibit the transport of soluble carbohydrate in the small intestine whilst protecting and

Hedera.
Geertje French

Honeysuckle.
Geertje French

strengthening the integrity of the epithelial barrier. An extra bonus is an increase in the good gut bacteria, *Lactobacillus*.

Honeysuckle would be a good plant to offer to horses with EMS/laminitis, best browsed fresh rather than cut down and offered in the stable. The fragrant honeysuckle flowers can also be given as a tea. Phytochemicals include quercetin, luteolin, kaempferol, ß-sitosterol, wogonin and other components important for alleviating any gastro-intestinal discomfort. As an additional extra, it has also been shown to have preventive effects on coronavirus disease in horses.

Holly (Ilex)

This is a highly potent pharmaceutical plant. Horses prefer the smooth or young leaves and will readily eat the young bark and dried leaves. If your horse is snatching at Holly or any member of the ilex family, he is searching out strong metabolic stimulants (polyphenols) called xanthine (chemically classed as a combination of caffeine, which are not permitted substances for horses racing or eventing) and followed by purine alkaloids (caffeic acid, 3, 4-dicaffeoylquinic acid, 3, 5-dicaffeoylquinic acid), flavonoids (quercetin, kaempfero, and rutin), amino acids, minerals (phosphorus, iron and calcium) and vitamins C, B1, and B2. Horses only require small amounts of chemicals from the leaves or stems and stabled horses may take some time to adjust from the relative 'sweet' tasting feed in hay and grain to the more bitter phytochemicals. The younger leaves are the most palatable and abundant in January–March; the older leaves are more woody and bitter.

Holly also contains high levels of an important antioxidant called caffeoyl, the action of which is to lower blood glucose. Ten leaves are sufficient to provide an adequate daily amount. Caffeoyl slows down the passage of food through the gastro-intestinal tract whilst the quercetin, kaempferol and rutin are excellent compounds for horses with ulcers.

Holly.
Geertje French

Knapweed.
Geertje French

Lichen.
Geertje French

Common rush (Juncus effusus)

Horses like to eat various plants at different times of the year; this might be because the plant contains higher levels of bitter, unpalatable secondary plant metabolites such as phenanthrenes, which are rare but important chemicals (antimicrobial and anti-cancer). Some horses will possibly have a nibble because they need to but in the summer months, most horses prefer not to eat but to gather amongst the clumps to breathe in the volatile organic compounds released into the air. Common rush has a sour and pungent smell, stimulating relaxation through the release of hexanal and acetic acid. It is described as a tall, soft rush grass, growing in large clumps about 1.5 metres tall in moist soil. Commonly found growing in humus-rich areas such as marshes, ditches and fens it is full of important antioxidants (triterpenes) that are antidepressants, anti-inflammatory and antibacterial, important for horses with Cushing's, abscesses, lethargy, muscle wastage and late coat shedding. This plant has a high triterpene content all year round, but high sugar content in autumn and winter, which may not be suitable for some horses – although ours are out 24/7 in a challenging environment. It is great for alleviating oxidative stress damage in skin and hoof. It also contains high levels of vitamin E and magnesium. Horses start to nibble at the seed heads in autumn and happily eat the plant to the ground through January and February. It is, however, classed as an invasive species and considered to be undesirable and unpalatable for livestock such as sheep and cattle.

Knapweed (Centaurea nigra)

Antioxidants are important compounds with health benefits, and some plants contain a wealth of them, common knapweed being one of the best. *Centaurea* species have been used in the treatment of renal dysfunction, inflammation (urinary tract and gynaecological), digestive and dermatological conditions. The extracted oils are full of polyphenols and sesquiterpene lactones and are anti-cancer, anti-diabetic, anti-inflammatory, anti-rheumatic, analgesic, hepatoprotective, antioxidant and antimicrobial. In the UK there are eleven varieties (which can be found through the wildflowerfinder.org.uk website) but the highest levels of antioxidants are to be found in Centaurea nigra and a cultivated variety (Orientalis) with a yellow flower. The flowers contain flavonoids and are a good source of free amino acids. Twenty free amino acids were identified: aspartic acid, asparagine, glutamic acid, glutamine, alanine, arginine, glycine, leucine, histidine, hydroxyproline, isoleucine, lysine, methionine, phenylalanine, proline, serine, threonine, tryptophan, valine and ornithine.

Leeks (Allium ampeloprasum)

Wild leeks (Allium ampeloprasum) are scarce in the UK (found in Wales, Cornwall, Somerset) and are thought to have been introduced into the UK and once used to identify Welsh soldiers in battle against the English. Other members of the allium family are wild garlic, spring onion, kurrat, salad leek and Persian leek.

As wild leeks are rare, replace them with cultivated leeks, spring onions and chives. However, don't be tempted to use white, red or brown onions, including shallots, as they are carrying compounds unsuitable for the horses' digestion. The green part contains a strongly anti-inflammatory compound (monoterpenoid) similar in action to the harpagoside found in Devil's claw.

There are many pharmacological evaluations to prove the effectiveness of Devil's claw as an anti-inflammatory and analgesic agent. One of its major mechanisms of action is its ability to inhibit the expression of cyclooxygenase-2 (COX-2) and inducible nitric oxide (NO), also involving the suppression of NF-kB activation, thereby inhibiting downstream inflammation and subsequent pain. However, as harpagosides are a prohibited substance under FEI rules adding a different but similarly strong natural alternative such as is found in the allium family might be a better way to reduce stiffness and inflammation.

Nettles (Urtica dioica)

According to Grassland Management for Organic Farmers the levels of the minerals potassium, phosphorus, calcium, magnesium and copper are significantly higher in nettles than in the commonly grown pasture grass perennial rye. The high levels of minerals and protein in nettles are thought to have an added antiparasitic effect as they boost the immune response to infestation. Stinging nettles contain an impressive array of phytochemicals of ethnoveterinary importance including phytosterols, saponins, flavonoids, tannins, sterols, fatty acids, carotenoids, chlorophylls, proteins, amino acids and vitamins. Nettles also contain the plant compounds beta sitosterol, trans ferulic acid, dotriacontane, erucic acid, ursolic acid, scopoletin, rutin, quercetin and p hydroxylbenzalcohol. They are pharmacologically active against all common ailments of horses including the big three – ulcers, arthritis and laminitis.

Horses like nettles best cut and dried; if you have a big patch, cut it down, spread it out and leave it to dry either in the field or on the yard and include a handful or two each day. Some horses will even nibble the flowers and tips from nettles growing in the field; they seem to relish the skill of removing something tasty from stinging or prickly plants.

Horses will eat it dry, so it's great to include in hay and makes a very nutritious tea to add to the winter food ration, instead of a mineral balancer.

Oak (Quercus)

Oak is an interesting choice for some horses; the tree has a wide and wildly varying range of important antioxidants and may be sought out for a variety of reasons. Oak leaves help to inhibit the uptake of iron. (Although iron is an essential mineral, as mentioned earlier, *too much* can be problematical.) A cell line was used to check for the inhibition of iron uptake by gallic acid sourced from wild blueberries, bark and leaves of oak, polyphenols and tannins, sourced from yarrow, thyme, oak, oregano, willow and chlorogenic acid sourced from blueberries and parsley. The results were as follows: 5 mg of tannic acid inhibited iron uptake by 20%, 25 mg by 67% and 100 mg by 88%. Gallic acid inhibited iron uptake by the same amount whilst chlorogenic acid was much lower.

The gallic acid content of oak leaves varies throughout the year being highest in May at 0.25 mg/g and lowest in September at 0.15 mg/g. Interestingly, if your horse prefers an autumn snack of oak leaves he may be looking for a glycoside hit: this anti-inflammatory, anti-obesity, anti-diabetic compound is at its highest in the autumn months at 12 mg/g. Tannins are at their lowest in

September, whilst proanthocyanidins are high at 10 mg/g, offering a heart and respiratory system health boost and protection against the formation of tumours.

Oaks have the reputation for being poisonous but contain many beneficial phytochemicals (*see* text on acorns earlier in this chapter). The acorns contain rapidly degradable tannins that are quickly taken into the bloodstream, whereas the leaves and bark contain tannins that are less able to be absorbed across the gut wall, increasing the benefits to the gut and reducing internal toxicity. Oaks contain more tannins than any other plant, meaning that the horse needs to eat less: 1 g will provide protection to the mucosal membrane against the effects of an increase in gastric acid production that can occur during times of stress. If your horse seems to be seeking out oak leaves and eating more than a few, he may be using the increase to reduce gastric acid production by the proton pump, repairing and preventing hypersecretion. Tannins also inhibit the production of pepsin, produced by the equine gut in times of stress. Horses with access to oaks produce proline, a protein, which protects them against the toxic effect of tannins, in other words, the horse becomes conditioned to eating food containing tannins. Horses that have access to some oak leaves will improve their use of protein and will also gain condition. Tannins reduce parasites, especially targeting nematodes or roundworms, the most common to affect horses from this group being the small redworm.

Peppermint (Mentha piperita) and oregano (Origanum vulgare)

Wild peppermint and oregano (also known as marjoram) are the best herbs to help protect the horse from the effects of translocating pathogens in the gut. Bacteria with translocating potential tend to colonise within the deep layer of the mucus gel of the crypts. The term bacterial translocation was first used in 1979, describing the passage of viable bacteria from the gut through the epithelial mucosa into the lamina propria and then to the mesenteric lymph nodes (MLN) to the liver and other organs.

Nettle.
Geertje French

Mint.
Geertje French

Oak.
Geertje French

Translocating pathogenic bacteria are in fact opportunistic and in the right environment will cross the gut wall barrier and cause disease in these organs, plus toxins produced by these bacteria will also cross the gut wall and have further negative effects on these organs.

Secondary metabolites contained in both herbs feed the gut bacteria that make up the 'resistome', which is the guarding mechanism preventing a translocating event.

Both peppermint and oregano are good herbs to cut and dry to use through the winter; cultivated varieties are as potent.

Rosemary (Salvia rosmarinus)

Rosemary is known for its antimicrobial, antiseptic, antifungal and anti-inflammatory properties. It can be a great herb to help horses suffering with arthritis and rheumatism. Rosemary is also known to cleanse the blood and it may help horses suffering from anxiety as it has a calming effect. Rosemary may also be used as a skin wash for horses suffering with mites or lice. For internal application you can either use the dried herb, or fresh – the latter being recommended as some of the properties may be lost during drying. Add a handful of chopped up rosemary to hay or to the ration. Mind you, some horses love it and some hate it. To make a tea tonic, boil a litre of water and pour over a handful of fresh leaves. Steep for about ten minutes and either offer as a drink or pour over hay. It is best to try it out by itself on your horse before adding to feed. It is not recommended for mares in foal or lactating mares as it may taint the milk and become unpalatable to foals.

Wild spinach (Chenopodium album)

The iron content of wild spinach is 151 mg/kg. This is compared to the content of some grasses as follows:

- Meadow fescue 132 mg/kg.
- Tall fescue 118 mg/kg.

Plantain.
Geertje French

Rosemary.
Geertje French

Rubus.
Geertje French

- Cocksfoot 104 mg/kg.
- Perennial ryegrass 151 mg/kg.

So if wild spinach were grazed as grass then it would be comparable to perennial rye. However, horses only select relatively small amounts to eat, if they are provided with the recommended wide range of alternatives. Therefore, depending on the species (there are some very large plants) one small wild spinach plant without roots would contain 15 g of iron.

Wild spinach also has some oxalic acid content, a substance about which there is some debate and also some confusion with the plants analysed from the 1996 papers referenced.[8] Wild spinach (i.e. Chenopodium album L.) came in at 1,100 mg/100 g and goosefoot (a common name given to Chenopodium album but here referring to cenizo (Texas sage) ranged from 361–2,027 mg/100 g, which is high. Within this paper and elsewhere we were unable to find any references in respect of oxalic toxicity in horses. There were, however, quite a few references relating to sheep and goats, the conclusion being that plants high in oxalic acid were often sought out by these animals and that over a period the rumen adapted with no ill effect.[4]

Pine needles (Lophodermella concolor)

Some horses enjoy a mouthful of pine needles and branches and they like to eat the bark of a fallen sapling, often in the late winter and into spring. There are various types of pine tree, of which the Sitka spruce is the firm favourite; our ponies wait until the green branches die away and then start their nibbling at the top (thinnest) of the fallen tree and slowly work their way to the bottom. We're not sure how, but eventually the sapling is entirely eaten or broken down into small pieces, though this might take a couple of years.

One of the major compounds found in the Sitka spruce (both live and dead) is stilbene glucoside, known to be a strong anti-ageing antioxidant, able to protect against liver damage and

Rosehip.
Geertje French

Stelaria.
Geertje French

Ragwort is toxic to horses.
Geertje French

help maintain healthy blood glucose levels. Another is resveratrol, which has many well-known clinically proven health benefits, helping to reduce obesity, cancers, metabolic syndrome, infections and inflammation. It's amazing what can be extracted from a seemingly dead bit of wood – we love the idea of nothing going to waste.

Pussy willow (Salix aegyptiaca)

When you are out on your daily exercise session, with or without your horse, look out for this bright and beautiful equine superfood! The pussy willow bud is jammed full of antioxidants that help reduce the effects of ageing – great for veteran horses. It contains diosmetin, isorhamnetin and glycosides, astralgin, quercimeritrin and quercitin-3, 7-di-oglucoside: all of these powerful but gentle antioxidants reduce the levels of circulating chemicals that cause inflammation, which increase naturally with age and are linked to the development of Cushing's disease. The way to introduce this plant is to start small; offer a small branch and see if your horse wants to try it out, only small amounts are needed and just a few willow buds are a great addition to the daily diet.

Purple orchid (Orchis mascula)

This plant also has several great sounding common names; adder's meat, bloody butchers, red butchers, goosy ganders, keck-legs, kettle cases and kite's legs.

It prefers non-acidic soils and is found in hay meadows, roadside verges, recent and ancient woodland, on chalky downland and grassy banks. It used to be a very common meadow plant in the UK and Ireland but, unfortunately, less so today.

It contains several potent phytochemicals, alkaloids, saponins, tannins, phenolics, terpenes, sterols and flavonoids and also contains high levels of natural alpha-glucosidase inhibitors, which delay and reduce the amount of starch that can be processed in the gut and transported across the gut wall. It is great for the prevention and management of EMS.

Seed head.
Geertje French

Silver birch.
Geertje French

Willow bark.
Geertje French

Every part of the plant is edible but you should allow the horse to choose his own, rather than just cutting one down yourself to offer in the stable.

Purple willow (Salix purpurea)

This is the most stable variety of all the willows, maintaining its salicylate and antioxidant content even in times of drought. It contains the highest levels of salicylates of the willows, calculated to be 4–8%, and the highest levels of antioxidants associated with the relief of inflammation and pain reduction. It is therefore the best of the willows for arthritis and pain relief.

A good foraging tip for purple willow is that it has the highest chemical phenolic content in the winter months and spring, slowly declining from the end of March until August/September, before increasing again for the onset of winter.

Willow (Salix)

Modern chemistry's unravelling of willow promises enough new medicines and materials to make even Hippocrates gasp. There is more to willow than aspirin and cricket bats. The Rothamsted Research Institute is the custodian of the UK's National Willow Collection. There are over 450 different species of willow, some ground-hugging, some shrubs, great for hedging, and others are trees.

As well as salicin (aspirin) the willow (Salix) contains 13% other anti-inflammatory agents, making this an extremely important plant for horses prone to laminitis. (The average anti-inflammatory compounds of all other shrubs and trees is calculated to be around just 1%.)

Willow also contributes to gut health. Adding willow to the diet increases the *Oscillospira*; these bacteria are important members of the clostridial cluster and make butyrate. In addition to being important for the prevention of inflammation, butyrate also has a role in strengthening the gut wall and increasing insulin sensitivity. Antibiotics and anthelmintics reduce or totally wipe out *Oscillospira*, making willow an important additive to horses that have been treated with either.

White clover (Trifolium repens)

Clover has had a bad reputation as a horse pasture plant, but it can be useful for nitrogen fixation and transfer. Transferring higher levels of nitrogen to neighbouring plants than red clover or lucerne, (approximately 40 kg N ha-1), white clover is especially useful for supporting herb or forage growth in mixed meadows or biodiverse pasture. It only needs to make up less than 15% of the pasture to succeed in supporting the health and continued productivity of the field, especially in relation to providing the horse with the NRC recommended levels of minerals. It also contains an extensive range of different phenolic and polyphenolic compounds such as saponins, flavonoids, clovamides and acids of phenol, all of which can support gut and respiratory health.

Referring back to the earlier point that clover generally has a bad reputation as a horse pasture plant, there are some toxicity concerns. Giant white clover (Trifolium repens var. giganteum) contains the lowest levels of cyanogenic glucosides (8.9% total phenolics) whilst red clover (Trifolium pratense) and Trifolium subterranean contain very significantly higher levels at 72.89% and 79.64% respectively. White clover (Trifolium repens) contains 10.26% concentration mg/g dry matter. Cyanogenic glycosides are a set of nitrile-containing plant secondary metabolites;

they synthesise cyanide (a highly toxic poison) upon enzymatic hydrolysis (cyanogenesis). We therefore need to be careful that our horses don't ingest the Trifoliums with a high percentage of these potentially highly toxic cyanogenic glycosides. Trifoliums are fine eaten by horses in small quantities and can be beneficial, but take care to curb the red and subterranean Trifoliums, as they can spread at a great rate. (Other sources of cyanogenic glycosides are found in apple pips, apricot kernels and peach pit among others.)

Trifolium subterranean has a specific characteristic in the geocarpy, the underground seed development. It can spread rapidly and thrives in soils where other species of trifolium wither. It is an excellent animal fodder and is often mixed with alfalfa to make it a sustainable feed. It is self-fertilising, meaning that it doesn't need pollination; the tiny flowers are hidden by the leaves, which not only protect it from bees but also from other predators.

Another factor to bear in mind is that Trifolium subterranean can contain high levels of oestrogenic compounds, which may interfere with fertility in mammals. There are some 800 chemicals within our environment that will never biodegrade, so will be forever polluting our environment, food chains and waterways. Unfortunately, oestrogenics, from the female hormone oestrogen, can be found in dozens of products that we use in our daily lives, from foodstuffs to plastics. These oestrogenics can interfere with the reproductive organs of the mare. It has been found that the stallion hormone testosterone may also be affected by the over-exposure to oestrogenics, through drinking water and other sources.

Yew.
Geertje French

Toxic plants to eradicate

Ragwort (Senecio jacobaea)

Ragwort is probably known as one of the most poisonous plants to horses, found in fields, meadows, and wasteland.

It may seem strange, but ragwort seeds have been found in the faeces of freely grazing horses who clearly survived the experience of eating them. This may be because seeds often leave the gut undigested and thus passed all digestive processes and could therefore not release their toxic substances. It was also not known whether the horses concerned had also eaten the plant's leaves and stalks. All of which leaves us with a conundrum. Did the horses ingest the seeds that had fallen from the husks to the ground, or had they perhaps been blown around and the horses ingested them whilst grazing other forage? This is

Young carrot.
Geertje French

the most likely scenario as it would seem unthinkable that the horses had ingested the seeds whilst they were in their husks attached to the plant, because that would mean the horses also ate the plants. Also, since the seeds appear in autumn, the plants would have been in a state of drying out, so does this mean that the toxicity of the plant had diminished because of the seasonal changes in its structure.

The general research into the damage of ragwort on horses and the toxicity level the horse needs to ingest for the poison to damage the liver, has been measured on the bodyweight ratio to 2–5% ingestion.

Ragwort contains the dreaded toxic pyrrolizidine alkaloids (PA). Although 5% – 10% of all flowering wild plants contain the same chemical, as to why the ragwort plant has increased levels is uncertain, but it is plausible that it needs these elevated levels of PA to defend itself against attack by fungi or herbivorous insects. Ragwort-loving bugs include six species of beetles, twelve species of flies, five species of moths, one aphid, three thrips (also known as thunderflies) and one mite. Fourteen species of ragwort-dedicated fungi are also able to increase the PA levels.

The reason why a horse might conceivably be attracted to the PA content of ragwort lies in his gut; PA is strongly antimicrobial and will quickly kill off an over-proliferation of bacteria linked to ill health. The ingested PA would promote the fungi and archaea in the gut whilst killing off the bad bacteria. A proliferation of bad bacteria is strongly linked to the over-consumption of starch raising the pH of the caecum and eventually causing hindgut ulcers. It's also worth noting that a horse given high levels of supplemented copper, especially if not in a bis-glycinate form, will be prone to a greater adverse reaction to PA levels in all plants. One of the problems with ragwort ingestion or other ways in which a horse ingests too much PA, is that the poison will have a detrimental effect on the liver, and this may not be discovered for weeks or even months after ingesting high levels of the toxin.

Although the findings are interesting, and we continue to follow any new research coming out, we need to make sure that our horses don't get the chance to ingest ragwort or in any way have its PA levels raised. The best advice is to clear your fields of all ragwort, root and all, and burn after removing. Keep an eye on regrowth. There are lots of different plants that contain much lower levels of PA, and still function in the gut to get rid of the bad gut bacteria in a less potentially toxic way.

Foxglove (Digitalis)

The foxglove is a very beautiful flowering plant, which is a great attraction to bees. However, if you see it growing in your pasture remove it root and all, making sure no seeds or parts are left behind. It contains a digitoxin that is highly poisonous to horses. It causes neurological problems such as staggering and depression and will show blood in dung. If you think your horse has eaten this plant, call your vet immediately.

Sycamore family (Aces pseudoplatanus)

Shrubs and trees belonging to the Sycamore family (Aces pseudoplatanus) are another highly toxic plant; the seeds are especially poisonous. If there are any types of sycamore growing in hedging or alongside pasture remove all parts and make sure there are no seed heads left behind on the verges of the pasture. It is the cause of atypical myopathy and can affect muscles and the heart, cause stiffness in the joints, lethargy and trembling. Call your vet if you suspect your horses have eaten this plant.

Deadly nightshade (Atropa belladonna)

Deadly nightshade is a purple flowering plant from the Solanaceae family (potatoes, tomatoes and aubergine also fall within this category). They all contain glycoalkaloids and tropane alkaloids. The compound atropine is used in eyedrops for humans with myopia. In horses it attacks the gastro-intestinal tract and causes convulsions, dilated pupils and can lead to the horse losing consciousness. Contact your vet immediately if you suspect your horse of having eaten this plant. Check your field and pastures for it, as seeds are often blown into them. Remove all parts of the plants found, including the root system, and check that there are no seeds left behind.

---

1. Lucke, M., Correa, M. G., & Levy, A. (2020). 'The role of secretion systems, effectors, and secondary metabolites of beneficial rhizobacteria in interactions with plants and microbes', *Frontiers in Plant Science*, 11, 589416. Sauer, S., Dlugosch, L., Kammerer, D. R., Stintzing, F. C., & Simon, M. (2021). 'The microbiome of the medicinal plants' *Achillea millefolium L. and Hamamelis virginiana L.*, *Frontiers in Microbiology*, 12, 696398.
2. Phytochemical balancers
    - Miller, J. K., & Poxton, I. R. (1999). 'The association of Clostridium botulinum type C with equine grass sickness: a toxic-infection', *Equine Veterinary Journal*, 31(6), 492–9.
    - Waggett, B. E., McGorum, B. C., Wernery, U., Shaw, D. J., & Pirie, R. S. (2010). 'Prevalence of *Clostridium perfringens* in faeces and ileal contents from grass sickness affected horses: comparisons with 3 control populations', *Equine Veterinary Journal*, 42(6), 494–9.
    - McCarthy, H. E., French, N. P., Edwards, G. B., Poxton, I. R., Kelly, D. F., Payne-Johnson, C. E., Proudman, C. J. (2004). 'Equine grass sickness is associated with low antibody levels to *Clostridium botulinum*: a matched case-control study. *Equine Veterinary Journal*, 36(2), 123–9.
    - Gilmour, J. S., Brown, R., & Johnson, P. (1981). 'A negative serological relationship between cases of grass sickness in Scotland and Clostridium perfringens type A enterotoxin', *Equine Veterinary Journal*, 13(1), 56–8.
3. Horsetail
    - Cramer, L., Ernst, L., Lubienski, M., Papke, U., Schiebel, H. M., Jerz, G., & Beuerle, T. (2015). 'Structural and quantitative analysis of equisetum alkaloids, *Phytochemistry*, 116, 269–82.
4. Wild Spinach
    - Guil, J. L., Torija, M.E., Giménez, J. J., Rodríguez-García, I. and Giménez, A., 'Oxalic acid and calcium determination in wild edible plants', *Journal of Agricultural and Food Chemistry* 44, no. 7 (1996): 1821–3.
    - Laghari, A. H., Memon S., Nelofar, A., Khalid Mohammed Khan, K. M., and Yasmin, A., 'Determination of free phenolic acids and antioxidant activity of methanolic extracts obtained from fruits and leaves of *Chenopodium album*', *Food Chemistry* 126, no. 4 (2011).

9.
Pastures – Paddocks, Meadows and a Walk Through the Seasons

The link between water and soil

Nature is its own efficient monitor, based on a circular process, but it needs to be harnessed. Therefore, there are a lot of nature-based solutions available and, by nature-based, we mean good-quality soil that is rich in all the vital nutrients to grow well-balanced feed crops – the foundation for all foods eaten by the horse and other ruminants. However, the capacity for soil to do this does not exist in isolation – it both *requires* watering and *filters* water and we can no longer rely on soil just *being* good soil, because the rain is polluted and therefore many of our water courses are polluted. In fact is has been found that the general drinking, river and sea water is now so polluted with excess chemical waste from drugs taken by humans and animals (this includes the contraceptive pill, steroids, chemical recreational drugs, GP or specialist prescribed medication, HRT, and all veterinary medications – wormers, steroids, fertility drugs, and so on) that on that basis alone we are slowly poisoning ourselves and our animals. Further to this, there may be a sense in which horse owners are unwittingly adding to the problem. All drugs pass through the body, do their work, or not, and they then become waste, which is released. Muck heaps are taken away and become part of the fertiliser manufacturers' system. It might be prudent to start looking at the percentage of drug waste to be found in the muck heap. If you multiply those muck heaps throughout the land you will soon find that the percentage of drug waste (even after all the processes are instigated to turn muck into fertiliser and soil) will be over the statutory limits set by the ministry of agriculture.

Another problem occurs when farmers let agricultural chemical products (which can include organic waste from, for example, extensive chicken, pig or cattle farming) leach into nearby rivers and waterways. This, of course, is a problem from the viewpoint of water itself, but it will also have an impact on the quality of the soil it irrigates. For this and other reasons, soil needs constant nurturing and monitoring.

Futhermore, the cocktail of chemicals we either wittingly or unwittingly let our horses ingest are rapidly starting to show some worrying results, as they lie at the heart of a number of health problems affecting our horses. Their entire physiological, neurological and metabolic systems will be irrevocably affected if we don't make a radical sea change and turn around in the way we feed and water our horses.

Arising from the pollution issue and other environmental factors is the unavoidable debate as to where our horses should be living. In a utopian society we would have them grazing the eternal meadows, grasslands, lowlands and highlands; we would afford the 5-star welfare package and entirely horse-centred treatment our equine friends deserve. Whilst, in practice, we may not

Mare and foal in the meadow.
Carol Hughes

be able to make it 5-star, we can care and use our best efforts to ensure that the happiness of our horses is enhanced by becoming knowledgeable about their dietary needs and how to create and enhance a stress-free environment.

Drinking water

We have already mentioned the importance of water quality in terms of the soil, but the importance of the horse getting enough good drinking water is sometimes underestimated or even overlooked.

A horse of 15–16hh, in normal exercise, will need around 30–35 litres per day to stay hydrated and horses in hard work, who lose a lot of water through sweating, will need considerably more than that – between 40–50 litres in normal weather conditions and, in hot conditions, up to 60–75 litres per day. Horses at rest will need about 20 litres of water daily and a lactating mare, because of the water she needs for her foal's milk, will need 25–30 litres per day. Horses who graze on healthy forage and grass, which can hold up to 70% moisture content, may not need as much drinking water as horses who are stabled, but their intake should still be monitored and a fresh, clean water source should always be available.

In hot weather all horses will need water constantly available to top up the moisture lost through sweating, as water has an important role to play in the control of body temperature. Furthermore, it is a major component in metabolism of the body. Without water there is no life, be it animal or plant life. The reason why water is so important to life is because it has many functions. And although a horse can go without food for a few days, if he is deprived of water, he will get dehydrated within 24 hours and this will put a huge strain on all vital organs and the intestinal tract, as all biochemical reactions within the body rely on the ingestion of enough water to function at an optimum rate. Water is also needed to help transport dry feed through the gut and it transports tissue fluids, solutes in blood, excretions and cells.

Water provision

Stabled horses need a fresh water supply in their stables, preferably with an automatic water dispenser; make sure to check the dispenser a few times a day, as bits of hay, straw or stable shavings can become a choking hazard. When this is not feasible the water can be put in a stainless steel trough with a plug to drain it for cleaning. Make sure the plug is underneath the trough so the horse doesn't pull it out and chew it up. Buckets placed on the floor are not recommended, as they can be easily kicked over or may become polluted by horse droppings or urine, ending up in the bucket, or a horse can injure himself by getting his feet trapped between the handle and the bucket. You can buy bucket brackets, from which you can suspend the buckets. Hang them in a place where you can see them from outside the stable to make sure there is always clean water available. Refill them three to four times a day (more often in hot weather), and clean them out properly every morning, taking out any bits of hay or straw. Keep an eye on the wear and tear of the buckets and replace any that start to crack or if the rims break up, as bits of plastic can get into the water.

In the field make use of a galvanised water trough placed where it can be filled up with clean tap or spring water. If this is not available, use water buckets that are hung on brackets at the fence. Ensure that all water vessels are kept clean and free from algae, as this can be a problem in hot weather, especially if water is left without being refreshed.

Galvanised auto system water trough.
Geertje French

When the weather is hot, make sure that water in the field is being topped up at least six times a day. In winter make sure that all outside water troughs are free from ice. In stables, lag pipes to prevent freezing. Don't let horses gorge on water after exercise as this can also cause stomach problems, including colic.

Flowing rivers or streams are potentially a good water source, but be careful if there is a lot of agricultural activity in and around the fields where your horses live because, as touched on earlier, heavy rainfall will cause leaching of fungicides, herbicides and fertilisers, which will end up in the water source. Water sources near heavy chemical industry should also not be used; stop horses drinking from such a source with fencing. Also avoid very shallow water sources, as the sediment of the bed will be ingested by the horse and can cause stomach upsets through ingestion of sand and bacteria. Take care not to let your horse drink from ponds, as they are stagnant and will harbour all kinds of pathogens and insects, so fence off any ponds situated where horses could get to them.

Actual pollutants aside, it is worth bearing in mind that 'clean' water can vary in what it contains in different parts of the country and this may have some impact on horses. On very chalky land the chalk will leach into rivers and streams and chalk has a high calcium content, of up to 20%. This is useful for horses who otherwise graze on land that is low in nutrients, or if the diet does not give an adequate calcium to phosphorus ratio. Water near the sea will have a higher than normal salt content and can become brackish in hot weather. Too much salt can cause kidney damage and diarrhoea.

Sick and healthy soil

Having recognised concerns about factors affecting soil quality, we need to ask the question as to whether sick soil contributes to the onset of some diseases in horses, for example to some types of laminitis.

Healthy soil has higher levels than unhealthy soil of the bacteria that support the production of interactive plant hormones, and lower levels of bacteria that increase plant carbohydrates and sugars.

We carried out some soil sampling and the first soil sample returned to us indicated a high level of *Rhizobiales* (17.5%) – the range is 3–18% across different fertilised/glyphosate-sprayed soils and organic untilled soils having the highest percentage.

Rhizobiales inhibit the growth of plant pathogens, promote healthy plant growth, clean up the soil of pollutants (*Cyanobacteria* are high in the gut of horses with laminitis) and are present in the microbiome of dogs and horses, presumably having a positive effect. Fertilisers and agrichemicals reduce *Rhizobiales* by lowering the pH of the soil. Speed of recovery is dependent on the field having some legume content, although it will recover without (the area of field we tested had no legumes, but had never been fertilised or tilled/ploughed).

The main health-promoting functions of these bacteria for horses are to supply nutrients and plant hormones and to reduce toxic plant pathogens. *Rhizobiales* come with a vast community of phages that kill susceptible bacteria, contributing to population turnover and driving selection for resistance, and they also provide competitive advantages and make the soil strong and resilient.

There are six main plant hormones with benefits to the horse. Indole-3-acetic acid (IAA) is an anti-tumour and anti-cancer agent, gibberellin helps in apoptosis (death of abnormal cells), abscisic acid (ABA) regulates glucose homeostasis, ecdysterones stimulate energy pathways and reduce adipose tissue and cytokinin works as an anti-ageing compound.

It is, then, a 'given' that the quality of the soil itself is a significant factor in growing the cereals, grains, hay, legumes, beet, linseed and carrots that our horses need. However, we cannot always know where the basic constituents (seeds, etc.) originated or how, for example, they have been fertilised. Therefore, look out for organically grown and sourced feeds. When the horse is given all the right nutrition from the ingredients that have been carefully thought about when drawing up a feed chart, he will undoubtedly thrive.

Growing your own

If you have any facility to grow feed of your own, you also have the opportunity to grow plant materials that are organic and high in nutrients, but there are a few things you need to take into account.

Before you consider buying a parcel of land, to use for either hay or grazing (or if you are going to re-sow existing land), it is vital to consider the quality of the soil since, as already mentioned, it is the health of the soil that will determine the quality of what is grown on it.

It is also important to know what kind of soil you have. With this in mind we will look at the different types of soil and what makes a good soil. You can buy soil-testing kits, but there are excellent companies out there, such as EquiBiome.com who will do all the hard work for you. They test under labroratory conditions, which are more reliable than self-testing. To find out if your soil is suitable for organic growing you will also need to have it tested.

Composition and different types of soil

Basic composition

Soil is made up from various components:

- Mineral matter, which derives from the breakdown of rock formations over many thousands of years.
- Organic matter, including both living organisms and dead organic matter.
- Soil air, which is not the same as atmospheric air. Soil contains more water vapour and carbon dioxide than air, and less oxygen. Water in the soil displaces the air held within the cell spaces in the soil. Soil that is very dense and water-absorbent, such as clay, can easily become waterlogged, preventing air within the soil being held by the cell spaces.

Since the constituent parts of the soil – cell structures, nutrient levels (copper, cobalt and other elements) – are constantly changing, soil can never be a static material. Other factors affecting structure include weather-dependent changes such as rainfall and erosion, and there are human influences including applied chemicals and the use of heavy machinery.

Soil water, from rain and dew, is important for plant growth. When soil becomes waterlogged and produces anaerobic conditions the organic matter content will decrease significantly, thus increasing the nitrate content and, rather than being taken up by plants the nitrate dissolves into the atmosphere.

Soil types

The soil type available to you will be determined by the terrain where you live. The general classifications are as follows: peat – sand – loamy sand – sandy loam – silt loam – clay – clay loam – silty clay loam – sandy clay – silty clay.

Some soils are better for pasture than others, but one of the main things to consider is how well drained the soil is. Very wet soil does not hold onto good nutritional values. Soils that are very sandy may also not be ideal for pasture. You can find what kind of soil you have on the Internet. See: Landis.org.uk, which gives you all the statistics on soil in England and Wales.

Healthy soil should contain a good balance of the following: oxygen – carbon – hydrogen – phosphate – calcium – magnesium – sulphur – sodium – chloride – phosphorus – nitrate – potassium – copper – iron – manganese – cobalt – molybdenum. These are ideal compositions; some soils may have all, some less, depending on where they are and the basic kind of soil.

Management considerations

As we will discuss in more detail later, horses are particularly susceptible to feed-related sickness stemming from the metabolic system and subsequently affecting their physiology, the central nervous system impacting on their mental health. These include conditions such as EMS, Cushing's, obesity, white line disease and the newly emerging equine atypical myopathy. This last one is on the increase and a review of previous scientific literature reveals that antioxidants were the only medical intervention to give a positive outcome.

These ailments can clearly be traced back to an unbalanced diet, which affects horses' gut to such a degree that it is almost inevitable that they could never be completely fit or strong, as their diets do not allow it. We can reverse this (to a sometimes greater and sometimes lesser degree) by focusing on natural healing medication and close monitoring of soil where horses graze and where hay may be grown. In other words, by looking at how our horses can be well cared for, not by making compromises, but by considering what they *are getting* and what they *actually need*. We all want only the very best for our horses – a natural desire – but sometimes our desires do not wholly match up with what our horses actually, not superficially, require.

A proportion of manufactured horse feeds lack the full range of high-quality micronutrients needed to support health and there is clearly a link between poor (mal) nutrition and disease but whilst equine scientific research has done its best to provide us with the basic understanding of how the addition of a vitamin and/or mineral supplement can improve and support health, it has limited information regarding the type of complex supplementation needed to avoid some of the modern and increasing diseases. Thus finding the right type of supplementation can be confusing to say the least. The shelves are overstocked with different supplements of every kind and it is difficult for the average horse owner to make sense of them all. In fact, many of these supplements are of a poor or variable quality meaning that the horse owner might be inadvertently giving less than is required to support health. Rather than reading the back of endless supplement packages to try to redress and balance the horse's diet, how much more rewarding to invest in your own field by improving the soil quality and microfauna (which in turn will improve the horse's gut bacteria), plant a range of wild flowers to further benefit health and biodiversity and learn to trust that your field can provide the vital nutrients and antioxidants he needs to stay healthy.

If you are a horse owner fortunate enough to have access to a natural micronutrient producing area (field), you may have to start off from a less than ideal point because, as mentioned, in recent years some fields have become almost a danger zone to horses suffering from the diseases previously mentioned, mainly a result of growing the wrong type of modern grasses and using chemical fertilisers and pesticides that not only leave a poisonous residue but also kill off the vital microflora in the soil and cause demineralisation.

Most horse grazing areas are currently deficient in minerals and micronutrients; a process of decline that started in the 1940s and has continued to worsen with the continuation of modern farming methods, the primary goal of which has been a high yield at the expense of high quality. Demineralisation began with the demise of the flooded water meadow system that was used throughout Europe for over 400 years as a remarkable system of remineralisation. Remains of this are found in many parts of the UK from Hereford to Staffordshire and to large acreages in the southern counties of Dorset, Berkshire and Wiltshire. You may even be using land with this type of system without knowing about it. Benefits from controlled flooding include the grass crop being available some weeks earlier than normal, and an increased hay crop. The demise of the flood meadow and destruction and silting up of the drainage channels has created a situation where water stagnates on flooded land and, rather than being a beneficial event, is now a bit of a disaster as stagnating water destroys the root system and the microfauna population of the soil. In a properly managed flood meadow system the water would come in at a trot and go out at a gallop, depositing mineral-rich silt on the way. Flood meadows evolved from the need to feed and sustain grazing animals through the winter months, provide early grass and then a hay crop late in the season and they offer an exciting opportunity to grow a huge range of beneficial plants. The late hay cut followed by grazing prevents domination by taller species (especially perennial rye), ensured a thick sward and re-seeding of the flowers. If you are fortunate enough to have access to land that resembles an old water meadow, this may be a good start and mimicking the old practices should be beneficial.

If the land includes a wooded area there are also great benefits available from woodland foraging for ailing horses and ponies – in fact the facility to eat from diverse hedge rows and trees is acutely important in order to maintain optimum health in the gut of all horses. In days gone by they were often turned out to scavenge through a scrubby wooded area under the direction of wise old horsemen. It is interesting, then, to discover that wooded areas contain some of the most significant plant compounds with medicinal benefits. Naphthoquinones are phenolic compounds common in nature, being secondary compounds produced by fungi and plants, within the bark of trees and in piles of dead leaves and woodland soil. Lichen found in trees and on walls also contains high levels – our herd will strip ours clear through the winter/spring months. Naphthoquinones have been heavily relied upon in traditional medicine throughout large parts of the world, including China, South America and Asia. They have very significant pharmacological properties as they are strongly antibacterial, antifungal, antiviral, antipyretic, anti-inflammatory and insecticidal. Naphthoquinones have been used in the development of nine synthetic drugs and their reported effects are complex as they bind to DNA and inhibit the processes of replication, interact with numerous proteins (enzymes) and change cell and mitochondrial membranes. They also interfere with electrons of the respiratory chain on mitochondrial membranes. They are great as a natural anthelmintic and as an antidote to malignant melanoma. The leaves of any tree will contain naphthoquinones and can be made into a poultice, by first making a tea, steeping it for a while, mushing it in the blender then applying on the area to be treated.

There are various other practices you can consider to help improve the quality of your soil and its produce.

Sow some wild oats – oat grass

We are often asked about the use of pesticides to control noxious weeds. The problem with using synthetic chemical pesticides is that they have a direct impact on the horse's endocrine system. Pesticides contain some pretty unpleasant hidden and inert chemicals such as phthalates, which are capable of and very likely to have a direct and disruptive effect on the horse's hormone balance and production. This not only increases the chance of the horse becoming obese but is also linked to the onset of laminitis and Cushing's.

Instead of using a pesticide, take a step away from our modern farming methods and begin to see yourself and your grazing land in a new light: see yourself as a conservationist and the land as a biodiverse environment, manage it with this in mind and your horse's health will improve visibly in a very short time. In modern farming terms any grass that is not related to high milk yields is classed as a noxious weed; this is fine if you see milk production as the end goal, but as horse owners we have a different agenda.

Currently our ecosystem is in jeopardy from the loss of many native plant species and the indiscriminate use of pesticides and synthetic fertilisers, so much so that there are now many government initiatives aimed at benefiting farmers and encouraging them to return to a more biodiverse method of farming. Invasive weeds such as docks, nettles, ragwort and thistles (and also the sycamore seeds that have caused such a problem recently) have less chance of survival or of being a health threat in an environment that encourages a wide variety of plants, grasses and flowers, as the soil will hold an increased population of microbiota which, in turn, increases a wide range of nutrients. This might mean that your mare's milk yield may well fall but her overall health and performance should rise significantly!

A horse is classed as a superorganism because he has a close and interdependent relationship with the bacteria that live in his gut; these bacteria in turn have a close relationship to the soil and with micro-organisms that exist in the rhizosphere of the plants they eat. The rhizosphere (roots and soil around the roots) contain algae, bacteria, *Cyanobacteria*, fungi, yeasts, myxomycetes and actinomycetes that are able to decompose almost any existing natural material. Micro-organisms transform organic matter into plant nutrients that are assimilated by plants. This is a wonderfully delicate environment into which the horse slots perfectly and it is a far easier method of grassland management than modern intensive methods. The clash between modern farming methods and what is considered to be useful for a grazing horse is clearly defined on the Defra website under the grass weed section, where almost all the indigenous grass species that we have analysed as having low sugar appear as weeds alongside methods of control with pesticides – *see* below.

Control and management

Wild oats can make a significant contribution to the overall health and well-being of the horse as they are full of vitamins and minerals. They also contain good protein, potassium and high levels of the vital but much depleted magnesium and a wide range of B vitamins, several anti-inflammatory antioxidants and beta glucans that stimulate the activity of macrophages, the immune cells that ingest and demolish invading pathogens. Macrophages also release cytokines, chemicals that help the immune cells to communicate with one another and they work as natural antibiotics against those bacteria that are resistant to modern antibiotics.

That said, DEFRA identifies wild oats as the most competitive of all weeds (wild plants). Quote: "Yield losses are greater the longer they remain in the crop, and just one wild oat/2m² causes a 2% decrease in yield. Therefore, the earlier a herbicide application is made the better. Earlier sprays not only give the greatest yield response, but also the highest level of control, since smaller weeds are more susceptible." Also, smaller weeds require a lower herbicide dose.

General weed control

A weed is a plant, just like any other, the difference being that weeds are those plants that are not desirable in the context of a healthy pasture, field or meadow. This undesirability takes on various significant forms. For example, as some weeds are toxic to horses, they need to be removed as soon as they appear.

Weeds that are allowed to get out of control in the field can start to damage soil structure and take over the land, as they become invasive when not controlled. They will also compete for the nutrients, water and light needed by grass to stay healthy. Becoming invasive can be driven by two natural processes. When you let weeds go to seed these will either drop to the ground or be blown across the field to spread even further. Also, some weeds have very fine and long root systems, so in addition to depleting the soil they will spread rapidly, with new plant formation. Weeds with deep root systems need to be dug out, as weed control solutions will not be able to reach that far down, giving the root plenty of opportunity to regrow in no time at all. For the reasons just mentioned, when pulling or digging out weeds, be sure to remove them *before* they get into seed production. Do not be tempted to try to mow the weeds or use a scythe, as both will only make it appear as if the weeds have gone, when actually their root system remains, which inevitably regrows the weeds.

There are chemical and non-chemical weedkillers on the market – if you intend to use them do your research and try to use organic non-chemical products to protect the soil against poisonous ingredients.

When buying hay, check that it is clean and weed-free.

Dealing with agrichemicals

Agrichemicals are chemicals used in agriculture such as pesticides, fungicides and inorganic fertilisers.

Four years of data from horses using the EquiBiome analysis has given us a unique insight into how the environment and modern management systems are impacting horse health. Using AI it has been possible to profile the gut microbiome of horses with EMS/laminitis/gastric ulcers and head-shaking: the common denominator is a reduction in alpha diversity and an increase in bacteria linked to environmental pollutants and the use of agrichemicals.

Agrichemicals reduce the stability of each individual complex, finely balanced ecosystem, directly affecting the health of each.

Antibiotics are excreted into the environment through faeces or urine in high concentrations and are then found in the soil and water, and ingested by grazing horses with the effect of reducing the numbers of good gut bacteria, whilst increasing the antibiotic-resistant pathogenic bacteria. Self-fertilising pastures may help improve the health of horses by increasing gut microbial diversity.

Action you can take

A herd of horses in a field or pasture, with a hedge, wooded area, or tree line, is a collection of interlinked ecosystems, including an above- and below-ground microbiome and host skin and gut microbiome. Each microbiome is a unique ecosystem, providing benefits (through microbial metabolic processes) to the other interlinked systems predominantly through nutrient and biochemical cycling.

Saprotrophic organisms in the soil break down organic matter into composites that increase fertility; the above-ground microbes providing nutrients directly to the plant and the below-ground microbes improving the nutrients to the plant roots. Oak trees have the highest levels of above and below and ground biotic interactions, although any tree or mixed deciduous hedge will increase nutrient availability.

The horse then acquires these nutrients through his own gut microbial community. The animal gut and plant roots share a similarly important function, that of nutrient uptake, though a major difference is that plants produce their own energy through photosynthesis (autotrophs) and animals must rely on energy captured by the plants (heterotrophs).[1]

Interaction between stress and the biome

There is plenty of published research on humans and other animals in relation to how increased social stress and conflict changes the biome, published in journals such as *Behavioural Brain Research*, but none yet on horses, although it is possible to look through the biome results coming back to us and make comparisons.

The main changes in the biome following social stress are:

1. A reduction in *Lactobacillus*, bacteria belonging to the friendly firmicutes. Many horses are indicating a reduction in the firmicutes. *Lactobacillus* is also included in the section on gut stress in the NGS test; many horses come back in the red, which means that there is a reduction of *Lactobacillus*. Provision of a *Lactobacillus* supplement is known to improve mood and behaviour in humans and animals.
2. Conflict and social interaction also change the bacteroidetes to firmicutes ratios, by increasing the bacteroidetes.
3. Levels of prevotella (a genus of Gram-negative bacteria) are an indication of dominance, the higher the levels the more dominant the animal/human is.

Plants that kill parasites and strengthen resistance to infestation

Plants with high tannin content may have either a direct toxic effect, killing the parasites, or may have an indirect effect by improving macro- or micro-mineral utilisation. Tannins are bitter; the bark of birch, hazel, horse chestnut, oak and willow have a high content but there are also more horse-friendly legumes such as sainfoin (Onobrychis) and birdsfoot trefoil (Lotus corniculates) with high tannins that can be grown within the pasture.

The plants just mentioned are valuable for increasing the absorption of dietary amino acids such as threonine, valine, isoleucine, leucine, tyrosine, phenylalanine, histidine and lysine. These make important contributions to the mineral content of pasture, which in turn is thought to be a contributing factor for increased resistance to worm infection, reducing the need for a synthetic wormer.

How to grow them

Sainfoin. This may be best grown as a separate area as it is a poor competitor with other grasses (except for meadow fescue and timothy) and legumes. However, it likes a pH of 6.2 and above and won't grow on acidic soil. The mineral content increases with each cut; it is very palatable and digestible, fantastic for horses stabled for long periods, a natural 'mineral balancer'.

Birdsfoot trefoil. This grows low to the ground, which makes it a poor competitor with tall grasses such as the modern perennial rye. It likes poorly drained soil with a low pH and is good at re-seeding itself. It is best established in a corner of the field, or on a sunny hillside, although once established it does spread well. It is very palatable and the strongest anthelmintic pasture plant.

Organic grassland

The ethos of being organic is that you rely on what is available rather than adding synthetic mineral supplements. Growing a variety of functional plants – grass, herbs and legumes – improves the root system, which helps to increase the mineral content of the plant. Even without fertiliser, sowing a mix of caraway, plantain, chicory, chervil (cow parsley), sainfoin and salad burnet at a ratio of 15% overall will provide enough minerals (NRC figures) for a horse in full exercise without the need to supplement. Growing herbs along with legumes reduces the grass growth later in the year, which is good for laminitic and EMS-prone horses.[2] Pasture can be fertilised with slurry (cattle excreta), which is known for its high mineral content, and one study found that mineral content in the herbs and functional plants increased following this treatment. Ideally, slurry from cattle that have been given drugs such as growth hormones, antibiotics, pain relief or other NSAIDs should not be used, although that information may not be readily available.

How safe is your grass?[3]

Most owners of laminitic/overweight/EMS or Cushing's prone horses will be actively involved in managing grazing and restricting turnout aware of the fact that grass and hay contain water-soluble carbohydrates in the form of simple sugars (sucrose, glucose, fructose) and also fructans that may trigger an attack. They may also be aware that sugar content tends to vary depending on the seasons and weather conditions and therefore they will spend a great deal of time selecting 'safe' grazing times to avoid sugar overload.

Clearly horses are designed to eat and digest grass but are also foragers of shrubs and herbage – a fact that many of us overlook. Furthermore, many of our UK native breeds are actually designed to thrive in harsh conditions on inferior pastures. Is there, in fact, some fairly accurate way of calculating sugar intake, depending on what type of grasses are grazed, so that owners can have greater peace of mind and are not continuously battling with their horse's grazing habits, especially if their breed or metabolic condition makes this a particular concern?

Intending to find 'safe' pasture Bangor School of Chemistry has been investigating the sugar content of some of our so-called inferior native species of grass compared to the more modern and most popular grass sown in the UK, perennial rye, which comprises a whopping 86% of grass seed sales. Since 2005, perennial ryegrass has been cultivated to have a high (80%) content of fructan whatever the weather or other environmental conditions. This makes sense to the dairy farmer who wants a high milk yield in the most economical way without feeding large quantities of hard feed, but makes it hard for horse owners who have been under the impression that fructan levels can vary and there may be safer times during which to graze horses. The idea behind the development of the high-sugar ryegrass varieties was that the rumen bacteria in cattle tend to preferentially metabolise the fructan leaving more amino acids available to travel through to the hindgut to be absorbed by the cow, resulting in better weight gain and better 'nitrogen use efficiency' (how nitrogen is absorbed into the bloodstream) in this animal, but making this grass entirely unsuitable for native horses/ponies.

There are two types of laminitis that may result specifically from over-grazing; one is endocrinopathic and the other is alimentary. Endocrinopathic laminitis is the result of a high fructose intake and alimentary laminitis is the result of an overload of fructans, which alter gut microbiota because they cannot be digested by the horse.

Fructose and fructan are digested in different ways: fructose is digested in the small intestine and is then transported into the blood in the form of glucose. As it hits the bloodstream the body immediately signals a release of insulin to take the glucose out of the blood as glucose is toxic to the vital organs. To protect the vital fight or flight mechanism the horse's system has a strict policy on glucose control (in terms of 'policing' it) and it is quickly either used or stored. Continuously high levels of glucose equate to a continuous release of insulin and the latest research from Chris Pollitt and Cathy McGowan (2011) revealed that high insulin levels will trigger an attack of laminitis.

Much of the grassland research in the UK has concentrated on feeding dairy cattle and growing turf for sports facilities and, although there are pony pasture types of seed available to buy, little has been done to analyse the fructose and fructan content of these indigenous grass species. Therefore, the initial project at Bangor University was to analyse the fructose content of a 25-year-old variety of perennial rye (Lolium *perenne*) in comparison to the more modern variety to see if the fructose levels had increased along with the fructans. At the same time the University would also analyse the fructose content of a range of old pasture grass species including Yorkshire fog, meadow fescue, cocksfoot, creeping bent, red fescue and several more. We have been very fortunate to have had expert help from Ianto Thomas at Ibers, who runs a global seed bank. He provided us with a number of validated grass species from his plant collection of over 25,000 original types that are stored on site.

The research project ran for a year from October 2012 and included seasonal comparisons of sugar content together with two-hourly comparisons of five native grass species and perennial rye. The first set of results received were quite remarkable, indicating that the fructose content of both the old and new varieties of perennial rye were high in fructose, but the new variety was even higher, with a 332mg/g fructose content in comparison to 0.52 mg/g in meadow fescue. Therefore, modern perennial ryegrass, the most popular type of grass grown in the UK, has the potential to give the laminitic-prone pony a double whammy of sugar in the form of fructose and also a high ingested fructan level.

Meadow fescue itself is actually 0.52 mg/g fructose, 0.26 mg/g glucose and 0.19 mg/g sucrose, whilst crested dog's-tail is 0.48 mg/g fructose, 0.23 mg/g glucose and 0.13 mg/g sucrose, which is too low to show on the chart. If given the choice of perennial rye over meadow fescue a horse will inevitably choose the sweeter variety and over-indulge on its sweet sugary content, whilst the meadow fescue will be far less appealing and the horse will eat more slowly and will more likely pick at other plants on offer as a healthy alternative.

Haylage

Here we look at the difference between haylage sprayed with homolactic and heterolactic inoculant and the difference between sprayed and non-sprayed. To define these terms, an inoculant is a product containing beneficial bacteria that stops the growth of mould and speeds up the fermentation process. A homolactic inoculant turns one glucose molecule into two molecules and a heterolactic inoculant converts one glucose molecule into lactic acid, carbon dioxide and ethanol.

1. Sprayed haylage has double the lactic acid content of non-sprayed. As lactic acid has been seen to cause dysbiosis leading to laminitis in horses, this may not be desirable.
2. Horses have their own lactic acid-producing bacteria, existing in a community that is self-regulating around a diet and the pH balance in the gut. Increasing the food containing lactic acid kills off portions of the biome that have existed in symbiosis, producing sudden changes in the microbial community and causing imbalances and inflammation.

Plastic-wrapped and open haylage bales.
Geertje French

3. The hindgut bacteria produce fatty acids that are absorbed and used by the horse for energy. The horse's fermentation vat (caecum) is designed to remain full, whilst digesting low-quality forage producing balanced proportions of different fatty acids. Providing some horses with a high lactic acid pre-fermented food will upset this process, changing the percentage and type of fatty acids produced.
4. Haylage containing a low dry matter will contain three times the amount of lactic acid compared to non-fermented hay.
5. Sprayed haylage will contain higher levels of WSC, sometimes double that of unsprayed – worth knowing if you are looking for low-sugar haylage.
6. 'Good doers' or natives are already very efficient at extracting energy from food. If the speed of the delivery (pre-fermented) and digestion are increased this will inevitably cause metabolic problems.

Mineral imbalance in hay or pasture

Some owners may be concerned about the possible effects that a mineral imbalance in hay or pasture may have on their horse's health, particularly in relation to laminitis, insulin resistance (IR) and EMS.

Analysis was done on the mineral content of thirteen grass species including three perennial rye varieties, two which were cultivated for high sugar content whilst the third was an older variety (forty years old). The remaining ten species were deemed inferior (as they had a lower sugar content) native grasses found in meadow and old lea pastures. It was found that the grasses varied immensely in mineral levels, but minerals were higher in those fields backing onto woodland and/or surrounded by a hedge.

The modern perennial ryegrass was highest in iron, lowest in magnesium and lacked many other vital micronutrients. The best balance appeared to be in the combination of all the species and the reasons for this are not only found in the soil, but in the rhizosphere and the hyphosphere of the plant roots, which is where minerals are organised into different groups and sub groups and absorbed.

The main group of minerals found in soil includes potassium, iron, magnesium, sulphur and calcium. The secondary group consists of hematite, limonite, goethite, gibbsite, and carbonates. The constituents of the primary minerals are by and large feldspars, micas and quartz. Each mineral has come from large rocks that have broken up and have become distributed throughout the soil. Depending on where the soil is to be found, the constituents can vary enormously from region to region. This also means that all the different soils have different levels off minerals. Roots extract the minerals, which are essential for the growth and health of the plant. The roots are also selective in what they take up. Although research into plant behaviour is a fast-developing field, we still don't know precisely why some plants take up larger quantities of selenium and copper, whereas other plants absorb higher levels of potassium or sulphur. Precisely how this works is still not entirely clear.

The rhizosphere is the area of soil that consists of the roots and contains a variety of micro-organisms called mycorrhizal (fungus-root). This is a rich area of nutrient manufacture and recycling, which directly influences mineral levels. The roots provide the fungi with glucose and sucrose; the grass roots send the sugars from its underground storage to the roots and out to the fungi. In return, the grass gains better access to water and the whole spectrum of minerals. Different grasses attract different communities of micro-organisms and create unique environments around themselves called hyphospheres, which is why it is so important to have a field with a wide variety of species.

As stated previously, horses grazing in a field surrounded by a hedge or in a field containing trees will obtain better and more balanced mineral levels from the grass than those without. Three of the best trees to have either in the hedge or field are white willows, silver birch and poplar; these trees encourage a varied community of micro-organisms into the grass, which will spread into the root systems across the whole field, provided the field contains a mixed variety of grasses.

Tree root systems are incredibly important for the health of horse pasture as they are far-reaching and can spread their good bacteria and fungi across the pasture to improve the mineral levels of the grazing horse. Grass mixed with trees is likely to be healthier than plain pasture, contain better nutrients, have faster growth and perhaps, more importantly, will have reduced sugar content as some of the sugar will go to the roots to feed the mycorrhizal where it will be converted to macro- and micro-minerals.

Fields (and hay for that matter) containing only one or two types of grass, particularly if they have been cultivated to hang onto their high sugar yield rather than translocate the sugar to the root system to feed the mycorrhizal community, will not contain the spectrum of minerals that a meadow type of pasture will.

Paddock management for obese/EMS/laminitic horses

When choosing grasses for horses mixed plant pastures are the best choice. If you are planning to re-seed your horse pasture to increase nutritional value and lower the carbohydrate/WSC intake, then a grass seed mix needs to contain old grass species, legumes and herbs. Good mixes to put together are listed below.

- **Grasses (59% of total mix).** Fescues (Festuca), cocksfoot (Dactylis glomerata), meadow grass (poa) and timothy (Phleum pratense) in equal amounts, so each individually would be 14.75% of the total.
- **Legumes (26% of total mix).** Red and white clovers, lucerne (Medicago sativa), sainfoin and birdsfoot trefoil. Clover content should be 5% for white and 1% for red. Lucerne should be 15%, birdsfoot trefoil 3% (tastes bitter fresh but very palatable dried in hay), sainfoin 2%. Sainfoin and birdsfoot trefoil will struggle to grow in low pH soils, so pH needs to be six and above. Legumes are high in tannins, which are important components of the diet for reducing worm burdens and feeding the good gut bacteria.
- **Herbs (15% of total mix).** Chicory (Cichorium intybus) 3%, chervil (Anthriscus cerefolium) 3%, ribwort plantain (Plantago lanceolata) 3%, salad burnet (Sanguisorba minor) 3%, caraway (Carum carvi) 3%. Although clover is often not considered a benefit to pasture, a legume of some sort is essential, both to maintain the nitrogen and minerals within the soil and to prevent the grasses taking over from the herbs. However, clover will tend to take over a pasture if the grass mix balance is too weak (i.e. low diversity of species). Also, if the paddock has compacted or heavy soil, improve the soil quality first by aeration and applying organic matter. The NSC levels in white clover are about half that for perennial rye, although some thought should be given to the variety of clover used regarding bacteria, virus and mould infections which cause photosensitivity in some horses. Therefore, choose a disease-resistant variety to reduce the chance of a bad reaction.

Grasses behave differently when in a pasture mix and it is important to grow grasses and plants that thrive and support each other. The mix above is tried and tested to increase macro- and micro-mineral levels, reduce carbohydrates and maintain sufficient protein, horses grazing on this type of pasture are unlikely to require supplemented food. Do not apply a nitrogen fertiliser to this seed mix as the balance of plants will change, reducing the herbs and legumes. By adding wild flowers in the mix, you help to add variety and diversity in the forage since many wild flowers can be eaten by horses. Buy only mixes that are safe for horses from your seed provider.

Unique metabolism of Spanish breeds of horses

Spanish horses in their natural environment feed on indigenous grass species such as rye. Rye is known to be high in sugars, and the relatively hot, dry climate of Iberia is likely to increase the sugar content of most plants – and horses from Andalusian/Lusitano/Spanish lines are extremely good at extracting sugar from their food. They have a unique microbiome profile, with a higher than normal percentage of two species of prolific sugar-digesting bacteria called Treponema bryantii and fibrobacter succinogenes. The difference in climate between northern and southern Europe may contribute to the presence of different bacteria species in these regions. Both species of bacteria have a metabolism called an orthogonal lignocellulose metabolism, meaning neither species relies on the release of enzymes from other bacteria before they can start digesting sugar. Instead, these bacteria manufacture their own enzymes and proteins for digesting *any* type of sugar and they do this at speed.

A horse with this type of microbiome will be very hard to keep in good health on any kind of pasture and may also struggle with hay. Both bacteria are acid-loving, which can lower the pH of the hindgut. A more acidic hindgut kills off the good gut bacteria and those that digest fibre more slowly. There is an increase in endotoxins and damage to the gut wall, inflammation, and mild/subclinical laminitis or 'footiness'.

Treponema comes from the syphilis family of bacteria and the best active plant compounds to reduce them are found in Jamaican sarsaparilla (Smilax officinalis), aloe vera and milk thistle. When you are wild foraging, oak leaves and ivy berries are also good antimicrobials that are active against treponema.

If you can lower the percentage of treponema then the gut microbiome is more supportive of those good gut bacteria that digest fibre more slowly and those that thrive in a less acidic environment.

Medicinal meadows

Meadows are now one of our rarest habitats and a priority for conservation and restoration within the UK's Biodiversity Action Plan.

The lack of meadow grazing is a problem for our horses as species-rich (biodiverse) meadows and roadside verges (those on quiet lanes, not ajacent to heavy traffic) provide our horses with anti-inflammatories, anthelmintics, anti-ulcerogenic compounds, antimicrobials plus an entire range of vitamins that match the requirements of the NRC.

Historically, medical science has demanded a single-target approach as verification or proof that a drug can do what it says on the packet. Multi-component medicine has been avoided and even frowned upon because science has lacked the platforms and tools to measure the effects. However, there is a growing awareness that complex problems such as those that relate to the immune response (allergies, inflammation, arthritis/rheumatics) require an equally complex multi-targeted medical approach. Plants are well equipped for this approach, although many meadows and grassland communities are losing important herbs and forbs with medicinal properties.

In the UK the best grazing areas for horses and most species-rich meadows are the upland hay meadow or MG3 grassland, which is found only in the north of the UK, often on wide grass verges. (The term MG3, designated by the National Vegetation Classification, refers to a specific vegetation type found in upland hay meadows. These meadows are characterised by a dense growth of grasses and herbaceous dicotyledons, reaching heights of 60–80 cm. The specific designation helps identify and classify these habitats for conservation purposes.) The most significant medicinal plant within this community is the great burnet, which is highly valued in many areas of the globe in respect of its phenomenal medicinal properties.

The great burnet contains very high levels of polysaccharides with multiple applications able to activate the innate immune system. Immuno-drugs including cytokines and antibodies, either organic or synthetic, have been used for this job, but with limited success and most have serious side-effects because they only act on single-target pathways, often causing death to cells around the area of disease.

Phytomedication

Plants work in different ways from prescribed medication; they interact with the body to renew, replenish, protect and strengthen. They have a shotgun effect – blasting out many health-promoting chemicals, rather than a single bullet dose of synthetic chemicals like drugs do. No living creature can do without them – as per the government promotion we need our five a day but your horse needs at least twenty-five, especially if stabled for long periods.

However, it is possible to use pharmaceutical drugs and biomedicine together as plants increase health before they target disease. Horses grazing naturally will have stronger digestive tracts, better immune systems (less arthritis and fewer chronic degenerative diseases) and better wound healing times than those who don't. On this basis it's extraordinary to think that many of the plants listed below are classed as noxious weeds and considered to be serious pests on grazing land, worthy of extermination in both the UK and USA.

Best plants to grow and supply for inflammatory diseases and ailments

1. **Borage (Borago officianalis).** This plant has among the highest number of sterols of all plants. Among them, campesterol (6.4% of total extract) and Y-sitosterol (6.3%) were found to be the major constituents, great for enhancing the activity of beneficial immune cells whilst inhibiting the response of those that cause inflammation and chronic disease. These increase the production of disease-fighting T cells by as much as 920% and have anti-inflammatory capabilities similar to the steroid drug cortisone, but with none of its negative effects. (Cortisone is used to treat joint pain, respiratory problems and is made into topical applications for wounds and mud fever.) Borage is high in gamma-linolenic acid (GLA), a type of omega-6 fatty acid found in various plants, which plays an essential role in normal bodily functions. GLA may help reduce inflammation, which can cause swelling, redness, and pain and contains very small amounts of pyrrolizidine alkaloids so is best given in small doses for short periods.

2. **Mallow (flowers and seeds).** Common mallow (Malva sylvestris) is a large flowering plant that grows in hedgerows and on roadsides and footpaths. It has been deliberately cultivated since Roman times for its anti-inflammatory properties. Its best use is as a coating for the mucous membranes, so it is good for horses with upper airway infections and gastric ulcers.

3. **Wild Radish (Raphanus raphanistrum).** Horses like the leaves and flowers, which are high in potassium, calcium and vitamin C, plus significant levels of phenols that help balance thyroid activity (both under- and overactive) and may help protect against the onset of Cushing's. The leaves also contain folic acid (B9); they are a great nerve tonic and muscle relaxant.

4. **Wild carrot (Daucus carota).** Also known by many other names, wild carrot contains high

amounts of quercetin (three times the level of a glass of red wine) and stimulates metabolic pathways associated with lipid and starch breakdown. It also contains anti-inflammatory phytochemicals and is especially good for horses with kidney problems such as increased drinking and urination. Horses like the young plants, flowers and seed heads – all are beneficial.

5. **Wild Mint (Mentha aquatic).** This is sweeter than common mint. This plant contains the highest levels of antioxidants with significant free radical scavenging properties, beneficial for chronic inflammatory conditions such as arthritis, gastric ulcers and airway inflammation.

Grazing habits

There are a number of factors that influence grazing habits and some of these have an effect on the land grazed.

Free-foraging horses

The feeding times of wild horses are longer than for wild cattle. Free-ranging horses eat for approximately 60–70% of their time, depending on availability of nutrients. (By contrast, domesticated horses spend far less time eating on improved pasture and even less time when stabled.) Feeding times are directly related to how much food is available; less availability in the winter means they are 'ribby' in the spring and ready to consume the higher-carbohydrate spring grass.

Clearly, feeding also stops at times so that wild horses can perform other important tasks such as resting (mares observed generally spent around 26% of the time resting, moving around, vigilance, drinking, comfort behaviour, social behaviour and alarm reactions.)

The natural digestive process and seasonal influences

Horses grazing naturally eat to maintain a high level of gut fill, so feeding consists of bouts of uninterrupted feeding separated by non-feeding intervals. Feeding doesn't occur randomly but is divided into meals. During meal times horses take short (less than ten-minute breaks) to look around, stand guard, or to walk over to see what their neighbour is eating. There are longer periods between meal times for sleeping and resting – the feeding habits are similar to deer. Meal lengths are affected by the time of day and horses prefer to eat during the day rather than the night, although stabled horses tend to eat throughout the night if they have access to ad lib hay.

As an average, meal times in April are around three hours and twenty minutes long, dropping to just one hour and ten minutes in October. The change in the length of the meal time is a result of the increase in the fibre content of the grass as the season goes on. In April though, the nutritive value (glucose/starch/protein) of the green shoots is high whilst the biomass is low, meaning that horses have to consume a greater quantity before the gut is full. Perhaps this partially explains why horses appear to gorge in spring and why grazing masks worn for long periods may cause a level of stress if the horse is turned out hungry. It might be better to feed a haynet of low-quality fodder before turning out.

Flies become a nuisance in the UK from the beginning to mid-June onwards, and in the fly season feral horses graze for much longer periods between the hours of 4 a.m. and 8 a.m. However, during times when flies are a nuisance, actual meal times are much shorter; horses stop feeding to rub themselves on each other and to groom each other, intervals between meals are longer and horses no longer feed until full and have longer periods of walking in between. The average feeding bout in between grooming and rubbing is around twenty-five to forty-five seconds, literally snatching a bite to eat.

This change in routine coincides with mid-season when glucose is still high and fibre content is also high enough to allow less time eating before gut fill level is achieved.

Seasonal disturbance by horseflies

As mentioned above, flies generally can be a nuisance for horses, interfering with their feeding habits, and horseflies are a major seasonal culprit. Horseflies are active between May and October from sunrise to sunset. In addition to simply biting, they carry viruses and bacteria that can cause disease in horses. They seem to prefer attacking bay, chestnut, black and dun horses above greys and their least favourite-coloured horses to bite are pale roans. They also prefer bachelor groups of geldings or colts to breeding or all female groups.

Some areas contain more horseflies than others; if you have a field that seems to be infested it is better, if possible, to put more horses in to decrease the attacks per horse.

Pyrethroids are thought to be effective repellents against horseflies but may have adverse reactions in some horses. Neurotoxic side-effects have been reported such as tremors, incoordination, elevated temperature and liver damage. Other side-effects include respiratory problems and skin rashes. The best natural alternative is found in grapefruit skin: soak the skin in boiling water, leave to stand for twenty-four hours, then strain and apply. It is safe to use continuously.

Damage to pastures caused by grazing horses

One of the things that can really spoil good grazing pasture is the damage to the grass and soil made by horses. If there are a number of horses using the field, activities like walking around, running, rolling and pawing can have a detrimental effect on the soil and the grass. The ground will get churned up, which will break up fragile root structure and leave bald patches that will need re-seeding. This is especially true of land that gets saturated during rainfall; this will not recover easily when there is lots of activity on the pasture.

It is always a good idea not to let too many horses use the field for grazing at the same time: when one group has had their fill move them to another field for relaxation and movement, before allowing the next group out on the field for grazing.

Also, ensure that the field is cleared of faeces every day. Another effective way to disperse faecal matter is by harrowing. This not only keeps the field clean but it will also stop the spread of worm infestation that may be present in the faeces for other horses to pick up – that is, it impairs colonisation.

Horses eating soil

Approximately 40% of the microbiome of a horse is made up of transient microbes (depending on how diverse his biome is) picked up from his environment. If the horse is stabled for long periods, the passage of good bacteria through the gut ingested from the grass, plants and soil may dwindle and the horse will seek out a top-up. Even horses out all the time will often dig up a patch of soil to eat, again to increase the population of important members of the biome. (*See* also the condition pica, mentioned under sodium in Chapter 7, in which eating soil may be a symptom of sodium deficiency.)

The bacteria most often required for top-ups are Actinobacteria, of which the average horse has seventy-five different species within the biome. Actinobacteria degrade cellulose, protein, fats and polysaccharides and help to maintain balance within the microbiome.

Note that all agrichemicals reduce the good gut bacteria within soil.

A walk through the seasons

Spring tonic

If your horse has had to spend more time in the stable through the winter months, then consider a spring tonic to give him a general health boost.

A recipe for this tonic is to mix dandelion root, nettles and marshmallow in equal parts and feed 30–40 g per day for three months.

If the horse has had any type of health problems through the winter, then add one part milk thistle for three to four weeks, to help support the detoxification process.

Horses with chronic health issues should have two parts gentian, nettle and marshmallow with one part turmeric and one part liquorice, steeped in boiling water for about thirty minutes, then added to hay or ration, fed at 30 g per day for two months.

Autumn – leaves and scent

Volatile organic compounds (VOCs) are particles released into the air by leaves and bark, soil and roots. Breathing in these beneficial autumn particles during a daily ride through a wood, alongside a hedge, or in trees growing in a park, will significantly increase the diversity of your own and your horse's nose and skin microbiome. Trees are especially beneficial as their microbiomes contain 200 species of beneficial *Clostridia*, supporting the immune system and reducing allergies. This needs to be done as frequently as possible to 'top up' your microbiome along with your horse's – from your skin the microbes find their way into your gut with the obvious multiple health benefits. Autumn changes some of the VOCs released by the trees and one of the most important antioxidants to be found during autumnal leaf senescence is vitexin; this helps reduce gastric discomfort (colitis) and specifically targets liver damage or injury from chronic colitis. And if your horse eats a few leaves, he'll be topping up on anthocyanins, ascorbate, carotenoids and alpha tocopherol.

Autumn foraging

Horses like eating berries, which are full of an antioxidant called anthocyanidins (they make up the berry colour); only small amounts are needed to benefit health. A good example is the bearberry (Arctostaphylos alpina) a significant protector of health, mentioned in *The Physicians of Myddfai*, a thirteenth-century Welsh herbal remedy book and, in the eighteenth century, by Carolus Clusius (doctor, scientific horticulturist and botanist), in the *London Pharmacopoeia* of 1788. It grows in the wilder parts of the UK, Europe, USA and Asia. Bearberry is used in Chinese medicine and, in parts of Europe, the leaves are officially classed as a phytomedicine. The Native Americans also used bearberries as tonics and as an alternative to tobacco. Cyanidins account for over 99% of the anthocyanin aglycones in bearberry, and it also contains quercetin (excellent and beneficial for the gastro-intestinal tract) and quinic acid. Quinic acid supports the synthesis of tryptophan and nicotinamide in the gastro-intestinal tract; both are important metabolites that modulate the gut bacteria, influence metabolism and the gut-brain axis, producing a feeling of calmness and well-being. They are okay for humans too. Happy foraging.

Autumnal benefits of seed heads

Seeds stay longer than fresh forage in the horse's gut and go through many digestive actions, some of which provide remarkable benefits to health. When ingested the seeds are abraded (the surface is worn away or damaged) and crushed by the grinding action of the teeth; they are then warmed up and made wet before being soaked in acid in the stomach and small intestine. Finally, they are colonised by the gut bacteria in the caecum and large intestine. Proteolytic bacteria adhere to the surface of the seeds and excrete enzymes as they digest the hard, outer surface. These enzymes have significant health benefits to the horse including the modulation of inflammation (gastric ulcers), reduction in swelling of the mucous membranes (helpful for gut wall integrity) and improving circulation.

Seeds that have gone through the gastro-intestinal tract of the horse emerge as faecal matter as waste. As is the case with bird droppings, the horse's droppings replant the seeds in the soil. It seems that some of these seeds have an enhanced rate of survival and growth, so perhaps the journey through the horse's gastro-intestinal tract may be of beneficial value. The following species of seeds were found to be more robust after their journey – an interesting research finding:

- 10,000 varieties of grass seed.
- 19,000 species of Fabaceae (legumes).
- 4,400 species of sedges and rushes.
- 1,265 species of flowering plants such as Cistaceae.
- 2,500 species of small shrubs and herbs including the common nettle.

Bracken in autumn

Bracken contains several toxic/complex chemicals, the main one being ptaquiloside, levels of which are high in the plant from late April, then diminish in July and are completely gone in October. Not all horses like to eat bracken but, for this reason, when they are partial to it, it is safer eaten in autumn. The very young fronds contain more of the toxic chemicals than the larger leaves, but cooking destroys these chemicals, making them safe to be eaten as a delicacy: boil for ten minutes, drain and leave to cool. (While bracken can indeed be toxic, the toxic dose has been estimated at 7–12 kg per day for the average 13–14hh pony. Signs of poisoning include trembling, shivering and collapse.)

As the plant grows and ages the toxic ptaquiloside is replaced by its final metabolites – pteropines B and F, which have been proved to have significant anti-diabetic and anti-obesity activities. Bracken also contains ecdysterones with similar glucose-lowering properties; ecdysterones stimulate the AKT pathway thereby increasing energy and metabolism. (AKT refers to a specific protein involved in transporting potassium. The AKT pathway is explained in detail in the next chapter.) Only a few mg of ecdysterones are needed each day; the horse will get all he needs in a snatched mouthful.

Brown bracken contains high levels of sitosterol and stigmasterol, both of which lower blood glucose levels and both also have an anti-inflammatory action – again only small amounts are needed.

Winter natural nutrition – the potential to help horses with Cushing's

Sedative stress and inflammation increase with disease and as the horse ages. Cyclooxygenase-2 (COX-2) is an enzyme found in horses that plays a crucial role in inflammation and pain. In horses with Cushing's, COX-2 is stimulated by oxidative stress and likely to be at a higher level in most tissues, leaving the horse more vulnerable and open to other health challenges such as respiratory, hoof, skin, and eye infections. Research has shown that a signalling pathway called nuclear factor erythroid-2-related factor-2 (Nrf2) gives protection against oxidative stress, especially in older horses, reducing the action and presence of COX-2 in the cells, thus diminishing the secondary effects.

Hawthorn bark is particularly high in a type of procyanidin, able to increase the action of the Nrf2 pathway, thus offering protection against some of the symptoms of Cushing's. The bark of hawthorn is also strongly liver-protective, important for those horses on long-term synthetic medicine. A horse needs access to only 250 mg of procyanidins per day, of which 74% will make it through the gut wall: hawthorn bark contains 20–55 mg/g dry weight procyanidins. The bark contains some similar procyanidins to the leaves, flowers and berries, but the expression of the most effective procyanidin B2 is around ten times higher in the bark, which is why only small amounts can make such a difference.

Winter diet of wild horses

At this time of year there isn't much about for freely grazing wild horses to eat, so what strategies do they have before spring brings in an abundance? In winter a high percentage of nutrients come from winter-flowering shrubs such as gorse. Feral horses also eat selectively from available high-nutrient grasses such as juncus or knotgrass (Polygonum aviculare). Wild barley and grasses from the millet family also have good protein and phytoecdysteroids, (great for the metabolism and the endocrine system). Feral horses will also eat lower value grass/plants to maintain a high gut-fill level, leaving it to the efficient gastro-intestinal tract to extract as many nutrients as possible from the food available. Lower value plants are actually very high in pro- and prebiotics, good for horses with gut problems. Feral horses choose high-quality low-fibre components and then dilute them with large amounts of over-mature leaves and stems.

The best wild antioxidants to feed horses in February

Vitamins A and E are often described as the most beneficial antioxidants for horses; ours get their daily dose from the newly grown tips of the whinberry bush or wild blueberry/bilberry (Vaccinium myrtillis). These shrubs grow prolifically over rocky outcrops and beside stone walls. The herd grazes the leaves, stems and fruit each year, eating from the lower slopes first before moving up the hill during the summer months to eat more of the bushes that, by then, will bear dark blue fruit.

Chemical analysis reveals that wild blueberry contains a 'medicine chest' of antioxidants to lower blood glucose, dilate blood vessels and sensitise tissues to glucose uptake. The plant is also high in vitamin C and chromium, and anthocyanosises, which are flavonoids, part of an antioxidant supergroup called polyphenols, well known for being anti-inflammatory, as well as for blood sugar-regulating properties.

---

1. Action you can take
   - Kienzle, E., et al., 'Field Study on Risk Factors for Free Faecal Water in Pleasure Horses', *Journal of Equine Veterinary Science*, Volume 44, 32–6.
2. Organic grassland
   - Pirhofer-Walzl, K., Søegaard, K., Høgh-Jensen, H., Eriksen, J., Sanderson, M. A., and Rasmussen, J., (2011). 'Forage herbs improve mineral composition of grassland herbage', *Grass and Forage Science*, 66(3), 415–23.
3. How safe is your grass?
   - De Laat, M. A., Van Eps, A. W., McGowan, C. M., Sillence, M. N., & Pollitt, C. C. (2011). 'Equine laminitis: comparative histopathology 48 hours after experimental induction with insulin or alimentary oligofructose in Standardbred horses', *Journal of Comparative Pathology*, 145(4), 399–409.
   - Eades, S. C., Holm, A. M., & Moore, R. M. (December 2002). 'A review of the pathophysiology and treatment of acute laminitis: pathophysiologic and therapeutic implications of endothelin-1' in *Proceedings of the 48th Annual Convention of the American Association of Equine Practitioners*, Orlando, FL (pp. 353–61).
   - Neville, R. F., Hollands, T., Collins, S. N., & Keyte, F. V. (2004). 'Evaluation of urinary TBARS in normal and chronic laminitic ponies'.
   - Williams, C. A., Kronfeld, D. S., Hess, T. M., Saker, K. E., Waldron, J. N., Crandell, K. M., & Harris, P. A. (2004). 'Antioxidant supplementation and subsequent oxidative stress of horses during an 80-km endurance race', *Journal of Animal Science*, 82(2), 588–94.

10.
Feed-related Diseases and Feed-related Behaviour

Obesity

There has been a marked and worrying increase in the numbers of overweight or obese horses, leading to health problems including EMS, laminitis, joint disease and Cushing's. Recent figures obtained from the Blue Cross suggest that at least 55% of horses are affected, and this number is expected to rise over the next few years. Obesity is seen as a disease of our time and the study of obesity in humans and animals is a new and emerging science. Recent research has revealed that adipose (fat) tissue can produce harmful and inflammatory chemicals that predispose to ill health and disease. EMS precedes many disease states and is a condition in which the tissues become insensitive to or unable to absorb glucose, creating abnormal glucose and insulin levels in the blood. Glucose is toxic in large quantities, and excessive insulin triggers laminitis.

Assessing obesity

Methods have been devised to assess degrees of obesity and these confirm that it is a condition that has crept into the horse population at a considerable speed, showing an unhealthy but steady propensity toward allowing horses to be overweight. By this we do not mean a horse who is a little heavier than perhaps he ought to be; we are talking about the serious implications and what happens to the horse's metabolic and hormonal, temperature and heart/organ health by allowing obesity to become a normalised condition. The forms of measurement most commonly used to indicate this area of concern are the crest score and the Equine Henneke Body Condition Score.

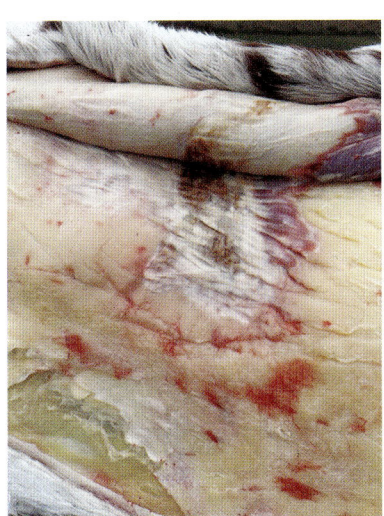

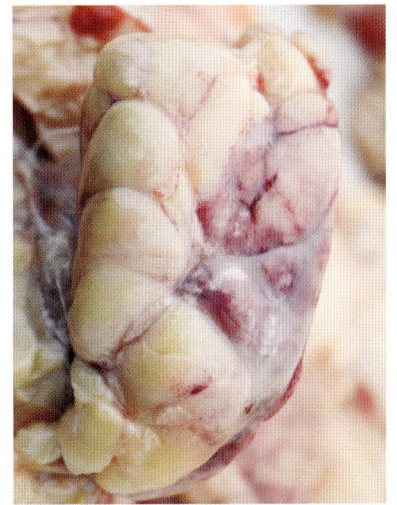

Left: Adipose fat and saddle damage.
Right: Fat nodules.
Below: Calcified fat.
All: Becks Nairn

Healthy Gut, Healthy Horse

Crest S=scores.
Drawing: Geertje French

Obesity crest scores

Obesity is an excessive accumulation of fat having a negative impact on health. The fat accumulates on the horse's neck ('cresty' neck) and around the shoulders and tail. There is now also evidence that fat globules appear in the blood and fat deposits are found around organs. Horses with fat making up 20–40% of bodyweight have a body condition score (BCS) of 7–9 and are classed as obese. (While a definition of obesity as BCS between seven and nine is crude, it is widely used.) In very obese horses, fat mass may even exceed 40% of bodyweight.

A scoring system for the neck can also be used to quantify obesity, as follows:

0. No visual appearance of a crest (tissue apparent above the ligamentum nuchae). No palpable crest.
1. No visual appearance of a crest, but slight filling felt with palpation.
2. Noticeable appearance of a crest, but fat deposited fairly evenly from poll to withers. Crest easily cupped in one hand and bent from side to side.
3. Crest enlarged and thickened, so fat is deposited more heavily in middle of the neck than toward poll and withers, giving a mounded appearance. Crest fills cupped hand and begins losing side to side flexibility.
4. Crest grossly enlarged and thickened, and cannot be cupped in one hand or easily bent from side to side. Crest may have wrinkles/creases perpendicular to topline.
5. Crest is so large it permanently droops to one side.

As 'cresty' necks get bigger (especially above 3 on the 'cresty' neck scoring system), adipocytes increase in both size and number triggering the release of pro-inflammatory agents causing whole body inflammation. As 'cresty' necks get hard (often indicating an impending laminitic attack) this is a visible indication that the adipocytes are now engorged and about to die. As they do so a flood of inflammatory chemicals is released. Adipocyte cell death may be as much as 300% higher in obese horses than in lean individuals.[1]

Equine Henneke Body Condition Score

The Henneke horse body condition scoring system was developed by Don Henneke during his graduate study at Texas A&M University in the early 1980s. The goal was to create a universal scale for assessing horses' bodyweight. The system evaluates the amount of fat on a horse's body using both visual appraisal and palpation.

A) Easy keeper. An easy keeper has a Henneke body condition score of equal to or higher than 6 and is described as 'over-conditioned'.
B) Medium keeper. Has a Henneke body condition score of 5, which he can maintain easily.
C) Hard keeper. Needs extra feed to maintain a body condition score of 6.

Since the gut microbiome plays an important part in nutrient extraction, what are the differences in the microbiome between the hard keeper and easy keeper groups? It was found there were differences relating to both metabolism (function) and structure of the microbiome.

Easy keepers have higher levels of Planctomycetes, known to proliferate in low-nutrient environments, which are antibiotic-resistant and cause inflammation in the gut.

POULIN GRAIN
BODY CONDITION SCORING CHART

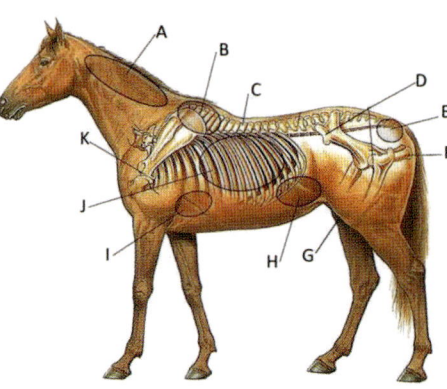

Areas of Emphasis for Body Condition Scoring

A. Thickening of the neck
B. Fat covering the withers
C. Fat deposits along backbone
D. Tuber coxae
E. Fat deposits around tailhead
F. Tuber ischii
G. Fat deposits on inner thigh
H. Fat deposits on flanks
I. Fat deposit behind shoulder
J. Fat covering ribs
K. Shoulder blends into neck

1. Poor
Animal extremely emaciated; spinous processes, ribs, tailhead, tuber coxae, and tuber ischii projecting prominently; bone structure of withers, shoulders, and neck easily noticeable; no fatty tissue can be felt.

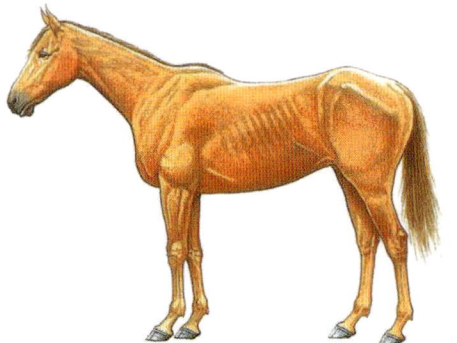 

2. Very Thin
Animal emaciated; slight fat covering over base of spinous processes; transverse processes of the lumbar vertebrae feel rounded; spinous processes, ribs, tailhead, tuber coxae, and tuber ischii prominent; withers, shoulders, and neck structure faintly discernable.

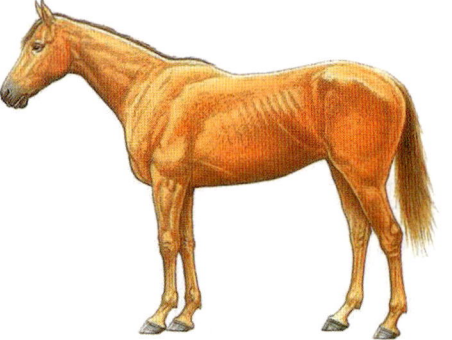 

3. Thin
Fat buildup about halfway on the spinous processes; transverse processes cannot be felt; slight fat cover over ribs; spinous processes and ribs easily discernable; tailhead prominent, but individual vertebrae cannot be identified visually; tuber coxae appear rounded but easily discernable; tuber ischii not distinguishable; withers, shoulders and neck accentuated.

4. Moderately Thin
Slight ridge along back; faint outline of ribs discernable; tailhead prominence depends on conformation, fat can be felt around it; tuber coxae not discernable; withers, shoulders, and neck not obviously thin.

Henneke score.

With kind permission from Poulin Grain USA

Hard keepers have a microbiome composition that highly favours plant fermentation, produces more methane (bloating), and has bacteria that are denitrifying, reducing available nutrients.

The differences in the microbiome were greater between the easy keepers and the medium keepers than between easy/hard and medium/hard. [2]

The EquiBiome analysis identifies the bacteria from these groups and provides a rehabilitation programme to restore a healthy biome.

Overview of some issues related to obesity

Obesity is found in all breeds, ages and status of horse. A brood mare will have trouble conceiving when she is obese; a competition horse and even those just used for little local shows will soon show exhaustion. Furthermore, there are specific and very damaging sicknesses a horse may develop when obesity becomes a serious medical problem.

Laminitis and obesity are both precursors to the feet becoming badly affected and rendering a horse crippled and in excruciating pain. Obesity/EMS and endocrinopathy laminitis have significantly increased in recent years. All three are part of a jigsaw puzzle, with all the pieces needed to make up the complete picture. We must be careful not to concentrate on one piece of the jigsaw above another or give one topic greater importance, which is an easy mistake in a complex problem. However, what is becoming increasingly very clear is that obesity/EMS/laminitis is a clash between the environment and the current management systems of the horse. A picture is now emerging of the existence of an intricate interaction and signalling system that exists between the host (the horse), the plants he chooses to eat and the microbial population in the gastro-intestinal tract that helps it to survive and adapt. Horses have between ten trillion and a hundred trillion micro-organisms in their gut and new technology has allowed us to know more about their role in equine health and disease. The gut flora of a horse refers to the diverse community of microorganisms predominantly bacteria, but also including fungi, viruses, and protozoa that inhabit the intestines of a horse grazing on a wilder environment of mixed moorland or old heathland, and are different from the gut bacteria (specifically the bacterial component of the gut microbiota) of a horse fed on more lush pasture and hard feed.

Starting to confront the problem

We must bear in mind that obesity is not an eating disorder to begin with; it becomes an eating disorder when it starts to affect the metabolic functionality of the horse. Obesity is a human-made sickness and this is mostly because many horses are fed on a trial-and-error basis. While it is true that finding the right balance of foodstuffs with the right nutritional value for each horse is in itself a puzzle, experience and some sound dietary knowledge go a long way in ensuring that each horse receives what he needs on an individual basis. We cannot afford to make foodstuffs for horses a generic affair; we have to continuously assess our horse's needs.

The answer to both problems of excessive fat and raised glucose/insulin levels is to control the horse's food intake and increase exercise, but it can be difficult to shift the abnormal fat pads on the neck, shoulders and around the tail and also to reduce insulin levels. The reason for this is that the adipose tissue is a separate organ and part of the endocrinopathic (hormone) system. Whilst this tissue exists it will continue to transmit information to the body concerning weight gain, energy levels and appetite, and will also predispose towards ill health and disease.

Human research into dealing with obesity concentrates on plant compounds with the ability to increase glucose uptake and diminish adipose tissue; this branch of health care is called functional foods. In recent years we have been investigating and analysing the plants eaten by native ponies allowed to graze freely over moorland country and pasture meadow and we have identified several active compounds with anti-obese and anti-diabetic qualities that are suitable to feed to insulin-resistant horses and those with EMS and laminitis. Ecdysterones (discussed in more detail below) have a long history of research in human and animal health and have several medicinal patents for use in weight control and diabetes in humans. Recently it has been found in plants growing in old pasture land, which horses will actively seek out to eat.

As part of our ongoing research programme into this problem, we have a herd of Welsh ponies in the mountains of Wales grazing on a mixed pasture of moorland, old grassland and woods. Some in the herd are from laminitis-prone stock but can happily graze freely at any time of the year without developing this terrible disease and they tend to put on muscle rather than fat. The ponies ate a wide range of different plants and shrubs and native grass species considered to be inferior by many of our dairy farmers. As mentioned earlier, growing modern perennial rye is fair enough if you want a high yield of milk but the effect of this on most horses is that they become too fat or, worse, develop laminitis. The modern perennial rye around 19–25% pure sugar and accounts for around 60% of grass seed sales in the UK – and even the grass varieties sold by many suppliers of pony paddock grasses are too high in sugar.

We found that our ponies' eating habits were more like deer than cattle and, on analysing the shrubs and bushes picked out as tasty morsels, these were found to contain very high levels of antioxidants, which would provide defence against a wide range of equine diseases and also have the effect of speeding up the metabolism, allowing for the development of lean muscle rather than fat.

The food horses and ponies naturally choose to eat (even when given ad lib hay) is very similar to the Palaeolithic diet, which has become so popular with scientists investigating type 2 diabetes and obesity in humans.

Fodder such as gorse and holly was given to animals in times gone by, even to dairy cattle when the addition of young holly tips to the diet was said to significantly improve the creaminess of the milk. An acre of gorse or furze was able to provide sufficient fodder for six horses, with half the protein content of oats. In factories producing gorse fodder it was usual practice to run the branches through stone mills or hit them with wooden mallets. The bushes were often deliberately burnt down to encourage new growth; the fresh sprouts of furze and grass providing easily accessible food for stock.

Our own investigations and analysis of gorse showed that it contained a very high level of saponins and phenolics with anti-arthritic, antiviral, and analgesic properties. What food do we give to our horses now that would provide the equivalent in antioxidants? Our research has indicated it is the woody shrubs, berries and twigs that provide a wide range of vital compounds with medicinal properties – even more than the usual and traditional herbs. Very few of us can go back to freely grazing horses, but it is now possible to buy the complete range of missing antioxidants, and anti-laminitic compounds, to ensure that your horse isn't missing out on them as preventatives against the development of fat pads.

The following sections outline some scientific studies of matters related to obesity and describe how their findings may help in preventing or dealing with this condition.

Comparison of ecdysterones to metformin

Ecdysterones can exert a glucose-lowering effect on hepatocytes and stimulate the secretion of insulin. A HepG2 cell line (a human liver cancer cell) was used for glucose consumption (GC) studies. At moderately high glucose concentration, the GC of HepG2 cells was increased from 44% to 77% with ecdysterones, which was comparable to that with metformin (a drug commonly used to treat diabetes). These results indicate that ecdysterones can exert a glucose-lowering effect in hepatocytes that is insulin-independent but has no effect on insulin release.

Ecdysterones, which can be extracted from spinach, have a positive effect on the stress-activated transduction pathways linked to inflammation. In one of the studies horses with chronic laminitis had three times the amount of free radical damage when compared to non-laminitic horses, even when they had not shown signs of the disease for the past two years. This is a similar figure to horses subjected to intense physical exercise in various studies.

Another compound (Carthamasterone A ecdysterones (CmA)) found in *Chenopodium alba* (white goosefoot) can also benefit EMS/laminitic ponies. In an independent study on weight loss, over a hundred ponies with a BMI (body mass index) higher than a 3 score were obese, had EMS with insulin resistance, and were prone to the potentially fatal disease of laminitis. After these ponies were given an optimum dose of CmA, 40% were scored with a BMI of 2 within two weeks, with 30% obtaining normal scores within three weeks and another 10% becoming normal within one month of the start.

Recent veterinary research found the presence of endothelin-1 in laminitis. Endothelin-1 is a vasoconstrictor and its production is inhibited by blocking certain binding sites with the ecdysterones along this important metabolic pathway. In a recent veterinary supervised dog trial nine obese dogs lost 8.9% of the target weight within a month when treated with ecdysterones in comparison to the national average, which is 3–5%. Ecdysterones are very dose-specific as they target the P13K/AKT signalling pathway; different strengths of extractions exert differing influences on the body. EquiBiome Microbia is a complimentary feed formulated for horses that contains a unique compound from a native plant accessible to freely grazing horses and is useful for horses with grass-related issues. It contains a dose to diminish the diameter of adipocytes thus affecting the inflammatory adipokines released from the adipose tissue.

The AKT pathway

AKT refers to a specific protein involved in transporting potassium (K). Ecdysone is a prohormone of the major insect moulting hormone 20-hydroxyecdysone, secreted from the prothoracic glands. It is of steroidal structure. Insect moulting hormones (ecdysone and its homologues) are generally called ecdysteroids. These compounds have well documented anti-adipocyte, anti-obesity and insulin glucose mediating properties, and there has been a recent rapid increase in scientific research and interest in ecdysones because they possess important pharmacological properties. Ecdysterones are hepatoprotective and immunoprotective, they are also able to enhance wound-healing and possess anti-cancerous properties (*see* ecdybase.org). Ecdysteroids are also being included as nutraceutical additives to food products to lower blood glucose and prevent the laying down of adipose tissue in mammals. Phytoecdysones act in a dose-dependent way and must be used together with other ecdysterones to improve pharmacokinetic activity in order to gain the diminishment of adipose tissue and promote healthy blood glucose levels in laminitic ponies.

Antioxidant activity

Compounds such as alkaloids, fatty acids, triterpenes and varied phenolic derivatives with anti-inflammatory bioactive capabilities are known as antioxidants. The structure-radical scavenging activity relationships of a large number of representative phenolic compounds (e.g. flavanols, chalcones, flavones, flavanones, isoflavones, tannins, stilbenes, phenolic acids and lignans) are beneficial to health and recovery from disease as antioxidants are cytoprotective, with particular effect on the cytokines (IL-1, IL-6, TNF and IFN). A rise in this group of cytokines significantly predisposes the individual to type 2 diabetes and insulin resistance and creates a perpetual state of inflammation and pain.

Gorse and blackberries in particular were found to have significant and potent levels of radical scavenger activity, as suggested by their high capacity to reduce the free radical 2,2-diphenyl-1-picrylhydrazyl (DPPH), and by their reaction with superoxide anion, peroxyl and hydroxyl radicals as well as with the oxidant species, hydrogen peroxide and hypochlorous acid. They also protected membrane lipids against peroxidation induced by the iron/ascorbate system, as evaluated by the formation of thiobarbituric acid-reactive substances (TBARs). Willow (Salix) contains 67% proanthocyanidins, which are a class of polyphenols. Research has shown that this class of antioxidants affects microcirculation and oedema and has an effect on oxidative stress – which has recently been shown to be a cause of diabetes mellitus in people and dogs. The phytochemicals in EquiBiome Microbia influence the glycaemic spikes encountered in ponies on high sugar intake diets. These spikes promote disease by increasing systemic glycative stress and vasculature oxidative stress and directly increase insulin levels, which has been shown to trigger a laminitic attack.

Overweight ponies

Fat ponies, genetics, alleles and more: veterinary science is in the process of developing tests to determine how susceptible your horse/pony is to laminitis/EMS. Will this prior knowledge make a difference to the type of horse or pony you will buy – i.e. is EMS on its way to being classed as a form of unsoundness?

If so, will breeders (especially of natives) aim to breed out or eliminate from the herd those individuals with the ob/ob gene, and will this action inadvertently have a knock-on effect to the breed's true and original hardiness and thriftiness?

Since manipulation of genes is an extremely complex issue, this is necessarily a complex

Feed-related Diseases and Feed-related Behaviour

Shetland pony.
Geertje French

question, the concern being that those same 'hardy' ponies might then also lose the ability to survive at times of low food availability on very low-nutrient forage. Might the ob factor then not be useful in these wild ponies? Circumstances would inevitably change when these ponies became stabled, as taking them away from their natural habitat would again make the obesity gene an issue as it would be unclear how to feed them properly to keep them on an even weight throughout the year. Therefore, is the process too complicated and uncertain, and would it be expensive? In the meantime, is it better to rely on common horse sense in regard to diet and exercise?

Welsh breeds, Dartmoor ponies, Morgans, Tennessee Walking Horses, Saddlebreds, Arabians and Paso Finos are thought to be particularly susceptible to EMS, and other native breeds (Highland, Dales, Connemara and Shetland) are under assessment. Affected horses and ponies appear to have high metabolic efficiency, meaning they require fewer calories for maintenance of bodyweight when compared to unaffected animals (i.e. they are 'easy keepers'). The breeds mentioned share key metabolic features of EMS, such as high insulin, an intense response to oral glucose, and elevation in serum triglycerides (fats).

Pony breeds have different responses to feeding than horses; some are natural gluttons (causing high insulin spikes) and have naturally higher insulin levels than horses (making continuous turnout difficult). Some ponies also have naturally high adiponectin levels. What makes a native pony unique is the ability to survive: we may therefore need to protect the 'good doer' and provide an appropriate environment for them. Perhaps breed societies ought to run different classes for ponies kept out in their native environment.

Survival metabolism – 'good doers' thrive on surviving

A 'good doer' is a pony or horse who can survive on 'fresh air', he is a survival expert but, with our modern management, whilst we may be providing our 'good doers' with a healthy environment it is also possible that, on the other hand, we may be predisposing them to metabolic dysfunction. 'Good doers' possess alternative energy systems to help them survive in harsh environments, so every now and then they need a harsh environment to re-establish or balance energy metabolism.

Such ponies (and cross breeds) possess an insulin-resistant genotype as a survival mechanism that makes them more likely to develop insulin resistance – a good thing as it helps them to survive their native harsh mountain/moorland environment. These ponies naturally have a higher level of insulin secretion and a slower glucose disposal rate, which is a positive adaptation for sparse food rations. During the harsh winter conditions when glucose is unavailable from forage, or scarce, the 'good doer' will switch to an alternative energy system to ensure survival and, as the available food changes from grass to shrubs and herbage such as gorse, tree bark and marsh grass, the metabolism will also switch to a more conservative system of energy use and storage that prevents any ingested glucose from entering the muscle and adipose tissue.

Deprived of glucose the tissues then start to use another energy supply (lipids/triglycerides) allowing the dwindling but precious sources of glucose to support vital organs. 'Good doers' have lower insulin sensitivity and higher insulin secretion plus high circulating levels of triglycerides. This tendency towards insulin resistance is a natural efficient adaptation that also involves the 'pay it forward' insulin system that exists in the gut.

The problems start when the 'good doer' clashes with the modern management system and change of environment, and switches to a diet containing too much sugar and starch from hard feed, high-quality hay and grass (especially perennial rye) with no drop in the quality of nutrients through the winter months. 'Good doers' are more predisposed than other types to laminitis, but any horse receiving more calories than required for work will store the excess as adipose tissue, and fat pads will soon appear as 'cresty' necks, tail pads, on the shoulders, around the sheath, etc. and have the potential to develop endocrinopathic laminitis.

Energy metabolism is so finely tuned in our native ponies and cross breeds that we may be underestimating the small changes and additions to the diets that may trigger energy/metabolic dysregulation. It is not always entirely clear why some horses need to have a poor diet through the winter months, but we may need to accept it as a normal event for these individuals. Or perhaps our modern management systems created a complete energy crisis of calorie excess when, for some horses, their metabolic system is totally geared to a calorie deficit.

Energy metabolism is complex but let's take another look at leptin.

Leptin is released from adipose tissue and is part of the process of energy and appetite regulation. Although more fat means more leptin, there is no defined point at which raised leptin levels then lead to leptin resistance, although it is speculated that high circulating levels of triglycerides are the trigger for this resistance.

In native horses feeding in a wild environment, they are often faced with a long period of low-calorie intake and starvation would be a much more common event than access to an unrestricted number of calories. Therefore, any system regulating feeding and bodyweight would need to be biased toward the acquisition and retention of calories. As mentioned earlier, 'good doers' are horses with a very finely tuned survival system biased towards acquiring calories, and our breed societies have ensured that our native breeds have hung on to this important genetic trait.

Metabolism is a regulatory system that must have some adaption capabilities to cope with sometimes harsh environmental conditions, including drops in temperature. A wild horse in January would need to have a system that could indicate and transmit information concerning fat reserves, and also a strong starvation signalling system indicating their calorie reserve, enabling them to stop all behaviours other than those that send them in search of food and to conserve energy.

Leptin seems to have all these characteristics and appears in many parts of the brain in a regulatory capacity and influences many important decisions relating to survival. This means that there must be a self-regulating cut-off mechanism to indicate dysregulation, thought to be the high levels of triglyceride. Triglycerides are the signal to say something is going wrong.

Natural nutrition to help reduce weight

An increase in the horse's body condition score indicates the likelihood of a decrease in the absorption or uptake of glucose through a loss of sensitisation in the tissues called insulin resistance. As body fat stores increase, there is a corresponding increase in the release of inflammatory chemicals from the adipocytes stored in the fat, the predominant/important three of which are TNF (tumour necrosis factor), IL-1 and IL-6. At the same time, the signalling chemicals associated with metabolism and energy are also changing. That these changes are starting to happen is indicated with a body condition score of 6 and above and they increase with age. Horses over ten begin to produce more insulin whilst losing their ability to absorb glucose and, if the horse isn't exercised or turned out on a low plane of nutrition, throughout the winter, he is even more likely to put on weight as he ages.

Being overweight causes more inflammatory chemicals to circulate, predisposing the horse to laminitis, arthritis and non-infectious respiratory disease. Being overweight also alters the speed and process of metabolism. The inflammatory chemicals TNF, IL-1 and IL-6 reduce the way insulin is absorbed into the muscles, liver and other tissues, and these chemicals also lower adiponectin and increase leptin.

The insulin, leptin and adiponectin signalling pathways are known to share certain downstream molecules, namely phosphatidylinositol 3-kinase (PI3K), protein kinase B (PKB), mitogen-activated protein kinase (MAPK) and AMP activated protein kinase (AMPK). Some plant chemicals (22-hydroxyecdysterone) also share these molecules and, if provided in the diet, will prevent them being used to signal for the overproduction of leptin and insulin. The same plant chemicals increase adiponectin production; adiponectin increases energy expenditure and fatty acid oxidation in the liver and muscles.

Nature has an abundant supply of 22-hydroxyecdysterone 2-acetate, including bracken, ivy, spinach (wild and cultivated) yarrow, anise hyssop, cow parsley, burdock and over ten thousand other plants. (Only very small amounts are needed.)

GLP-1 pay-it-forward mechanism

Some horses are hungry all the time and will do absolutely anything for food; the desire to eat is stimulated by gut hormones, and an imbalance is thought to contribute to 'hungry horse syndrome'. Hormones use feedback loops or circuits as methods of maintaining the balance between stimulation and over- or under-stimulation. The hormone that creates a desire to eat is called ghrelin and the one that prevents the desire becoming too strong is called GLP-1. Being hungry all the time can suggest an imbalance of ghrelin, which may show as a rise in the adrenocorticotropic hormone (ACTH) levels. Imbalances seem to be common but respond well to the addition of polyphenol compounds. The highest levels of plant chemicals to help restore balance of the gut hormones can be found in wild marjoram (Origanum vulgare), which can be found growing on chalk and limestone grasslands in summer, with pink blush flowers appearing between June and September. The cultivated varieties are also good to use.

Hedges for overweight or EMS/IR horses

Essentially native to the UK, wild barberry (berberis vulgaris) bushes were commonly grown as hedging in medieval times but were almost eradicated in the eighteenth century because of an infestation of puccinia graminis (commonly called 'rust') originating in the barberry but then passed on to wheat and oat crops. For this reason, barberry is best planted as part rather than a whole hedge, thus reducing the opportunity for this disease to develop. If you are able to do this, it may be beneficial to overweight and EMS/IR horses.

The main chemical is berberine, strongly antimicrobial against *Staphylococcus*, *Streptococcus*, *Salmonella*, *Klebsiella*, *Clostridium*, *Pseudomonas*, *Proteus*, *Shigella*, *Vibrio*, and *Cryptococcus* species. Berberine has also been investigated and given approval as a natural alternative to metformin, being able to reduce blood glucose and improve insulin sensitivity. You can buy berberine as a supplement, but if you grow barberry as part of a hedge the horse can have the benefit of the other chemicals it contains. Barberry has a 71% phenolic content, from this there are 2.6% alkaloids (antimicrobial), 4.9% flavonoids (antiviral) and 0.3% saponins (antiparasitic).

A horse needs around 1.5–3 gm of berberine a day and, although the roots contain the highest levels, the fruits come a close second, then the twigs, whilst the leaves contain the highest levels of flavonoids and saponins. Barberry contains at least twenty-two different alkaloids, making this a brilliant medicinal shrub to grow for horses. It would be the plant of choice for its antiviral properties against the common and prevalent viruses.

Insulin-resistant metabolic syndrome (IRMS)

Insulin resistance is a condition whereby the body's cells don't respond effectively to insulin, the hormone responsible for regulating blood sugar levels. Insulin-resistant metabolic syndrome is a cluster of risk factors that often occur together.

Dietary intake for horses with IRMS should not only be about the restriction of some foods but must also be about unrestricted access to foods that benefit the gut bacteria and increase glucose sensitivity.

Energy metabolism is one of the most complex systems in the body (equal in complexity to the immune response); it relies upon a precise and continuous inter-organ communication system to maintain the balance. Chronic obesity/EMS is defined by a low-grade inflammatory response (circulating chemical messengers that bring about devastating changes in the foot; laminitis) and can simply be described as a breakdown in normal communications.

The breakdown has the following visible signs:

- An increase in appetite: the horse/pony starts to gorge on his food and seems to be permanently hungry.
- Decrease in energy: sluggish behaviour and movement generally becomes stilted and flat.

○ Hard 'cresty' neck – the fat pads become harder and larger as insulin resistance increases.

It is easy enough to see these outward signs or symptoms but one of the primary instigators of all is an organ that is unseen but is probably the most important. The gut microbiota can and do contribute to the onset of metabolic disorders and cause low-grade inflammation in intestinal and adipose tissue, muscles, liver and the brain, and also alter the glucose and energy balance.

As the horse eats, the gut has several sensing mechanisms (including quorum sensing by gut bacteria) with reference to the type of food being eaten and uses hormones and afferent nerves to inform the liver, adipose tissue and brain of the nutritional status. The liver, brain and adipose tissue then generate signals through the autonomic nervous system relating to the amount of food eaten, likely energy expenditure, and whether storage facilities are needed. Glucose in the blood is very tightly controlled as it can be damaging if too high and the horse has a set of mechanisms to clear plasma glucose as quickly as possible.

EMS and IR are exacerbated by dysfunctions in nutrient sensing in the gastro-intestinal tract, triggered by the gut bacteria, especially those that generate inflammation, which disrupts the sensing system of the gut.

Including the right material in the diet will have the effect of changing the gut microbiota composition by favouring bacteria that pass on health benefits to the host whilst reducing those that cause inflammation.

Plant material reinforces the gut barrier and promotes gut hormones that control appetite, glucose homeostasis and systemic inflammation.

The best proper hard-to-digest (prebiotic) hedgerow foods to eat to prepare for the spring are gorse, hazel, willow and any type of fern or lichen.

The desired end result can be presented as follows:

⇩ Appetite ⇩ Fat mass ⇩ Glycemia ⇩ Lipemia ⇩ Metabolic endotoxemia ⇩ Insulin ⇩ resistance ⇩ Glucose tolerance ⇩ Inflammation.

Insulin resistant 2

Not all obese horses are insulin resistant, but those who score 7 or higher on the Henneke scoring system and those with a higher than 3 'cresty' neck score are classed as obese and are said to have EMS with a high potential to develop IR. The blood tests for raised glucose levels/insulin resistance can be inaccurate and a better method may be to measure the microbial activity using a simple faecal test. Using a machine learning framework,[3] it is possible to identify the phyla of gut bacteria that increase as blood glucose levels rise, and decrease as blood glucose levels drop, meaning that the gut bacteria in some way, are controlling the amount or levels of glucose in the bloodstream. Gut microbiota may also play a key role in controlling obesity through their effect on food digestion, nutrient absorption and gut health. In horses there seems to be a link between raised proteobacteria and raised blood glucose levels, and the same core bacteria ratios also exist in horses with colitis. Flavonoids help reduce the numbers of proteobacteria in the gut, reducing blood glucose at the same time. The best plants to provide for this are chamomile (Chamaemelum nobile), wild celery (Apium graveolens), and wild mint (Mentha arvensis).

Colic

Colic is not classified as a disease: it is caused by different factors taking place in the gut. Therefore, in equine veterinary medicine colic is used as a general term to refer to acute abdominal disorders and visceral abdominal pain. It's a digestive syndrome that can indicate various symptoms of differing severity, including obstructions, inflammatory processes, or strangulating obstructions. Causes of the symptoms can vary from issues such as compacted feed to gas, which shows in the stomach being distended. It may also arise because the intestines are twisted or because movement of foodstuff in them is inhibited by inflammation or internal damage. It is a condition that, in some circumstances, can have fatal consequences.

Colic can present in different ways. The horse may suddenly be in pain and 'panic', which can take the form of either shutting down and having trouble getting up after lying down (or do so repeatedly) or he may continually nose his stomach and trying to kick it. The horse may also lose control of himself and become aggressive, lashing out and not wanting to be touched, especially in the abdominal area. He may start sweating excessively and his heart rate may become elevated, or he may have trouble passing faeces. His facial expression may show flared nostrils, wrinkled lips or nervous eyes. If you think you horse has colic you need to keep him warm and get him to walk and phone your vet immediately.

Treatments and surgical interventions are available, but there is a high morbidity (death rate) associated with colic. Reducing colic episodes is crucial, and it's worth examining and understanding any predisposing or other factors, that might help to prevent or reduce the onset of a colic attack.

Evaluated risk factors can be put into three basic categories: horse-related factors, management-related factors, environment-related factors. The most common risk factors are diet-related (which come under the umbrella of management), either because of changes to the concentrate or fodder consumed by the horse, or a decrease in water intake.

The role of the equine gut microbiome in colic episodes

As explained earlier, the gut microbiome is a complex system composed of millions of microorganisms that work together to ferment indigestible fibres in the large and small intestines. In the equine gut, it's like a large metropolis, teeming with life – a bustling community of microorganisms that play a vital role in horses' growth, development and health. These microbes give new meaning to the term 'crowded house', with an estimated 10^{15} organisms and 1,500 different species all vying for space. Foals get their first taste of the microbial world at birth, when they acquire their first microbes through direct contact with the mother and their environment.

The first settlers of the equine gut are strict anaerobes like *Bacteroides* and *Clostridium*. The microbiome's development is influenced by many factors, including diet and age. Colostrum, milk, and even the incorporation of fibre play a role. A study on foals and their mothers found that the microbiome becomes more stable around day 50 post-partum, coinciding with the introduction of the adult diet well before weaning. As horses age, the diversity of species within the microbiome decreases. Older horses have fewer bacteria than their younger counterparts. The ageing process also reduces microbial diversity, and in one study, the *Proteobacteria* phylum was more abundant in older horses than the control group.

With new techniques, such as sequencing the 16S ribosomal RNA gene, it's possible to learn more about the functionality and abundance of these micro-organisms and their interaction with their environment and the host (the horse). Studies have shown that these minuscule ecosystems inhabiting our horse's gut are incredibly intricate, with each segment serving distinct functions. For instance, the large intestine boasts a plethora of microbial activity, while the stomach and small intestine are relatively less populated. The gut microbes play a crucial role in breaking down indigestible fibres, a process that is particularly crucial for horses, who rely on fermentation in the colon and caecum to break down food. These bacteria act as little superheroes, breaking down cellulose and hemicellulose to create short-chain fatty acids (SCFAs) like propionate, butyrate, and acetate. Among these SCFAs, butyrate is a key player. It helps maintain a healthy gut by reducing inflammation and even plays a role in the development of the horse's immune system.

It's important to note that the gut microbiome is a constantly changing ecosystem, with different bacterial species competing for resources such as food. All these interactions are dependent on the chemical nature of dietary compounds and could influence health, according to the different SCFA profiles that each individual manifests. The diet is the main factor that contributes to gut microbiome modification in horses. Recent studies have shown that the composition of the intestinal microbiome changes during and after a colic episode, but it's currently unclear whether this is a cause or a consequence.

Studies and findings

Most studies on microbial composition in adult horses have been based on stool samples, which are representative of the microbiome in the large intestine, particularly in the caecum. In healthy adult horses, the microbial profiles are mainly composed of bacteria from the phyla *Firmicutes* (44%) and *Bacteroidetes* (38%), followed by *Spirochaetes* (2.5%), *Fibrobacter* (2.0%), *Proteobacteria* (0.8%), and *Tenericutes* (0.5%). However, other studies have shown that the most abundant phylum in healthy horses is *Bacteroidetes*, followed by *Firmicutes*, *Verrucomicrobia* and methanogenic archaea.

Other studies indicate that, in healthy horses, the most prevalent phylum is *Bacteroidetes*, followed by *Firmicutes*, *Verrucomicrobia* and methanogenic archaea. Conversely, certain studies suggest that *Firmicutes* surpass *Bacteroidetes* in a 4:1 ratio, contradicting the current 1:1 ratio data. These discrepancies could be affected by various factors such as location, breed, diet, gut segment, differences in DNA extraction methods, and the sequencing platform used.

Changes in the microbiome's composition, known as dysbiosis, have been associated with diets high in concentrate, poor-quality forage, stress, confinement, fasting and age, among other causes. Recent studies have linked alterations in the gut microbiome of horses to colic because changes in the abundance of certain bacterial groups that play an essential role in maintaining a healthy gastro-intestinal tract have been observed.

Dysbiosis, or the loss of microbiome homeostasis, is linked to the onset of certain diseases in both humans and animals. It is categorised by an imbalance (too many, too few or missing altogether) of bacterial species, as seen in inflammatory bowel disease, metabolic syndrome, irritable bowel disease and chronic relapsing *Clostridium difficile* infection.

Recent research in humans has established a significant correlation between irritable bowel syndrome (IBS) and the gut microbiome. One study showed that transferring faecal matter from individuals with IBS to healthy mice resulted in disease-related changes, including compromised intestinal movement, increased intestinal permeability, and heightened sensitivity.

While limited, a study on the connection between the gut microbiome and colic in horses noted an increase in *Clostridium phytofermentans* and *Bacteroides sp.* during colic episodes in Thoroughbred horses compared to samples collected post-episodes. Also, colicky horses had higher levels of *Clostridioides difficile* compared to their healthy counterparts. The use of antibiotics was found to promote the rapid growth of harmful bacteria, leading to dysbiosis, diarrhoea and colitis when administered orally to horses.

Faecal transplants from healthy donor horses have highlighted the link between microbiome composition and disease (a phenomenon also observed in human patients). Horses with colic showed decreased species diversity and variations in bacterial abundance compared to healthy horses. The *Firmicutes: Proteobacteria* ratio was associated with colic onset, with a higher ratio linked to reduced colic probability. However, another study indicated an overgrowth of lactic acid-producing bacteria and a decrease in methanogenic archaea in colicky horses.

These findings highlight a crucial link between the gut microbiome and gastro-intestinal disorders in horses. Understanding the impact of microbiota on conditions like irritable bowel syndrome and colic can help drive the development of innovative treatments and preventive measures. The intricate relationship between the gut microbiome and digestive disorders continues to unfold, offering new insights and potential solutions for managing these conditions effectively.

Understanding the delicate balance of bacteria in the gut microbiome is crucial for maintaining overall health in horses. Referring back to the *Firmicutes: Proteobacteria* ratio, those bacteria that decrease in number produce butyrate, which promotes health in the gut, whilst those that increase are lactic acid-producing bacteria, effectively causing an environment of acidosis in the hindgut. However, whilst this appears significant, the exact relationship and its link to colic incidence is still being researched. In addition to this ratio, the presence of specific bacteria such as *Lachnospiraceae* and *Lactobacillus*, known for their ability to produce lactic acid, can also play a role in gut health. Conversely, a decrease in methanogenic archaea has been observed in certain cases, highlighting the complexity of the microbiome and its impact on digestive health. By delving deeper into these microbial relationships, we can gain valuable insights into predicting and potentially preventing colic episodes in horses.

Possible precursors to colic

Research indicates that sudden dietary changes can lead to an increased risk of colic within four to six days, because of altered fermentation patterns and metabolic disorders. The sudden introduction of high levels of soluble carbohydrates can overload enzymatic degradation in the small intestine, leading to microbial fermentation in the large intestine. This fermentation causes an accumulation of lactic acid and gas by bacteria such as *Lactobacillus* and *Streptococcus*, causing a drop in hindgut pH.

Grass-fed horses tend to have higher levels of certain bacteria families in the hindgut, whilst grain-fed horses show a decrease in *Fibrobacter* abundance. Pregnant mares are at a higher risk of colic because of changes in feeding management during the peri-partum period, leading to alterations in colon pH and hindgut microbiota. It has also been noted that post-partum mares developing colic had a higher relative abundance of *Proteobacteria* 1–76 days (an average of 17.5 days) before the onset of the colic episode.

Onset of colic

Gut blood flow is reliant on a group of chemicals called prostanoids, known to be the creators of inflammation. Lack of blood flow to the gut is the first step to the onset of colic. The gut needs a good blood flow and, if this is disrupted, twists and rotations are more likely to happen. Bute is often given for pain and inflammation but blocks production of these chemicals immediately, causing disruption to the gut and tissue damage, and also interferes with the healing afterwards.

One of the reasons why the gut needs a good blood flow is to control hindgut fermentation and volatile fatty acid production. In the event of gastro-intestinal injury, prostaglandins have been shown to be necessary for the restoration of mucosal barrier function, and bute prevents the production of prostaglandins.

We also know that bute prevents the production of COX-1 and COX-2. COX-2 is the better chemical to bring resolution of pain and inflammation, however in the gut it plays an essential part in health rather than playing a role in inflammation. Also, for some reason, the gut needs both COX-1 and COX-2 to stay healthy, especially within the jejunum and the pelvic flexure of the large colon. The best plants to maintain blood flow to the gut whilst taking bute are Espinheira Santa (*Maytenus ilicifolia*) and cat's claw (*Uncario tomentosa*).

Factors that may cause colic and how to work on prevention

Greedy feeders bolt their food, meaning that they may not chew enough to moisten the food. This will end up as compacted and cause a blockage within the gut. It may be useful to place large stones in the feeding trough of such horses so that they are forced to eat at a slower rate. If you give your horse sudden access to large feeds such as lush grass, starch-rich cereals, fruits that have fallen from the tree (such as apples, pears or plums), on which the horse can gorge himself, he may develop colic because the stomach does not get the time needed to digest the food stuffs properly. Other factors include mouldy foodstuffs – it is imperative not to put fresh feed into a barrel where there is still old food residue, as this will become mouldy and thus contaminate all the food. Working your horse on a full stomach is another precursor, as the horse has not had time to digest all that food. It is better to spread feeds over smaller portions given at intervals during the day. When a horse becomes exhausted the intestinal tract will not be able to work at its optimum rate, so the slower the digestion the more quickly food gets trapped or compounded.

Horses thrive on routine, so feed at regular times every day of the week. Regular exercise not only ensures good muscle development; it also keeps the intestinal tract moving properly. If your horse is moved to a different yard, make sure that he continues on the feed he is used to, and if you want to change the diet, do this over a period of a week to ten days, so the horse and his intestines get used to the new feed.

Hay needs to be clean and as fresh as possible, as old hay also harbours bacteria that can cause mould to develop. Haylage, once the bale is opened, needs to be consumed within a few days, as the heat at the core of the bale quickly becomes a breeding ground for bacteria and mould spores.

Ensure that your horse has time to cool down after strenuous exercise before feeding or giving water, and make sure that the water is not too cold.

If your horse needs to be on long box rest, stop feeding starch- and carbohydrate-rich feeds, as he doesn't need the energy. Also, because he lacks exercise, the intestinal tract will also slow down. He will do well on good-quality hay and alfalfa.

Clostridium colitis

This condition is caused by a disturbance or imbalance in the bacteria of the gut creating an increase in the numbers of the genus *Clostridia*. Rapid changes in diet, loss of appetite, stressful events such as travelling, competition, isolation, antibiotics, anthelmintic use and hospitalisation are common causes of this type of imbalance. *Clostridia* are present in the stable and in the field environment and can persist even after the use of disinfectants; they are especially prolific in the soil, but also live in the grass. *Clostridia* are common – some are permanent members of the core gut community; the good *Clostridia* species do good (supporting immune function) but most ingested *Clostridia* species pass harmlessly through the gut and out in the faeces. However, when the microbial community has been disrupted and when the conditions are right, *Clostridia* remain in the gut, multiply and produce toxins that cause ill health in horses.

Cited as a cause of grass sickness, colic, tetanus, laminitis, colitis and diarrhoea, *Clostridia* are important pathogens. The EquiBiome test can identify all the species of *Clostridium* currently linked to equine diseases and make management and dietary recommendations to avoid ill health. Using metagenomic shotgun sequencing, new research has discovered hundreds of new species, many of which are pathogenic. As *Clostridia* are so important to horse health, we are now collaborating with microbiome experts to identify as many species as possible to increase the existing list in the EquiBiome report.

Enteritis

This intestinal problem presents itself when there is an inflammation of the intestines. It may be caused by poor feeding, a viral infection, parasites present in the intestine or malevolent bacteria. A sudden change in diet, mould found in hay or other foodstuffs and overfeeding may also cause problems. Enteritis will manifest itself through diarrhoea, scouring or loss of appetite. It usually clears up by feeding the horse only good-quality hay and fresh water for a few days, but if symptoms don't clear up, please contact your vet as the horse may become dehydrated.

Polysaccharide storage myopathy (PSSM)

There are emerging links between the gut/dysbiosis and PSSM. Horses with PSSM have lower levels of bacteria associated with and responsible for energy, muscle mass and muscle strength. In horses these are:

- *Lactobacillus iners* (Y16329), *Lactobacillus-hayakitensis* (AB267406)
- *Lactobacillus equi* (AB048833)
- *Lactobacillus fornicalis* (Y18654)
- *Bifidobacterium bombi*
- *Veillonella montpellierensis* (AF473836)

The gut bacteria maintain skeletal muscle mass. *Lactobacillus*, *Veillonella* and *Bifidobacterium* produce acetate, propionate and butyrate, and these metabolites produce muscle mass, increase muscle strength and ensure the health of several important energy pathways. However, the use of antibiotics completely wipes out all the named bacteria.

Laminitis

Visual signs of a pro-inflammatory state preceding laminitis

- Prominent growth rings on the hoof wall.
- Dished hoof wall with flared out long toes (and often low compacted heels).
- Low grade seedy toe, sub-solar haematomas that may lead to an abscess.
- Crumbly white line.
- Flaky soles and hoof edges broken away.
- 'Sore feet' in the front feet.
- A shortened gait that doesn't improve with exercise and worsens with fast and hard work. (More evident particularly on hard ground.)
- The radial pulse of the hoof is fast when the inflammation is acute. There is a line of heat radiating from the hoof.

This is the hoof of a laminitic horse who also suffered with ulcers, showing severe inflammation on the pastern and hoof ridges.

Becks Nairn

Timeline of laminitis – onset

The following is a timeline to damage and expected damage to the structures of the foot, as associated with the root causes.

Starch/grain overload laminitis

Undigested carbohydrates pushed from the small stomach into the hindgut can cause a rapid change in the gut bacteria and a drop in pH, the lining of the gut then disintegrates and toxins are absorbed into the bloodstream, causing a massive inflammatory reaction.

Time to destruction and separation of the basement membrane is twenty-four to forty hours.

Time to the inflammatory response in the feet causing more damage is seventy-two hours; during this phase a chemical is released in the feet, which is linked to the degeneration caused by arthritis.

Fructan overload laminitis

The mechanism of action is unknown, but time to destruction and separation of the basal membrane is twenty-four to thirty-six hours.

Toxaemia/systemic laminitis

Inflammatory response syndrome laminitis is caused by an infection or toxaemia.

The time to destruction and separation of the basement membrane is eight to twelve hours, during which there will also be a rapid loss of shape and arrangement of the sensitive lamellae.

Time to massive inflammatory response in the feet ranges from one and a half to three and sometimes five hours.

Endocrinopathic laminitis

This is high-insulin laminitis. The mechanism of action is uncertain, but insulin is thought to change the circulation to the foot, causing vasoconstriction. In this form there is a much slower onset of damage, no separation of the basement membrane, and no massive inflammatory response either in the feet or in the gut. Lameness results from the lengthening of the secondary epidermal lamellae, caused by stretching rather than separation of the basement membrane. Some 28% of ponies are considered to have a higher-than-normal level of insulin and are said to be predisposed to this type of laminitis.

Time to onset of laminitis from abnormally raised insulin levels is thirty-six to forty-eight hours.

Mechanical onset laminitis

This is caused by uneven weight-bearing or concussion. It is distinct from other forms of laminitis until the later stages, when there is evidence of secondary inflammation and vascular disruption, thought to be caused by inadequate blood flow to the tissues of the foot.

Time to onset depends on the loading and level of concussion, but is within twenty hours.

Genetic laminitis

This is a genetic defect of the P63 gene, otherwise known as tumour protein and/or transformation-related protein. This gene purifies or 'cleans up' after illness or disease; in humans a defect causes cleft lip/palate, whilst defects in animals cause severe deformities of limbs and hooves. In horses it is also in charge of forming the detail of the hoof wall and is linked to the formation of bone and lamellae. The lamellae of the chronic laminitic horse is lacking in the expression of this p63 gene compared to normal control horses and this is thought to be directly linked to the abnormal growth and development seen in the chronic laminitic hoof. Shortage of P63 causes a change in the size, shape, and organisation of the adult lamellae cells.

The differences in P63 expression between those horses with laminitis and those without were seen in all areas of the hoof tissue and lamellae but were more obvious in the lower and outer regions of the hoof. The five horses used in this trial had chronic laminitis with distal displacement of the phalanx (sinking). Replacing the tissue lacking in p63 using stem cell therapy has now been suggested as a veterinary treatment to prevent the long-term damage and deformation of the hooves of those horses prone to repeated bouts of laminitis.

Laminitis and 'cresty' neck

The 'cresty' neck is not just a layer of fat; it is a hormone factory manufacturing at least ten different types of hormones that set in place several mechanisms that eventually lead to the catastrophe of laminitis. In humans, adipose tissue around the stomach has been found to contain large amounts of chemicals that are inflammatory in nature, and the same chemicals have been found in the 'cresty' neck and tail fat pads of horses. These inflammatory chemicals have a massive impact on health, with multiple complex interactions between glucose and lipid metabolism, control of appetite and energy levels to name just a few.

Countdown to catastrophe

The first stage of the breakdown is the release of a chemical (MCP-1) from the fat pads to attract and recruit white blood cells (monocytes) from out of the bloodstream into the adipose tissue. CP-1 is responsible for recruiting MCP-1; both can be found in blood tests but it may not be seen until obesity has been present for some time. (This chemical is also breed-specific to natives and cross-breeds. The monocytes cause the fat cells to grow and to swell, hence the hardness of a 'cresty' neck before an attack of laminitis.

Stage two is the setting up of a low-grade inflammation throughout the body: to achieve this effect the monocytes convert to macrophages and to a chemical called TNF-1, both alter the normal metabolism and signal the release of triglycerides from the adipose tissue, which is a normal response to infection, inflammation and disease. Low-grade inflammation results and chronic insulin resistance sets in.

Stage three is the release of yet more insulin to deal with the transport of triglycerides, whilst in the adipose tissue IL-1 and IL-6 are produced and have a negative impact, producing greater insulin resistance. These immune cells also influence the appetite and energy levels by producing the hormone leptin. This hormone is often measured in a blood test as it is indicative of insulin resistance.

The final stage in the process is endocrinopathic laminitis caused by:
o   High levels of circulating insulin (above 200 micro iu/ml).

- A disrupted glucose supply to the foot.
- High levels of triglycerides/lipids cause an altered blood flow to the foot.
- Pro-inflammatory chemicals TNF-1, IL-1, IL-6, which are also influential in many disease states in humans, are anticipated to be part of the final breakdown of the hoof.

Treatment

Giving Danilon/bute to horses with laminitis is the quickest way to ease the pain but unfortunately, this popular and commonly used drug has no effect on the high levels of circulating inflammatory chemicals. The inflammatory chemicals are responsible for damage done to the sensitive laminae, which peak at twenty to forty-eight hours after the onset of lameness. Whilst bute makes the horse and owner feel better, there is sadly no resolution to the damage continuing unabated in the feet. The horse still needs extra doses of antioxidants to minimise and mop up the effects of the circulating inflammatory chemicals that bute is unable to change or effect, the symptoms of which are Obel grade 1 laminitis (paddling or lifting one foot then the other; short stilted gait in trot).

Horses with the carbohydrate overload type of laminitis will have raised levels of IL-1 IL-1ß, IL-6, IL-12p35, COX-2, E-selectin and ICAM-1 and, whilst the bute will mask the pain, it does not alter the cocktail of deadly chemicals the laminitis episode has released, which are rapidly causing devastating levels of breakdown.

A mixture of five of the strongest plant anti-inflammatories are required to dampen down, buffer and reduce the effects of all the chemicals released. These are usually found in the bark or more woody part of the plant or shrub and the best to use include curcumin, uncaria tomentosa (cat's claw), rubens fruticoses also under smilax rotundiflora in the brier family (brambles, horsebrier and greenbriar) and Espinheira Santa (Maytenus ilicifolia).

Apart from curcumin, plants containing high enough levels of these chemicals are not the easiest thing to source and administer and they should be ground finely and mixed with 20 ml of omega-3 oil and syringed in three times per day. However, freely foraging horses will find enough in wild barberry, blueberry and white willow. (Manufacturers do put this cocktail in an inexpensive product called Rescue Remedy.)

Polyphenols and endocrinopathic laminitis

High concentrations of insulin trigger IGF-1 receptors that exist in lamellar tissue.[4] This causes out of control cell proliferation and the elongation of the lamellar tissue that is a common feature of laminitis. Plant polyphenols block the action of the IGF-1, preventing the onset of laminitis. (They also have other health benefits – *see* Five reasons why a horse needs a daily supply of polyphenols, later in this chapter.)

A polyphenol is a chemical found in the outer layers of the leaves and stems of most plants. Polyphenols can also be aromatic, and found in the flowers and the fruits or seeds of wild plants. There are over 8,000 different polyphenols, all of which are easily absorbed through the equine gastro-intestinal tract, especially in the fermentation vat called the caecum. In humans, the polyphenol contribution to health is noted and consumption of tea, wine, fruits, vegetables and extra virgin olive oil are encouraged and promoted as an antidote to many diseases including type 2 diabetes, insulin resistance and obesity.

The following are some thoughts from equine nutritional scientists about polyphenol consumption in horses. Rather than referring to horses' natural habitat as an important and rich source of polyphenols, some scientists prefer to rely on human intervention. Horses generally consume bland diets, especially if offered only hay and pasture. Tasty treats spice up the menu. Instead of reaching for peppermints, though, consider brightly coloured fruits, vegetables and even berries so that horses reap the rewards of polyphenols. However, many books on equine nutrition omit any mention of polyphenols at all and antioxidants are only really mentioned as synthetic additives, the main ones being vitamins E and C.

Going back to the subject of pasture, a field or diverse meadow designated a site of special scientific interest (SSSI) will yield an estimated 500 different polyphenol compounds, whilst the average equine pasture provides only thirty to forty.

Bioactive substances such as polyphenols can potentially have both a positive and negative effect on health. This is because a diverse pasture will provide a diverse range of polyphenols (positive), but if more are added synthetically to the diet the optimum range of a type of polyphenols might be exceeded (negative). Therefore, they are best provided fresh from the field or from clean, good-quality hay. One of the old rules of feeding used to be to feed good-quality hay with the seed head intact and the colour of the flowering head retained. This will provide a range of polyphenols to the diet and is a simple and effective way to ensure your horse gets enough polyphenols from a high-fibre forage.

Some benefits of polyphenols additional to their role in treating endocrinopathic laminitis are mentioned later in this chapter – *see* Five reasons why a horse needs a daily supply of polyphenols.

Laminitis turnout time

According to an analysis by Bangor University, it's 1–2.00 pm for a paddock containing Yorkshire fog and 2.24–3.24 pm for perennial rye and meadow fescue. These are the times of the day with the lowest fructose and glucose production for these grasses in any weather between the months of June and September.

Fructose concentration differed within species of grasses as follows:

64–135 mg/g in perennial ryegrasses.
52–114 mg/g in meadow fescues.
48–57 mg/g in crested dog's-tail.
40–48 mg/g in Yorkshire fog.

Glucose concentration varied ranging from:

2–12 mg/g in perennial ryegrasses.
0.3–14 mg/g in meadow fescues.
2–8 mg/g in crested dog's-tail.
0.2–8 mg/g Yorkshire fog.

Yorkshire fog is quite bitter in taste, more so in late summer, hence less desirable to eat, and this may not be a bad thing for the horse.

Five reasons why a horse needs a daily supply of polyphenols

Polyphenols were mentioned earlier specifically in connection with endocrinopathic laminitis, but they can be useful in a number of circumstances:

1. **To protect against diseases and allergies.** The highest levels of polyphenols are found in the bark of trees, where they protect the tree against disease. When horses eat young trees or tree branches or strip the tree of bark the polyphenol content ingested by the horse provides similar protection against disease. Pharmaceutical research looks to tree bark above all other plant material in the search for new drugs to treat cancer.
2. **To provide pain relief.** Polyphenols are anti-inflammatory; those providing the strongest pain-relief are sourced from plants with red or black fruits such as blackberries, wild blueberries, sloes and hawthorn. These polyphenols are called proanthocyanidins – the strongest are found in the fruit and young bark.
3. **As a supply of prebiotics.** If you are feeding a prebiotic supplement as part of your horse's diet the polyphenolic content is likely to be zero, manufacturers preferring the following, which have none: gum Arabic, fructooligosaccharides (FOS), Xylol oligosaccharides (XOS), polydextrose, mannooligosaccharides (MOS), galactooligosaccharides (GOS), pectin and psyllium. However, you can get good prebiotics by letting your horse eat bark. Horses love to eat young trees, which have a high polyphenol content in the form of lignin which, including its polyphenol content, is an important prebiotic. Fir, hawthorn and copper beech have the highest content. Your horse can seek out such sources for himself, as horses are excellent self-medicators.
4. **To protect against hindgut ulcers and colitis.** Glycoside polyphenols from hedera, meadowsweet, cloudberry, heather and many others plants are extracted by microbial action in the large and small intestine and are rapidly absorbed by the cells of the gut wall, where they are used to reduce inflammation (colitis).
5. **As an antimicrobial.** Some polyphenols have a strong antimicrobial action and will reduce bad bacteria in the gut; ideal for horses with runny poos. The best sources are from the Epilobium family (great willow herb) or Calluna vulgaris (common heather/ling).

Three feeding suggestions for horses prone to laminitis and/or EMS

1. Try not to become too fixated on the 'one' popular additive of the moment but provide a wide variety of herbs, shrubs and hedgerow plants (at least twenty-five per day). If you can't grow them cut them from the hedgerow (if you want to buy some in a pot follow the link www.phytorigins.com.)
2. A wide variety of plants will provide small amounts of different chemicals, which will interact with the digestive system and the endocrine system to reduce the triggers of laminitis. Twenty-five different varieties would be the usual minimum, but reduce to just three if your horse is on box rest. If he is on restricted exercise, then cut a branch of fresh gorse and or fresh willow every day – both are strongly anti-inflammatory and will help to reduce pain.
3. Purple willow has the highest levels of the anti-inflammatory and analgesic compound called

salicin, which is kinder on the system than salicylic acid, also found in willows. The salicylic acid is ten times lower than the salicin in purple willow. This plant is easy to spot in the spring as the catkins are red or purple; it's a small shrub usually 1–3 m high and common in Europe and America. (It can also be used as a good hedging plant.)

Changes in the nerves of the laminitic horse

Laminitis causes a change in the nerves themselves as they respond to the stress of the laminitic event. During a laminitic event the nerves in the last cervical vertebra of the neck, situated deep between the shoulder blades of the horse, are changed and actually suffer damage rather than just becoming inflamed, which makes the pain of laminitis difficult to control. The injury to the sensory nerves can be a reason why laminitic pain becomes chronic, with the horse suffering from repeated bouts of lameness even after the original bout of laminitis has been resolved. The nerve injury also causes a change in the behaviour of horses causing them to become withdrawn and spend a longer time at the back of the box.[5]

Herbs offer a good alternative to bute, as many can reduce nociceptive pain. The best nerve pain relieving plants are those containing high levels of triterpenes and quinovic acid glycosides, such as turmeric and rosemary.

Offering a cocktail of antioxidant plants helps to alleviate the damage of laminitis as it affects many structures including the circulation, hoof tissue as well as the unmyelinated nerves.

Ulcer syndromes – EGUS and SEGUS

Another field of research that has found traction over recent times is the worryingly high incidence of EGUS (equine gastric ulcer syndrome) and SEGUS (squamous equine gastic ulcer syndrome). Gastro-intestinal ulcers are brought on by several coinciding and conflicting factors. Feeding an ineffectual type of diet plays a significant role in the development of both EGUS and SEGUS syndromes. Up to 90% of sports horses and 70% of domestic horses are all suffering with the same problem. As we have mentioned before, the high percentage incidence tells us that the majority of horses do not get the right amount fibrous content in their ration. This is of great concern. We must not normalise the problem and just mask it with antacids or other gastric ulcer preparations. The horse needs us to use our reasoning when it comes to trying to reduce and hopefully illuminate feed and/or stress- related gastric ulcerations. The solution is simple. Give your horse continuous feed – day and night access to fibrous roughage. Your horse, if at all possible, needs to be able to go outside for at least two-thirds of his day. Where there is space and some grazing, the horse will feel entirely in his element.

Nonetheless there are more things that can be done to lessen the suffering from these conditions and use remedies that are non-invasive whilst avoiding those that are chemically incompatible with the condition. These are extremely painful diseases and cannot be ignored or masked with a never-ending cycle of medication. A good diet with a variety of plant materials will go a long way in rescuing a very damaged stomach lining and small intestine ulcerations.

Using AI, EquiBiome has detected a gut bacteria profile of horses with ulcers, a predominant feature of which is high levels of biofilm bacteria producing inflammatory and neurotoxic chemicals. The outward signs of gastric ulcers are easy enough to see: poor performance, reduced appetite, a generally altered temperament leading to being difficult to ride, bucking, refusing at jumps, weight loss, teeth-grinding, colic, diarrhoea, crib-biting, box-walking and weaving, to name but a few.

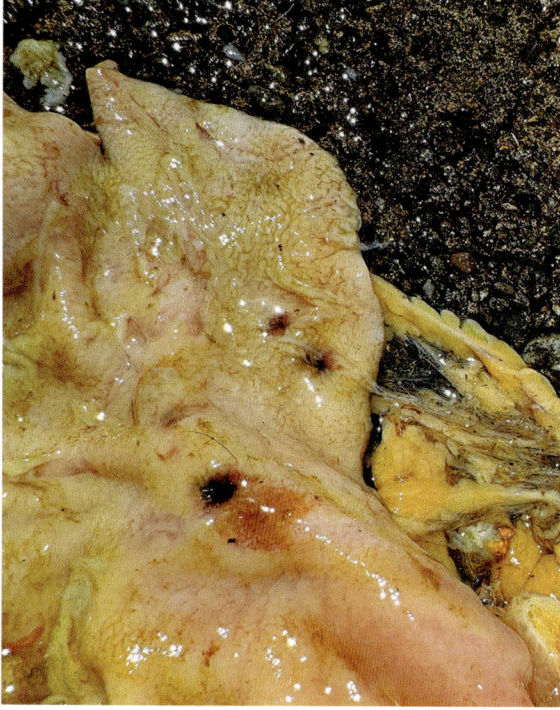

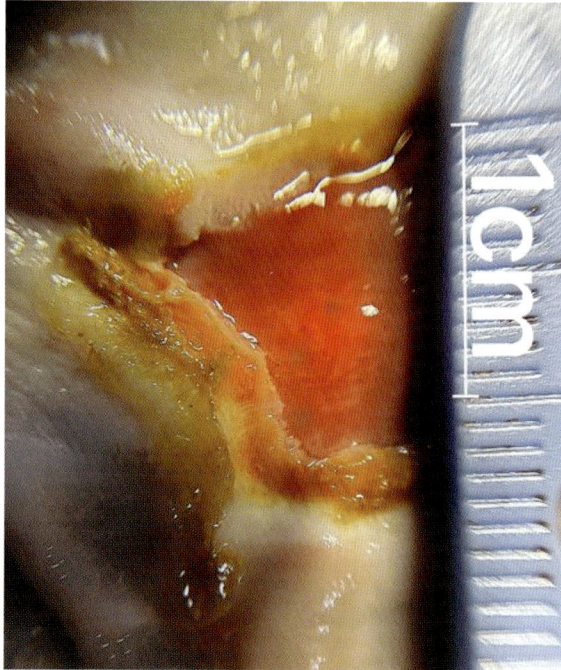

Above: Fresh ulceration.
Becks Nairn
Below: Old ulceration.
Becks Nairn

Above: Close up of ulceration.
Becks Nairn
Below: Ruptured spleen of a horse with laminitis and ulcers. Three-year-old Thoroughbred.
Becks Nairn

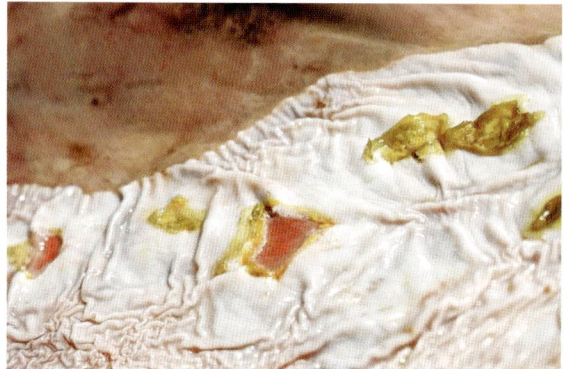

The reasons why horses get gastric ulcers are easy enough to understand. Most of us are familiar with the causes: diet, as in restricted feed or water intake, inappropriate exercise, stress (whether in the stable or during transportation), bacteria and the use of non-steroidal anti-inflammatory agents. Most of us begin with an assessment of the symptoms and follow with a treatment strategy which, if under veterinary care, will usually begin with a course of omeprazole – easy enough you might say. Unfortunately, it is not that easy because, for many of us, success lies in the development of a long-term management strategy, and this requires a deeper knowledge of the internal workings of the gastro-intestinal tract, to provide ongoing care, prevention, and protection of the gut wall.

How to start treatment

The easiest place to begin is to look at the battle front, the place where the problems start. Start by looking at EGUS as an imbalance between the aggressive factors above the protective factors; once the protective layer of the gut wall is disarmed then ulceration can and will occur. Protective factors are: mucus production, bicarbonate, prostaglandins, good blood flow, nitric oxide (NO). Aggressive factors are: gastric acid, Helicobacter Pylori and other pathogenic/biofilm bacteria, NSAIDs, oxidative stress and VFA production.

Good gut health begins with a strong, healthy gut wall barrier, including the tight junctions in the squamous mucosa and mucosal membrane, which protects the gastric tissue from the gastric acid, plus a good production of bicarbonate to neutralise the acid as it touches the gut wall. The imbalance begins when the host (the horse) produces inflammatory chemicals or toxins which stop, prevent or restrict mucus production, making the gut wall cells prone to gastric acid damage. Successful management and treatment require us to look at the lines of defence and how to improve, maintain and strengthen them. One of the best wild plants for strengthening the defences is shepherd's purse (Capsella bursa-pastoris). If you can grow it in the paddock and include it in the hay, only a small daily amount (3 g) will protect the gastro-intestinal wall. Another effective plant is mallow root (Althaea officinalis).

Plants high in quercetin will not only treat the ulcer but relieve the pain and rebuild the gut wall. Such plants include Plantago, wild brassica including wild water cress, holly and hazel leaves and Queen Anne's lace. (Plantago is also fantastic when mixed with honey and applied to a wound; a combination of the two ingredients does a deep clean and leaves no scar tissue.)

Managing the cause

Give oil twice daily for the added anti-inflammatory protection of omega-3 and -6 and make sure the horse has access to some sort of forage throughout the day. The other most important action to take during times of stress, travel and restrictions to grazing is to provide protection and buffering to the vulnerable top part of the stomach by feeding an antacid product containing bicarbonate of soda or calcium carbonate. These can be effective but short-lived, with the effects said to last for maybe only an hour, therefore it may be better to buy the antacid in syringe form and give it whilst travelling rather than making it a permanent addition to the feed. More long-lasting antacids are dihydroxy-aluminium sodium carbonate, aluminium phosphate and magnesium carbonate; these both neutralise gastric acid and protect and coat the mucosal lining of the stomach. Some products may also contain threonine and glutamine which are compounds known to increase the integrity and quality of the stomach wall and help produce mucus, which is the body's natural buffer against the effects of hydrochloric acid.

Many products that are antacids also contain probiotics and prebiotics.

Yea-Sacc is a probiotic yeast culture based on *Saccharomyces cerevisiae* strain 1026. It's specifically selected for its positive influence on animal performance. With a low inclusion rate and extensive research supporting its effects, it is ideal for beef, dairy, calf, and equine feeds.

Prebiotics are food for the friendly microbial populations that live in the hindgut rather than the stomach. Seaweed extracts are becoming an increasingly popular addition to gut soothing products, being reportedly able to lower gastric acid production, but are more likely to be beneficial to the health of the hindgut and for their nutritional benefits, especially the B vitamins.

The standard solution – treating the ulcers

There are several medications or rather 'soothers' which may be recommended by your vet for gastric upset relating to ulcers, a common one being Gastroguard. Some of these treatments can be costly and not always the solution to the problem. In some instances, the product can bind irreversibly to the acid pump, preventing the production of gastric acid and altering the overall pH of the stomach, meaning that the stomach ulcers are worse after the end of the treatment. It is, in effect, a 'plaster' rather than a cure. Other than Gastroguard, the following medications are commonly prescribed:

- Generic omeprazole is cheaper than Gastrogard but it has the same action and thus the same consequences.
- Ranitidine is a histamine H-2 receptor antagonist that inhibits gastric acid production. Ranitidine is also known to give false positives for methamphetamine on drug tests and its use is not recommended for some competitions.
- Cimetidine is also an H2-receptor antagonist but must be withdrawn at least two weeks before some competitions, such as horse racing.

Recent discoveries

It is estimated that between 70 and 90% of horses are affected by gastric lesions including those in the colon (hindgut ulcers) and, as mentioned earlier, it is thought that the majority of ulcers result from modern management methods of travelling, training, feeding and stabling. Any horse who is without food for more than four hours will have a low pH in the stomach (greater acidity), which is damaging to the walls of the top (non-glandular) portion of the stomach, whilst horses with a constant supply of feed have a much higher (better) pH and less chance of suffering from EGUS. Foodstuffs vary in pH balance; coarser materials form a mat in the upper portion of the stomach and mix with saliva to keep the pH in that region around 6 to 7 (more alkaline). Medium-density foodstuffs are located in the middle zone of the stomach, and this area has a pH of 4 to 5. High-density fluids are in the lower portion of the stomach and the pH is more acid at 1 to 2.[6] The lower portion of the stomach is protected from acid production by a mucous coating, whilst the upper (non-glandular) portion of the stomach is not intended to be exposed to stomach acid. Hydrochloric acid is secreted continually by the gastric glands, which are located in the lower portion of the stomach.

The discovery of this layering effect helps explain why exercise tends to increase the frequency of gastric ulcer formation in horses. Monitors implanted in working horses revealed that the contractions of abdominal muscles forced the lower pH liquids from the lower portions of the stomach up through the coarser foodstuff layers, exposing the non-glandular portion to the corrosive acids. Even abdominal muscle contraction secondary to anxiety caused the same reaction.

Acid secretion is up or down and is regulated by food intake. The stomach acts as its own pH meter and is stimulated by histamine, which releases hydrochloric acid, from the parietal cells. Blocking the H2 (histamine 2) receptors suppresses gastric acid production. Within the pyloric gland mucosa, unique cell types that are located very close to each other constantly 'test' the pH of the stomach and react in such a way as to keep the pH in the correct range.

The type of food eaten also has an effect, for instance feeding alfalfa and oat straw significantly raises the pH level, whilst feeding high-grain diets produces volatile fatty acids and lactic acid, both of which easily damage the upper portion of the stomach causing pain and inflammation. All these events cause the body to release stress hormones and chemicals that ultimately lower the pH of the stomach and thus damage the lining.

Another major cause of ulcers in horses is the use of NSAIDs given as pain relievers and anti-arthritics, the most commonly prescribed one being bute. NSAIDs prevent the production of prostaglandin, which is a key ingredient in the protection of the stomach. Long-term use of any NSAIDs in the horse is considered to be detrimental to gut and liver health, but balance is the key and if a horse is so lame he is unable to walk around the box, then most owners would agree that the primary concern is to make him comfortable as quickly as possible and consider ulcer medication alongside.

Recent research has suggested that NSAIDs may be implicated in the development of hindgut ulcers in the prescence of bacterial infections. Until the mid-1980s, it was felt that stress, NSAIDs, poor eating habits or all of these factors working together led to the development of gastritis and ulcers. Since that time, evidence has been mounting that *Helicobacter pylori* has a major role in causing these diseases The most recent research has indicated that the most common cause of ulcers and cancer in humans is infection with *Helicobacter pylori*.

The first signs of ulcers can be nothing more than subtle changes in attitude or behaviour of the horse, i.e. sluggish movement, lacking in energy or becoming more nervous and spookier and resenting having the girth tightened. Other signs include a change in the amount of food usually eaten, chewing wood in the stable or fencing (not trees) and the onset of wind-sucking. Also, mild colic-like symptoms, turning round to look at his flanks, lying down and urinating excessively, sudden loss of coat condition such as coat looking slightly raised and flat-coloured (i.e. lacking shine).

New studies on ulcer treatment with natural compounds

As explained in the section Natural medications – the other side of the coin (*see* the final section of Chapter 5), there has been a huge increase in the potential of using plant-sourced compounds to treat a wide range of conditions and, in this context, there a specific interest from vets in the use of plant compounds for the treatment of ulcers. Brazil and Japan lead the way in human research and have developed a primary healthcare product as a natural alternative to Gastrogard, generic omeprazole, ranitidine and cimetidine, which has now been adapted for use in horses. The study concluded that the lyophilised extract represented a more powerful gastroprotective effect than cimetidine. This study also observed an increase in gastric juice volume and effect on pH identical to that of cimetidine.

Scientific studies of Maytenus ilicifolia

According to some studies, the plant Maytenus ilicifolia presents a potent action against peptic ulceration and gastritis. Other research reports that the action of Maytenus ilicifolia in peptic ulcer and gastritis involves more than one mechanism (albeit not conclusively elucidated) by a specific active ingredient, but by different phytocompounds. It was shown that both the tannins, especially epigallocatechin, and essential oils, especially fridenelol, are responsible for part of the gastroprotective effect.

Maytenus ilicifolia is grown as a medicinal crop to provide an efficacious dose and it provides a multi-targeted approach for the relief of ulcers. Studies *in vitro* showed that inhibition of gastric acid secretion occurs by inhibition of H+, K+,-ATPase, which is the final step of acid secretion and therefore one of the most important steps in the gastric acid secretion process.

Its use in medicine has been well-documented with no fewer than eleven patents lodged in South America, America and Japan for a variety of medical uses including the treatment of gastric ulcers and as a gastro-protective medicine, a gastric anti-inflammatory and an antibacterial agent.

In controlled studies researchers and vets have found that Maytenus ilicifolia grown as a medicinal crop produces similar but better results in the prevention and treatment of gastric ulcers than omeprazole, cimetidine and ranitidine (*see* below). It also has a positive effect on hindgut ulcers.

It has low toxicity, does not alter gut microbial flora even in long-term use and as it has a reversible action it does not permanently damage binding sites, ensuring a healthier stomach pH. The advantages of using anti-ulcerogenic plants instead of a synthetic drug are that plants have many synergistic chemicals and are generally able to provide analgesic, antibacterial and anti-inflammatory actions plus many flavonoid-rich antioxidants to aid healing. It was shown also that both epigallocatechin (tannin) as fridenelol (essential oil in Maytenus ilicifolia) account for much of the protective effect of the gastric mucosa. It is a fraction of the cost of Gastrogard with a ¼ daily dose recommended for prevention during stressful times and competition. It is a palatable and easily digested compound that can be included in the normal feed ration.

Over long periods of treatment with a maintenance dose 3 g daily of Maytenus ilicifolia a potent gastroprotective action is observed with no changes in pH. This observation can be confirmed. It was also shown that both epigallocatechin (tannin) and fridenelol (essential oil) account for much of the protective effect of the gastric mucosa.

Comparison of Maytenus ilicifolia with other drugs used for treating ulcers

Comparison with cimetidine. The anti-ulcer activity was initially studied by using necrotising agents such as aspirin, indomethacin (NSAID), reserpine and immobilisation at low temperatures.

It was demonstrated, by studying these models and the lyophilised Maytenus ilicifolia extract, that there was a marked gastroprotective effect. The study concluded that the lyophilised extract represented a more powerful gastroprotective effect than cimetidine. This study also observed an increase in gastric juice volume and effect on pH identical to that of cimetidine.

There is also a study that states that the anti-ulcer activity is primarily due to tannins and catechin derivatives. Later studies showed that the anti-ulcer actions of tannin and catechin derivatives are enhanced by the presence of components of essential oils, and friedelin fridelol, suggesting that more than one component has a gastroprotective effect.

Evidence of synergistic effect between the components of Maytenus ilicifolia was corroborated in another study, which demonstrated that, when used separately and in models of ulcer induced by indomethacin, the tannins did not show activity.

Another study demonstrated that the ethanol extract shows activity similar to blocking H2 as cimetidine: it inhibits the increased production of HCl by the oxyntic cells of gastric fundus induced by histamine. This corroborated previous studies, which demonstrated that epigallocatechin-3-gallate inhibits stress ulcers induced in rats by immersion in cold water for prolonged periods. This effect was blocked by the addition of pro-oxidants, suggesting that the antioxidant activity of epigallocatechin-3-gallate is part of its anti-ulcer activity.

Comparison with ranitidine. In studies involving the infusion of leaves, both orally and intraperitoneally, using ranitidine and cimetidine as positive controls, Maytenus ilicifolia was demonstrated to have comparable activity (higher in some cases) than the control drugs.

Comparison with omeprazole. In this study gastric ulcers were induced using indomethacin rather than by the usual necrotising agent ethanol. Indomethacin is a COX inhibitor and its application induces the appearance of severe lesions. The use of this non-steroidal anti-inflammatory inhibits the formation of prostaglandin and produces severe bleeding lesions. Prostaglandins are responsible for the stimulation of mucosal mucus and bicarbonate and for the increase in mucosal blood flow and they limit back diffusion of acid into the epithelium. The researchers found that the flavonoid-rich fraction of Maytenus ilicifolia was 6.2 times more potent against the use of indomethacin than ethanol. This suggests that the action of the Maytenus ilicifolia is strongly involved in the cyclooxygenase-prostaglandin system to promote gastro-protection. The study concludes that as well as having gastro-protective abilities Maytenus ilicifolia has a proton pump inhibitory effect.

The evidence for bacterial infections as a cause of EGUS in horses

Until the mid-1980s, it was felt that stress, NSAIDs, poor eating habits or all of these factors working together led to the development of gastritis and ulcers. However, more recent research has been directed at the relationship between the presence of ulcers and bacterial infections. Evidence has been mounting that *helicobacter pylori* has a major role in causing these diseases. The most recent research has indicated that the most common cause of ulcers and cancer in humans is infection with *Helicobacter pylori*.

Ulcers underwent examination in the glandular part of the equine stomach to determine whether there was a link between the presence of *Helicobacter pylori*, *Helicobacter equorum* and EGUS. The study concluded that there was sporadic infection with *Helicobacter pylori* in horses with gastric ulcers and *Helicobacter equorum* was found in a faecal sample of one horse without ulcerations.

A further study also examined lesions in the glandular part of the stomach. Lesions located in this region were found in 58% of 162 hospitalised horses and 47% of 345 racehorses, and acid exposure would not be the primary causative factor here. In humans and many animals including dogs, sheep and cattle, infection with *Helicobacter pylori* bacteria is a major risk to the development of glandular stomach ulcers and cancer.

However, the conclusion of this study was that *Helicobacter pylori* could not be verified as being involved in the formation of lesions of the glandular stomach of the horse. An emerging pathogen *Escherichia fergusonii* was found in one case of gastric erosion. These bacteria were found intercellular, but what was not known was whether this was a primary or secondary infection. As very limited amounts of bacteria were found in the glandular region, detection of a moderate to high amount of any bacteria at a glandular mucosa level is significant and further studies need to be undertaken to clarify whether gastric infection by *E. Fergusonii* is an important part of the EGUS syndrome.

In a study looking at several tannins contained in Maytenus ilicifolia these were tested against *H. pylori*. The most active is epigallocatechin-3-gallate, the minimum inhibitory concentration of which was 8 μg/ml. This study also induced an experimental infection with *H. pylori* in gerbils. Both a fraction of tannins and gallic catechists as epigallocatechin-3-gallate were effective in eradicating infection in all treated animals, whilst it persisted in controls, suggesting greater efficiency of the tannins *in vivo*. There was also a significant reduction of inflammatory changes, foci of haemorrhage and ulceration in the treated animals.

Head-shaking

Trigeminal-mediated head-shaking is linked to a nerve-like pain causing loss of performance, poor quality of life and even eventually euthanasia. Symptoms include violent vertical shakes, snorting, rubbing of the nose and many anxious facial expressions, including grimacing, flared nostrils, wide eyes and flattened ears. In a recently published paper, a disruption of the gut bacteria is described, indicating an increase in the percentages of methane-producing bacteria.

Developing a microbiome profile for head-shaking horses

In a recently published paper Aleman et al. (2022)[7] described a disruption of the gut bacteria with an increase in the percentages of methane-producing bacteria called *Methanocorpusculum*, in the microbiome of horses with head-shaking. The study used ten horses, five with trigeminal mediated head-shaking (TMHS) and five healthy control horses.

In 2022 we conducted our own microbiome study, selecting fifty-four horses with head-shaking symptoms, twelve with severe symptoms (unrideable) and the rest with mild symptoms (could be ridden with care) and we compared this group to seventy-five healthy horses.

Following the microbiome analysis of all the horses, we then used ML and AI (Agxio.com) to look for patterns within the large datasets produced by genomic sequencing. The use of AI means a better identification of patterns within the large datasets that couldn't be seen with the human eye. The AI picked up a pattern within the horses with head-shaking symptoms with 100% accuracy as follows.

The gut microbiome profile of a head-shaker:

- Lower alpha diversity (alpha diversity is the number of different species present in the gut microbiome); a healthy horse has 1,000–1,500. Those with head-shaking symptoms had between 750– 800 different species.
- Higher levels of pathogens associated with colitis and inflammation of the gut.
- Higher levels of *Clostridia* – a large family of well-studied gut bacteria in the horse. Species within the *Clostridia* phyla have been linked to colitis (Uzal & Diab 2015),[8] diarrhoea (Båverud, 2004),[9] liver disease (Navarro & Uzal., 2020),[10] lockjaw/tetanus (Dean, 2017)[11] and botulism (Swink & Gilsenen 2022):[12] *Clostridia* have also been named as a possible pathogen in grass sickness (Garrett et al., 2002).[13]
- Higher levels of a toxin-producing bacteria called *Cyanobacteria*.
- There were low to non-existent levels of *Gemmatimonadota*. These microbes are very common in unpolluted water and healthy soil; they can be easily killed off in treated water and unhealthy/compacted soil.
- Higher levels of antibiotic-resistant *Staphylococcus*; an emerging cause of serious infection in horses, the bacteria residing in the mucosa of gut/nose/lung etc. These bacteria can come into the equine environment through the water supply or from the sludge produced from the treatment of water, which may be sprayed back onto the land, to find its way back into the water supply. High oxidation treatment seems to be the most successful at reducing levels of antibiotic-resistant *Staphylococcus* but chlorination, ozonation and ultraviolet radiation can actually increase levels.

Healthy horses had exactly the opposite profile: there were no differences found in the methane-producing bacteria identified by Aleman et al.(2022)(*see chapter endnote 7*).

Plants to help alleviate head-shaking

There are several features common to the dysbiosis seen in the microbiome of horses with head-shaking, including:

1. Higher levels of antibiotic-resistant *Staphylococcus*.
2. Higher levels of *Cyanobacteria* – a waterborne pathogen.
3. A reduction in beneficial bacteria that come into the microbiome from healthy soil, having a protective role on the health of the horse.

Considering (1) as a priority, antimicrobial resistance (AMR) is one of the greatest threats to human and animal health in the twenty-first century, although antibiotics remain important for treating both minor and life-threatening bacterial infections. Animals and humans are reservoirs of AMR, but equally antimicrobial-resistant bacteria are commonly found in the environment, especially in water and animal feeds. It should not therefore come as a surprise that horses will be exposed. *Staphylococcus* is a commensal-bacteria to the equine skin, mouth and gut and only causes health problems when present at higher-than-average levels. As AMR has long been considered to be a serious health problem; in recent years the search has been on to find novel antibiotics from nature that will be effective on antimicrobial-resistant bacteria. The plants most likely to be useful for horses with head-shaking are a combination of antimicrobials from thyme (Thymus), sage (Satvia), wild garlic (Allium sativum), great pig nut (Bunium bulbocastanum), and least mallow (Malva parviflora).

Myofascial and fibromyalgia pain[14]

Fibromyalgia is a common complaint in humans, as is myofascial pain syndrome. New research indicates the onset of both may originate from an imbalance through the microbe-gut-brain axis. There are multiple links and similarities between fibromyalgia and myofascial pain syndrome, although symptoms relating to active trigger points may be different in fibromyalgia. Myofascial pain syndrome involves mainly pain originating in a muscle whilst the pain from fibromyalgia is often widespread through the body and may include joint and gastric pain. Myofascial trigger points have been detected in horses. Myofascial trigger points in both horses and humans are defined by the following symptom criteria: abnormal spontaneous electrical activity, spike activity and local twitch responses at the trigger point site. Fibromyalgia and myofascial pain syndrome causing chronic back pain has been researched in depth, the cause was hypothesised to be the result of a trapped nerve and acupuncture was the recommended therapy. There are now a growing number of acupuncture practitioners who specialise in work on horses.

Symptoms of fibromyalgia in horses

These include chronic pain signs and impaired performance, bloating and abdominal pain. Also muscle soreness (tying up), joint pain, severe nerve pain and tenderness and excessive sweating. Cranial nerves can be affected, causing facial nerve paralysis, head tilt, laryngeal dysfunction and difficulties in swallowing (choke).

Fibromyalgia is frequently seen in racehorses (most of the symptoms coming under the banner of poor performance syndrome) and it accounts for at least 25% of racehorse loss each year, especially prevalent in National Hunt horses.

The role of the gut bacteria in fibromyalgia and myofascial pain

The microbe-gut-brain axis is crucial for creating and maintaining the health of the entire body. If the balance within the gut bacteria community is altered, through diet, environment or stress, the result can be an increased production of chemicals that affect the nervous system, promoting pain and sensitivity.

The gut profile of horses with chronic pain/fibromyalgia/myofascial pain

Gut bacteria can produce secondary metabolites (chemicals) that support good health or are detrimental to good health. Too many bacteria producing toxic/harmful chemicals will alter the homeostasis (health balance) of the whole horse and will cause symptoms to appear in other organs of the body away from the gut as they react to higher levels of chemicals that aren't good for them. Although all the bacteria listed below are part of the core family of microbes present in most horses, an increase of any within those listed causes an imbalance within the community that can have devastating effects on the homeostasis of the gut and the rest of the body.

1. *Eubacterium*, *Faecal bacterium prausnitzii*, *Ruminococcus*, *Clostridium* and *Actinomycetaceae*. These bacteria reside predominantly in the small intestine and whilst hippuric acid production is a normal and important part of equine metabolism, an excess (that can be measured in urine) is an indication of an unnatural (detoxification) process by the gut.
2. Higher percentages of *Fusobacteria* nucleatum and faecal bacterium cause an increase in 2-Hydroxyisobutyric, this is the most damaging of the three chemicals to be produced, the other two being hippuric acid and lactic acid. 2-Hydroxyisobutyric acid is chemically similar to lactic acid.
3. Higher levels of *Fusobacteria* only occur in horses under stress (competing) and a higher percentage of *Fusobacteria* is also linked to colic and colitis.
4. Higher levels of lactic acid-producing bacteria such as *Lactobacillus*. Lactic acid is part of many metabolic and biochemical processes in horses and especially relates to the muscle i.e. tying up (rhabdomyolysis) and PSSM; it is also mentioned in the onset of hindgut acidosis and laminitis.

Long-term changes

If the gut imbalance isn't rectified then the persistent, chronic noxious stimulant produced by the metabolites mentioned above can sensitise the nervous system and eventually make three long-term changes that cause chronic pain to perpetuate. These changes to the nervous system are:

1. The growth of extra nerves.
2. Nerves that increase their area of innervation (creating oversensitivity to touch).
3. The nerves become more sensitive to the pain stimulus.

White line disease

We have looked at the link between chronic disease and a suppressed immune system, mostly the result of a combination of the lack of fresh antioxidants and a mineral deficiency in the diet, together with the increasing resistance of bacteria to antibiotics. A large number of horses now have an immune system that is compromised and open to many chronic diseases and infection states. We know that bacteria are resistant to many drugs, but fungi are also resistant and many are emerging as major causes of equine disease. Most fungal and bacterial infections are largely opportunist, causing infection when the host's (horse's) defences are breached. White line disease (seedy toe) in horses is an example of this; it is a disease caused first by a compromised immune system followed by a secondary breach of the immune defences by several opportunist fungi and bacterial saprophytism. The fungi are namely *Scedosporium brevicaulis*, *Scedosporium prolificans*, *Scedosporium apiosporium* and *Pseudallesceria boydii*.

The mineral sulphur plays an important part in equine health, supporting the immune system, being a key constituent of some important amino acids and a cofactor for enzymes that trigger various chemical reactions. It is also a key constituent of keratin, from which the white line is mainly built. The amino acids that build keratin are highly prone to oxidative damage caused by high circulating free radicals, compounded by low levels of plant antioxidants whose job it is to neutralise the damage. A lack of sulphur in the diet can therefore compromise the health of the white line, both in terms of less robust construction and reduced defences.

It is better to provide sulphur in the diet rather than providing the amino acids with which it is associated because it is impossible to monitor the amount of oxidative damage to the white line at a micronutrient level. However, the horse will convert the amino acids from the sulphur as needed and will convert the rest to antioxidants such as glutathione.

A dietary lack of sulphur will also contribute to high insulin levels (laminitis/EMS) and compromise adrenal hormones (Cushing's) and, as mentioned above, low levels of sulphur also weaken the immune system by providing low levels of antibodies. The most noticeable feature of white line disease is the hypertrophy or enlargement and weakening of the cells, causing defects in the elastic barrier line. These changes were considered by the researchers to be similar to laminitis – often mild laminitis goes undiscovered but causes a similar change in the hoof, creating fissures to appear. It may be that this then allows the fungi to take the opportunity to breach the immune system, take up residence and cause the catastrophic breakdown often seen in this disease.

Cushing's disease

Cushing's disease, named after the neurosurgeon who first described it, is the common name for pituitary pars intermedia dysfunction (PPID). It is described as an enlargement or a tumour of the pituitary gland, which causes an increase in the excretion of pro-opiomelanocortin which, in turn, raises ACTH levels and creates an increase and an imbalance in the levels of several important hormones, particularly relating to the change in seasons (it is worse in July and into the autumn and goes into regression in the winter months, for reasons explained later in this section).

Cushing's is a complex disease with a number of symptoms and is closely associated with other conditions such as laminitis (as will be evident in the following text). During the early stages of the disease, the symptoms can be sometimes very hard to detect and the age onset may have a genetic component. Although there is currently no actual cure there are a number of ways in which it can be managed to reduce its speed of onset and effects, which we will discuss here. Whilst some of these methods involve scientific testing and providing appropriate medical intervention, avoiding an inappropriate diet is crucial, and there are a number of plants and herbs that can have a highly beneficial effect.

The incidence of Cushing's disease is on the rise among horses (Ireland & McGowan

2018).[15] In quite recent times (30–50 years ago), native ponies and cross breeds in particular were expected to reach their thirties in a healthy state, and whilst there were cases of Cushing's, they were relatively infrequent compared to the present day. Whilst this increase is attributed in part to advances in veterinary diagnosis, it is also the case that increasing numbers of younger horses are diagnosed with the condition(van der Kolk 2004 & Frank 2006).[16]

Some horses are genetically predisposed to Cushing's; in these horses onset of the disease can start as early as the age of seven (Schott, 2002 & McFarlane, 2007)[17] affecting males and females to the same extent. Despite the common occurrence of Cushing's there is limited knowledge about the frequency, distribution and control of the disease.

Scientists have hypothesised a link between Cushing's in horses and Parkinson's disease in humans (McFarlane 2007) (*see chapter endnote 17*). Environmental exposure to insecticides – specifically permethrin – has been identified as a potential causative agent to Parkinson's, with a 28% to 62% increase in the risk of developing the disease (Van Maele-Fabry et al., 2012).[18] As well as being a component of many lice treatments used on horses, almost 70% of permethrin is used as an insecticide on corn, wheat and alfalfa, increasing the risk of contamination from the diet even if the horse is not given a topical treatment for lice.

Glyphosate, another commonly used agrichemical herbicide, has been the subject of debate concerning its safety, particularly in relation to its effects on animals and once again to potential links to human diseases such as Parkinson's. Its impact on the liver has been discussed in Chapter 3. There is a lack of specific grazing restrictions in respect of glyphosate, raising concerns given the mixed reports on its toxicity in horses. Some studies suggest that glyphosate exposure can lead to symptoms such as anorexia, lethargy, vomiting, diarrhoea, and hypersalivation in animals, and it may interfere with reproductive health. Also, glyphosate is classified as an endocrine-disrupting chemical (EDC), which implies it can affect hormone production and function, potentially leading to broader systemic health effects. This may be significant in regard to Cushing's, which is caused by the degeneration of neurons that influence hormone production.

Although Cushing's and Parkinson's are anatomically distinct in many ways there are two very clear similarities, the first is the dopaminergic neuronal damage in Cushing's and Parkinson's and the second is the link between even very limited exposure to pesticides and the significant reduction in dopamine production in the brain of humans and mammals.

However Cushing's is on the increase and is up to twenty times more prevalent in horses than Parkinson's is in humans and recently, with the early testing available for raised ACTH levels, more horses are being diagnosed as having Cushing's at increasingly young ages (although younger horses showing some signs of the disease are often described as having pre-Cushing's).

Onset

The onset of Cushing's is likely to be a complex interaction between the environment and genetic makeup, particularly in relationship to how well horses age naturally and the degree to which oxidative stress damage in Cushing's might be considered part of the normal ageing process. However, recent early diagnosis based on raised ACTH levels should raise the owner's readiness to question whether this represents the early stages of a chronic degenerative condition, or whether it could possibly be a response to the environment, or even an environmental pollutant.

In this age of social media perhaps this is the perfect time for concerned owners to begin an epidemiological log of populations of horses deemed 'at risk' either at an early age or who have a history of raised ACTH levels before the onset of the major signs of Cushing's. Is it possible for some horses, especially those under the age of twelve, to have a raised ACTH level without actually having Cushing's?

Cushing's disease in older horses is usually accompanied by a long list of other symptoms which we will mention shortly. However, in recent years many horses have been diagnosed as having Cushing's without the full-blown symptoms listed, but with raised ACTH levels, what might cause this to happen? Is there possibly another reason for horses – particularly younger ones – to have raised ACTH levels without having full-blown Cushing's?

As we know there is a link between full-blown Cushing's in older horses, EMS and IR and the common denominator between the three is obesity (Cushing's horses are often obese, 'good doers' who suddenly go thin with the onset of the disease). As explained earlier, a horse with a body condition score of between 7 and 9 is said to be obese, and horses who are obese have fat pads and 'cresty' necks, which are made up of adipose tissue. As we now know, the adipose tissue is a hormone factory linked to the immune system and we are now only just beginning to understand what these hormones and signalling chemicals (cytokines) do. One chemical that is released from adipose tissue is interleukin-6, which can significantly raise ACTH levels because it has a direct influence on the hypothalamic-pituitary-adrenocortical pathway. A diet based mainly on cereals or high carbohydrate hay/grass-based diets can also raise ACTH levels by raising the insulin levels (post-prandial) after a feed; the higher the insulin response from the ingestion of certain carbohydrates the higher the release of cytokine chemicals such as the interleukins from the adipose tissue which, in turn, results in the raising of ACTH. (Some easily digested carbohydrates will raise post-prandial insulin more than others.)

Symptoms

As mentioned above, there can be many symptoms associated with Cushing's. In the later stages, abnormal and excessive hair growth are two of the most common symptoms, the most significant and the one that is unique to Cushing's is the change in coat growth, either in the form of very long hair or excessive hair growth with poor shedding. The changes in coat length are 95% specific for the diagnosis of Cushing's, especially in native ponies. The changes start with delayed coat shedding, with patchy hair that is a lighter colour than the rest of the coat. The lower legs are the first area to retain the hair, and the leg hair becomes longer and thicker. (It's worth noting here that many native ponies foaled in the late summer do not shed their coat until June.) The next most significant symptom that contributes to a diagnosis of Cushing's is the loss of muscle along the 'topline' back of the horse, followed by muscle wastage and atrophy, weight loss, laminitis, depression and lethargy.

Active laminitis or previous signs of laminitis represent the next most common Cushing's symptom seen in native ponies. However, in horses, abnormal hoof growth is noted more often than laminitis, and often the owner has been unaware of these pathological changes. This highlights the importance of education around recognising the whole range of symptoms and how important it is to spot these early to help manage the disease. Since owners generally notice their charges ageing at around nineteen years, which might be a contributory factor in the misreading of Cushing's symptoms (Welsh et al., 2016).[19]

Other symptoms include:

- Low lymphocytes in the blood, insufficient to protect against infections.
- High neutrophils in the blood, meaning the horse is currently trying to fight off an infection.
- High levels of cortisol in the blood – the body produces cortisol in times of stress.
- Excessive urination is caused by high levels of cortisol lowering other levels of hormones that control urination. Suppression of hormones also causes an increase in thirst and the horse will drink more.
- High levels of cortisol also suppress the immune system and may also be the cause of low protein in the tissues. The horse becomes susceptible to chronic infections; wounds take longer to heal; there is an increased chance of eye infections and an increase in hoof abscesses.
- Elevated liver enzymes found in the biochemistry section of a routine blood test. Aspartate aminotransferase (AST) values of 693 IU/L, alkaline phosphatase (ALP) approximate values up to 204 IU/L, gamma-glutamyl transferase (GGT) with approximate levels of 46 IU/L, and succinate dehydrogenase (SDH), with approximate levels of 10 IU/L.
- A change in metabolism. The horse will go (in a very short space of time) from being an 'easy keeper' living on 'fresh air' to a horse who consumes more calories whilst suddenly losing weight.
- Increase in sweating.
- High insulin levels are routinely recorded in horses with laminitis who also have Cushing's, and hyperglycaemia (high blood sugar) and glucosuria (high glucose in the urine) are also common.

Summary of symptoms of advanced Cushing's

These include:

- Longer retention of a winter coat caused by changes in the melanocyte stimulating hormone (MSH).
- Horses with advanced Cushing's are more prone to laminitis because hyperadrenocorticism causes changes in circulation and loss of protein in the hoof tissues, which lowers the threshold for laminitis.
- Changes in body condition:
  » Horses lose muscle whilst retaining the fat pads and start to look pot-bellied. This is because the spine, which needs to remain strong and stable, is no longer supported by the reduced muscle whilst, at the same time, the fat pads are mostly deposited and around the flank and belly.
  » Excessive urination is caused by high levels of cortisol lowering other levels of hormones that control urination. Suppression of hormones also causes an increase in thirst and the horse will drink more.

- » The horse becomes susceptible to chronic infections; wounds take longer to heal; increased chance of eye infections and an increase in hoof abscesses. The cause is high levels of cortisol, which suppresses the immune system and may also be the cause of low protein in the tissues.
- » Lethargy and increased pain resistance.
- » Increase in sweating.
- » Seizures and eye lesions.
- » Mouth and foot ulcers.

A broad picture of likely progression

Advanced Cushing's is associated with the development of an abnormal growth which has made permanent changes to the metabolism and hormone levels. This is described as neoplasia, but some scientists have termed the seasonal changes associated with pre-Cushing's as being hyperplasic in nature, suggesting that the seasonal hormonal changes may start with a normal event but, in some horses, become more pronounced and progress into advanced Cushing's when, for some reason, the swollen tissues become a tumour and the condition becomes permanent. The changes to the coat, mentioned earlier, will also become evident.

Also to be noted are changes in metabolism. It was found that horses who have suffered with obesity issues, are then prone to develop EMS and insulin resistance and often go on to develop Cushing's. There are some significant changes to consider between early Cushing's disease and advanced development. First there will be a drop in temperature followed by a drop in energy levels, and then the horse will need extra rations, as there will be a demand for calories to maintain weight.

The horse will go (in a very short space of time) from being an 'easy keeper' living on fresh air to a horse who consumes more calories whilst suddenly losing weight. Fat pads on the neck, around the sheath, the eye socket and the tail can be signs of either EMS or Cushing's. *The Veterinary Clinicians' Guide* recommends testing horses with fat pads for EMS and IR if they are under ten years of age and for Cushing's and IR if they are above this age.

Warning signs

- ○ Cushing's enlarges the pituitary gland, increasing pro-opiomelanocortin release and raising ACTH levels. However, some horses under twelve may have high ACTH levels without Cushing's (which poses the question as to the cause, especially in younger horses) whilst some horses show raised ACTH levels without full Cushing's symptoms. Although these variations illustrate the complexity of the condition, the raised ACTH levels should be investigated, since they are concerning in themselves. (ACTH levels are discussed in more detail later.)
- ○ Cushing's, EMS and IR in older horses are linked by obesity; obese horses have adipose tissue producing hormones affecting ACTH levels. For example, adipose tissue releases interleukin-6, influencing ACTH levels through the hypothalamic-pituitary-adrenal pathway.

Diets high in cereals or carbohydrates can raise ACTH by spiking insulin levels post-feeding, leading to cytokine release and ACTH elevation, so it's crucial to manage the diet to regulate ACTH levels. (Easily digested carbohydrates can also trigger higher post-prandial insulin responses.)

Scientific research and testing

The following laboratory tests are those most frequently used to detect early stages of Cushing's – although they are not recommended in subclinical cases when a horse has no definite or observable symptoms. (This has not always been the case and tests for raised ACTH in the past have resulted in young horses with no other symptoms being prescribed the drug pergolide.)

The basal ACTH test

ACTH is produced by the pituitary gland and it stimulates the adrenal glands to produce cortisol. Cortisol helps the horse's body to respond to stress, helps reduce inflammation, and regulates blood glucose.

This is the most popular and well recognised test for diagnosing Cushing's; it is relatively simple to conduct and requires just one blood sample from the jugular vein.

Factors such as stress, illness, pain, season, age, sex and body condition score will increase ACTH concentrations, so it is essential that the test results are interpreted with care to avoid/reduce the chance of a false result, either positive or negative.

There are also differences that should be taken into account between breeds, with Shetland and Welsh ponies, cob breeds, Arabs (and donkeys) having a higher and more prolonged peak in ACTH concentrations during late summer and autumn compared to Warmbloods or Thoroughbreds. Cobs, Arabs and donkeys also have higher levels in May (Kirkwood et al., 2022).[20]

The late summer/early autumn is thought to be a good time to test as horses affected by this condition have the exaggerated seasonal variation, resulting in significantly elevated concentrations of ACTH compared to healthy counterparts.

Interestingly, these breeds with higher levels of ACTH do not have a higher incidence of the disease itself. If the results are inconclusive, a Thyrotropin-Releasing Hormone (TRH) stimulation test (*see* below) is recommended because of its higher accuracy.

Making sense of seasonal variations of ACTH

We mentioned earlier that raised ACTH levels could be a precursor to Cushing's. The question was posed as to why a horse with EMS tested in June and July is likely to show a positive reading for Cushing's and the same horse tested in April would show normal ACTH levels. A trial by Donaldson et. al. (2005)[21] tested the ACTH levels of horses in September, January and May and found that the ACTH levels were higher in September, but that still posed the question of what happens in the remaining months of the year; which month is the best for an ACTH test? ACTH levels during August, September and October are significantly higher than in all other months. The lowest ACTH levels are found in April (ACTH levels are very much lower in this month). Three-quarters of (healthy) horses and seven out of eight EMS horses with blood taken in September were above the reference range of 9–35 pg/mL (picograms per millilitre).

Horses with EMS had higher ACTH levels in August (4 out of 7), in September (3 out of 7) and in October (3 out of 9). In these months the percentage of horses with ACTH levels above the Cushing's cut-off level of 70 pg/mL was no different between the controls and horses with EMS.

The conclusions from the research trials were that blood test results taken in late summer and autumn should be interpreted with caution and that an adjustment table needed to be developed following further trials. A later trial was undertaken by Copas & Durham (2012)[22] using a selection of hospitalised horses with and without Cushing's, resulting in a seasonally adjusted upper limit for ACTH of 29 pg/mL between November and July and 47 pg/mL between August and October.

ACTH levels from an earlier trial by Place et. al (2010)[23] were 18 pg/mL in February, March and April which is well below the 29 pg/mL given as a reference level in the 2012 trial. In fact the only three months the ACTH levels went above 29 pg/mL (discounting the higher levels August–October) were in June, July and December for the EMS horses.

Insulin levels varied significantly throughout the year and between horses but remained continuously high in the horses with EMS despite a reduction of carbohydrates and an increase in exercise. Interestingly, thyroxine levels fell in the horses with EMS during September.

The EMS horses from the 2010 trial all indicated raised levels of ACTH above the controls; these horses also had higher though very variable levels of insulin. Therefore, based on an ACTH test only (no other symptoms present), do horses have EMS rather than Cushing's. Given the wide variations of insulin levels throughout the year, is a raised ACTH therefore a better predictor of EMS?

Insulin dysregulation test

Insulin dysregulation can complicate the treatment of Cushing's, with higher rates of failure. The test can be done at the same time as the TRH stimulation test and it is useful for vets in the field to check the insulin levels at the same time as the ACTH.

Insulin is injected into the jugular vein and blood samples are collected just before and thirty minutes after this; blood glucose levels and peripheral tissue insulin resistance are then calculated.

A diagnosis is made on the blood glucose concentration of the thirty-minute sample being higher than half the baseline, indicating a less than 50% decline of blood glucose (Horn & Bertin, 2019).[24]

Testing for insulin resistance

Some horses with Cushing's have insulin resistance and some don't, so it is important to test for and consider both situations. A horse may have insulin resistance because of the Cushing's or because he is overweight, and it is so important to manage the diet of horses of this type as they become very prone to laminitis. Some obese horses with EMS then go on to develop Cushing's and the first symptom in this transitional period is a change or loss of energy – they become noticeably lethargic and suddenly require more calories in order to maintain weight.

It will be seen from the potential connection with these other conditions that testing horses suspected of having Cushing's for insulin resistance may also provide information useful in confronting other challenges. One example of this is as follows. (Although it focuses on the treatment development and treatment of laminitis, which is dealt with in more detail later in this chapter, it also shows another potential link between that condition and Cushing's.)

Insulin resistance increases the risk of laminitis and although this is usually linked to overweight horses, not all fat horses are affected – sometimes thin or normal-weight horses can be prone. Knowledge of why this happens is limited, but in case your horse is affected and is not responding to management or medication here are three potential reasons why:

1. Some horses have an abnormal response to fructose that damages the liver causing hepatic insulin resistance and laminitis. With these horses it is important to remove as much fructose from the diet as possible – i.e. test hay and grass for fructose content, soak hay and severely restrict grazing.
2. Cortisol and insulin are released from adipose tissue around the liver (all horses have adipose tissue here, even the leaner ones, this fat produces quantities of detrimental hormones including leptin) causing local damage to the liver leading to insulin resistance, which is also known as peripheral Cushing's.
3. If your horse has continuously high levels of insulin he may have a pancreatic disease causing the liver cells to secrete insulin in response to even slight increases in blood glucose.

If this is the case with your horse, take the following steps. Severely restrict fructose and starch intake and increase antioxidants to increase glucose uptake in the body. Identify the grass species on your paddock, as the fructose content is much higher in some species and safe grazing times will vary. For hard feed and chaff check both the carbohydrate and sugar content with your feed manufacturer. (It's worth mentioning that manufacturers list the sugar content in percentage as added, but don't list the carbohydrate levels.) It is certainly important to go through all the food intake of a horse with Cushing's to restrict the sugar and starch intake and find any hidden starches such as the corn oil coating on some brands of chaff. As horses with Cushing's are prone to laminitis it is important to restrict grazing on grasses with high fructose levels. This is especially so in the early summer and early autumn grazing periods, as the grass it particularly high in sugar in those months. If the horse also has laminitis then grazing at these times should be cut out all altogether and only resumed with caution when the hoof has become more stable. Laminitic horses need a lot of box rest and preferably to lie down as much as possible to take the weight from the affected leg. (It is also the case that horses who suffer with both leaky gut and Cushing's disease should not be allowed to graze on lush grass or given any feed with high starch or sugar content.) It is important to test for IR as well as Cushing's in older horses because insulin resistance causes the laminitic attacks to be more frequent.

Insulin test findings: the importance of accuracy

High insulin levels are implicated and associated with diseases such as laminitis, osteochondrosis, EMS and Cushing's, therefore an accurate reading of insulin levels is vital in order to treat, avoid, or prevent. Tests showed that as insulin levels in the blood rise there is an increase in lameness in a horse with laminitis or who is prone to laminitis; even slight hikes in insulin can cause 'footiness'. Scientists found that as insulin decreased the horse became sounder. All of the EMS (with high insulin level) horses chosen for the study had a 'cresty' neck score higher than 3. The relationship between high insulin levels and laminitis was first recognised in 1986 and a high insulin level was calculated at >100 µIU/mL (normal range, 8–30 µIU/mL). Having said this, horse owners should be aware that insulin tests may be inaccurate as per a report from 2011.

Most commercial kits used by labs in measuring insulin are human diagnostic assays but are used because of the anticipated similarity in the behaviour and characteristics of insulin across different mammal species. Because of the increasing importance of accurate insulin measurements by research and equine veterinary science, some equine tests have been developed and are available, but this has led to different and varied standards being accepted as normal or high in insulin, making comparisons between laboratories impossible. Within the individual tests precision and accuracy are also vital, but research has indicated that out of six equine commercial assays all but one failed to produce an accurate reading when compared to the gold standard method of gas chromatography MS or LC-MS. The most accurate test had to be adjusted away from the manufacturer's instructions and one of the most used equine tests performed poorly, delivering continuously high results depending on the dilution of the serum – although this may differ from lab to lab. Furthermore, the results from one commonly used test were described as 'spurious', which is a strong way of saying 'not what it purports to be', or false or fake. Our advice for horse owners is: don't be misinformed, ask the vet which test he uses and how accurate is it likely to be. In 2014 research indicated that the difficulties in producing an accurate test for insulin levels in horses still existed; this published paper reports that horses are highly likely to be misdiagnosed as having high insulin levels, and recommends the use of liquid chromatography or mass spectrometry. This equipment is very specialised and sensitive, and we are currently using it to develop an accurate test for the antioxidant status of horses. (We also use it to analyse the biochemicals contained in plant material.) Horse owners should be aware that most labs don't have this equipment. In the light of this information horse owners wanting to manage high insulin levels should try to reduce their horses 'cresty' neck size, as a higher than 3 score is indicative of EMS and high insulin levels.

Nitric oxide deficiency

Most chronic degenerative diseases such as EMS, Cushing's, arthritis, colic, endotoxaemia, joint disease and COPD could be the result of the deficiency or loss of nitric oxide. In 1992 nitric oxide was named 'Molecule of the Year' because it caused such major advancements in many clinical treatments. There are currently over 130,000 published papers devoted to understanding its role in health and disease. Nitric oxide (NO) is a gas produced naturally in the body and serves as one of the most important signalling molecules in the physiology of mammals. It produces relaxation and increased blood flow, and nutrient and oxygen delivery. It also controls inflammation in the bloodstream and prevents abnormal activity. In fact it was first tested on horses with laminitis in the 1990s to increase blood flow to the foot before the lack of oxygen to the delicate structures of the foot could cause the typical symptoms and catastrophic breakdown. The use of glyceryl trinitrate patches or nitro-glycerine to treat laminitis was controversial at the time and one of the leading laminitis authorities (Chris Pollitt) reporting to *The Horse* in 1997, had this explanation of how and why nitro-glycerine might affect laminitis:

> Nitric oxide (NO) is now known to be the universal and most potent of natural vasodilators. It is manufactured from arginine, a simple amino acid, by all the cells lining all blood vessels (the endothelial cells). GTN (glyceryl tri-nitrate or nitro-glycerine) acts as a source of nitric oxide and acts very quickly to dilate.
>
> When endothelial cells are being ravaged by an episode of septic shock or endotoxemia, they tend to give up their NO and cause a rapid fall in blood pressure (terminal, irreversible shock). When horses sick with colic reach this stage, their mucous membranes go bright red, and then they die. Horses with carbohydrate overload are also endotoxic, and it is my hunch that the vasodilation that always coincides with the development of anatomical destruction of the lamellae is mediated by NO. This is speculation on my part. If I am right, it means that vasodilators like NO are contraindicated during the fever, and developmental, stage of laminitis. I have no problem with GTN patches, along with other vasodilators like isoxuprine and ACP, when the metabolic crisis is over and the foot is trying to heal.

In 2005 there was a consensus that 'In clinically healthy horses, digital arterial blood flow and digital venous plasma nitric oxide concentrations did not change significantly with application of the GTN patches/ointment.' (This was from a BEVA/AWF practice-based study on the factors affecting return to soundness in acute pasture-associated laminitis, N. J. Menzies-Gow, K. Stevens, A. Barr, I. Camm, D. U. Pfeiffe, C. M. Marr.) The clinical relevance of this is as follows. Although GTN patches have been used as a method of decreasing vasomotor tone and improving digital blood flow in horses with laminitis, this study provides evidence in healthy, conscious horses that this treatment is not effective in altering digital blood flow.

There followed a host of supplements containing nitric oxide for horses. There was also a trend towards supplementing equine diets with L-arginine to increase the production of nitric oxide, but research soon discovered that, during inflammatory conditions such as laminitis and Cushing's, dietary supplementation with L-arginine actually contributed to further deficiency. It was then left to researchers of human medicine to discover that inorganic nitrates from leafy green vegetables were the best way to restore nitric oxide balance and prevent further degeneration and deterioration of conditions such as laminitis, arthritis and Cushing's. The best wild plants for horses containing adequate levels of nitric oxide are wild mustard (Sinapsis arvensis), lamb's quarter and fat hen (Chenopodium album), chasteberry (Vitex agnus-castus), hawthorn (Crataegus), self-heal (Prunella vulgaris) and willow (Salix).

Red blood cell levels

One of the many different symptoms seen in horses with Cushing's is a depletion of red blood cells, which will cause low blood cell levels. This can occur because of the chronic state of inflammation that exists in horses with Cushing's or because Cushing's is degenerative and one of the components of degeneration is that the red blood cells are destroyed faster than they are made. Red blood cells can be provided with protection by plant chemicals known as betalains, delaying the ability of free radicals to destroy or deplete production. It takes around one hour for the ingested chemicals to reach the blood cells and the protection lasts for around eight hours, protection being greatest at the three-hour mark. Red blood cells protected by betalains have an enhanced resistance to free radical induced haemolysis directly linked to the amount ingested, suggesting that a regular daily amount is required. The source plants are best given as a fresh cut stable selection twice daily, or grown around the side of a track system with daily access. The best plants containing both betalains and other compounds to help with Cushing's are Chenopodium album (wild spinach) and Amaranth (a horticultural plant with the common name 'love lies bleeding'). Higher levels of betalains are found in the seeds of both and these can be easily harvested and dried to take you through the winter months. Daily amounts are 3 g seeds twice daily or one large whole plant without roots provided daily. Don't cut the whole plant up, but leave it in the stable for the horse to nibble what he needs.

Treating and managing the condition

Medicinal treatments currently relate to management rather than actual cure of the condition. We will discuss these before looking at other management practices that may reduce the chances of onset or unnecessarily rapid development of Cushing's.

Pergolide

Pergolide (sold under the brand name Prascend among others), is an ergoline-based dopamine receptor agonist used for managing the symptoms of Cushing's disease. In a 2002 study, pergolide was found to be more effective than cyproheptadine in reducing symptoms, including ACTH levels, in horses with Cushing's. However, since pergolide only controls the condition without curing it, as horses age, further degeneration is likely.

A subsequent 2009 study examined changes in various organs of thirty-two horses with Cushing's compared to twenty control horses. Noteworthy findings for horses over fifteen years old included:

- Enlarged adrenal glands resulting from cell overproduction.
- Liver damage and hepatocyte degeneration.
- Kidney inflammation.
- Lung inflammation.
- Thickening of heart muscles and increased lipofuscin pigment.

As is evident from these findings, the study linked Cushing's with organ degeneration, attributed to inflammation and oxidative stress from high hormone levels.

Pergolide and competitions

As mentioned earlier, Cushing's used to be diagnosed mainly in older horses but now younger horses (sometimes as young as seven) are increasingly being diagnosed, with a common secondary problem of muscle wastage and weakness, which may easily affect the performance in competitions. The proposed explanation for these changes occurring is the very well-documented NF K-B pathway which is linked to increased stress, oxidative damage, bacterial or viral antigens, and general inflammatory responses of the body. Cushing's affects and atrophies type 2a and 2b muscle fibres, both of which provide the explosive movements needed for jumping, dressage, and galloping and, if undiagnosed, may account for poor performance syndrome in many horses as symptoms may only be slight at the beginning of this chronic syndrome. There seems to be no significant difference in the *size* of the muscle fibres after treatment with pergolide. This means that, although pergolide (which is currently banned from use during competition by the BHA and FEI) may lower ACTH levels, it will not cause a reversal in the muscle fibre degeneration, so horse owners are advised to be watchful for loss of muscle mass and energy, especially when the loss of muscle seems to be accompanied by an increase in fat, which has a softer appearance.

Vitex agnus-castus (chaste tree)

Is there a way to enhance nutrition in horses with Cushing's to minimise damage to vital organs such as the liver, lungs, and heart? As explained earlier, plants are commonly used in healthcare as free radical scavengers, reducing oxidative stress effects. Many Cushing's-afflicted horses are on restricted diets, potentially lacking essential antioxidants to counteract degenerative effects. The plant Vitex agnus-castus (also known as chaste tree and abbreviated to VAC) has a history of use for Cushing's and could potentially extend the life of and safeguard an ageing horse, emphasising the importance of using the correct plant part for optimal results.

Plants, rich in antioxidants, like VAC, known for treating conditions impacting dopamine production (such as Cushing's) may protect organs. VAC, abundant in gallic acid, has been used for treating Alzheimer's and Parkinson's in humans and preventing amyloid fibril formation, an early sign of both diseases. Gallic acid helps control stress-induced chemical release, which elevates inflammatory hormones, negatively affecting organs. VAC contains potent free radical scavengers, particularly beneficial for the kidneys and liver. In managing chronic incurable diseases, symptom control and damage limitation are crucial to prolonging health and quality of life. According to a WHO report, high-quality VAC can achieve this goal. It has a 2,000-year history of use in humans and horses for hormonal imbalances and chronic diseases.

In horses, the two main uses of VAC are for Cushing's and for hormonally challenged mares, but this versatile and most important of medicinal plants has other uses; it has significant anti-inflammatory and antimicrobial actions, depending on which part of the plant is used. To use VAC against Cushing's it is essential to use the part of the plant containing the phytochemicals that act on dopamine production. Successful treatment depends upon the amount of diterpene contained in the fruit of the plant. If other parts of the plant are used, then the levels of this particular diterpene are diluted. Plants grown specifically for treatment (medicinal use) or interaction in this way will contain more of this important diterpene phytochemical. To achieve this, the plant will be grown outside of its comfort zone or 'stressed' to produce more. Growing a plant essentially for drug use requires quality control to produce an efficacious dose and the plant must be grown in a strictly controlled environment. If a horse has Cushing's, it is vital for success that the part of the plant that is used is of the most benefit but very often, when buying the raw ingredient, it is labelled simply as Agnus Castus without a mention of whether it contains whole plant or parts of the plant.

VAC contains many phytochemicals that interact with and target the endocrine system in several complex ways. For mares with temperament problems, it is okay to use the whole plant but for horses with Cushing's, the fruit is the most important part. Each part of the plant contains important phytochemicals that are suitable for and most effective against different dysfunctions. The leaves contain thirty-one different compounds from the fruit and woody stems, whilst the major antioxidant compound in the leaves has a strong antimicrobial action against *E-coli* and *MRSA*. The flowers contain phytochemicals that act as probiotics, and anti-inflammatory compounds that are as strong as aspirin and are useful against laminitis caused by SIRS.

It has taken a very long time for our company EquiBiome to source a supplier of VAC who understands the need for quality and provenance of the VAC used for the Cushing's products we produce, and it is also tested again for quality using high-performance liquid chromatography to ensure that it contains an effective dose. More than five hundred studies have been done on the quality and type of phytochemicals contained in VAC and, so long as a manufacturer sticks to the guidelines and buys good-quality raw ingredients you can be sure of success when using it.

Diet-based ways to prevent or control Cushing's

As horses age they are more likely to put on weight, developing fat pads and 'cresty' necks. In fact horses with a body condition score greater than 7 and a 'cresty' neck score of 4 or higher are considered by some researchers to already have EMS leading to insulin resistance (also known as peripheral Cushing's) and leaving the horse more vulnerable to developing full Cushing's. The consensus from other researchers is that owners often underestimate their horse's weight and make 'thinner' and thus inaccurate calculations based on this even if using a weight tape, mostly by waiting for their horse to breathe in before measuring. Owners also know that committing their horse to a weight-loss programme can be difficult and onerous – especially difficult areas from which to shift fat are the neck, hindquarters and around the tail.

Knowing how to adapt the diet to avoid fat pads developing is important for all owners of mature horses (especially the non-TB types) who seem to put on weight more easily because of a change in metabolism as they age. Taking a different approach to the diet of a mature horse who puts on weight easily will help to avoid and protect against the early onset of long-term chronic health problems such as Cushing's. To get started on a dietary change it's important to understand about fat pads.

Fat pads are special tissues/cells grown from the bone marrow, requiring extra blood vessels and a platform for attachment as well as storage space for extra lipids. The adipocytes in fat pads are formed from cells called blast cells – immature cells found in bone marrow. Since they are not fully developed they do not yet carry out any particular function within the body, in fact at this point these cells could potentially do other jobs, i.e. be recruited as osteoblasts to help bone density or help rebuild ligaments and lubricate joints.

So, if your horse is putting on weight, he is manufacturing adipocytes in preference to cells with more important functions, such as those that strengthen bones and joints. Raised ACTH levels also affect the recruitment of blast cells, causing more to be chosen and grow/develop as adipocytes, and raised ACTH is one of the first diagnosed symptoms of early Cushing's so if your horse has high levels, it is even more important to make dietary changes.

With Cushing's, it's crucial to manage the diet to regulate ACTH levels. Avoid large, high-carbohydrate meals of hay and grain to minimise the post-prandial release of insulin which will raise ACTH levels – i.e. feed little and often. Our further recommendation would be to feed a wide variety of plants, shrubs and hedgerow herbs (at least twenty-five different plants) containing the major antioxidants needed to help digest the carbohydrates in the diet. Some plant antioxidants will shrink the adipocytes and in turn prevent the release of IL-6 and other signalling hormones, which will help to lower the levels of ACTH. This is especially important in younger horses who may not have any symptoms of Cushing's other than a raised ACTH level.

Since adipocytes have a defined life-cycle: a beginning (when and how many are formed), a middle (when they are mature) and an end (when they die), it is possible to give multiple nutrients to interact with each part of the life-cycle to prevent them being formed in the first place, then to prevent them from maturing and ultimately to speed their early death. Understanding how nutrients can interact in this way is a much smarter way of managing your horse's diet than by calorie counting.

One popular additive to the diet is cinnamon, but how can it help to protect the middle-aged and veteran horses from chronic diseases such as Cushing's? The answer is that it has a direct action on the growth of adipocytes and the sensitisation of tissues to respond to insulin, but this is only one part of the life-cycle of the adipocyte. If your horse is responding to cinnamon that's fine, but if he needs more help, look at the list below of other plants that are necessary to ensure a good metabolism and protect against the development of unwanted fat.

List of beneficial plants in order of the adipocyte life-cycle

Stage 1 – plants to prevent adipocytes from forming
This is especially important in horses with raised ACTH.
- Any member of the Chenopodium family (wild spinach). The UK has around twelve different varieties; the rest of the world also has plenty as Chenopodium album is one of the most invasive weeds.
- Wild blueberries – these small shrubs are very easy to grow in heathland areas; horses will eat the fruit, flowers, and leaves, the leaves being the most important.
- Willow leaves and twigs – a wild replacement for cinnamon.
- Wild pear – this makes a wonderful hedgerow shrub or tree; you may have some already but haven't noticed as the fruits are so small.
- Wild brassicas – watercress and bog rosemary. The latter is the county flower of Kirkcudbright, Ceredigion and County Tyrone. Horses love the flowers most of all.

Stage 2 – to prevent the adipocytes from maturing
- Hawthorn – found in most hedgerows and has many other benefits so this is certainly a definite one to include.
- Any of the Lamiaceae family to include wild mints, flowering nettles, salvias, scabious.

Stage 3 – plants to aid in the demise and diminishment of adipose tissue
- Wild spinach (Chenopodium), wild blueberry leaves, wild garlic.
- Lichens and mosses. Many are edible for horses. Reindeer moss is one; our horses are able to access this plant from the surrounding stone walls and the granite outcrops.

Finally, once the adipocytes are under control, you may find the horse will, for a time, be interested in eating twigs, leaves or bark from a variety of trees or hedging. This is to help get rid of the lipid stores as they are released from the adipocytes (lipolysis).

We have mentioned throughout this section a number of plants that can be beneficial in preventing or help to control Cushing's and our overall recommendation is that the horse has access to a wide variety of plant species and is turned out in a paddock with low-quality indigenous grass to reduce sugar to safe levels, of which at least half and preferably two-thirds are other plants and that he also has access to trees, shrubs and bushes.

Some of these beneficial plants are endangered species and it is such a pleasure to help restore them to the meadows of the UK whilst at the same time being of benefit to our horses' health. Remember that the horse only needs small quantities of each plant – sometimes only a couple of snatched mouthfuls – and also remember that some of these beneficial plants contain quite potent phytochemicals and, in the wild, the horse will make his own choice and take only small amounts from a wide range of similar plants, each containing the compound he needs.

Equine metabolic syndrome (EMS)

Equine metabolic syndrome causes a dysfunction or alteration in circulation. It is a common condition affecting 18–27% of the equine population, and predisposing the horse to laminitis. For a number of years there has been an interest in how altered blood flow affects the feet during laminitis, but little evidence for how the dysfunction occurs owing to difficulties in obtaining the right sample material. Vets used to give acepromazine (ACP) to horses in the earlier stages of laminitis in the hope of achieving an increase in blood flow to the foot.

In the study referred to below, the altered blood flow was found to affect not only the feet, but also the arterioles of the facial skin arteries. The six horses used in the study had body condition scores average 3.9, had previous episodes of chronic metabolic/endocrinopathic laminitis and higher than normal triglycerides and insulin levels.

Circulation is part of metabolism, and organs and other structures of the body rely on blood to deliver nutrients and healthy blood vessels constrict and open to meet demands and delivery of nutrients, therefore control of blood flow and delivery are tightly governed by signalling chemicals. The digital pulse felt in laminitis is a consequence of the shutting down of the circulation to the foot, though prior to this study the increased pulses were thought to be part of the mechanics (backing up) or an increase in blood pressure. It was not known that the veins themselves shut down, stimulated by the action of a hormone. This is important information for those managing the increased pulses because management can now be aimed at the hormone responsible.

The horses in this trial on endocrinopathic laminitis all had an altered circulation, presenting as a lack of ability to open the small blood vessels, especially in the foot and as far away as the face. The trial used a drug, Phenylephrine, and tested the effects of a natural hormone, 5HT (serotonin receptor), which has been found to increase during laminitis attacks and is responsible for the release and control of many important hormones, including those responsible for inflammation.

The trial concluded that, in chronic EMS, all-over body circulation is reduced, with further sensitivity to constriction in the veins of the foot. These veins showed a high sensitivity to increased 5HT and responded by shutting down. This was a new finding; previously small blood vessels have been examined, but not the veins.

The study concluded that failure of the blood vessels to dilate leads to an increase in capillary pressure, oedema and lack of oxygen supply. The trial proposed further investigation to include retinal vascular lesions. There is also an urgent need to define biomarkers to determine the level of circulation changes; this will better define the risk and progression of the disease, including the level of degeneration of the foot. Using vasodilating drugs has had previously only limited success, possibly because of lack of knowledge of endothelial disease. It is possible to use vasodilating herbs and plants which target 5HT, but these must be used with precise knowledge of the chemical cocktails they contain.

Adipose tissue in horses with EMS

Adipose tissue is different in horses with EMS. With EMS the adipocytes (fat cells) are enlarged and swollen (hypertrophied). EMS is defined by an inability of the horse to regulate blood insulin levels (insulin dysregulation) and an increase of regional fat deposits – the 'fat pads' to be found at the base of the neck, shoulders, and tail. Swollen adipocytes cause an increase in the release of leptin and inflammatory cytokines (*TNFα*, *IL1ß* and *CCL2*) compared to adipose tissue samples from healthy horses. The horses with EMS in a study were defined as those at two years of age of a susceptible breed (native British breeds) with a body condition score between 4 and 5, fasting basal insulin of 20 µIU/mL, current or historical laminitis, plasma ACTH within the seasonal reference range and a pituitary histological score between 3 and 5.

How to bring about reduction in adipose tissue

This is best done by feeding plants containing multiple chemicals that have a shotgun effect on the dysfunctional physiology associated with EMS. With complicated and complex syndromes, the remedy must be as complex to help restore health and balance.

The best plants are any from the Amaranth family, common examples being spinach and quinoa. The leaves, stems and roots of all species contain alkaloids, saponins and sterols. The roots contain ecdysone and ecdysterones, the action of which is to shrink adipocytes. The seeds contain saponin and the fruit contains two oleanolic acid-based saponins. The whole plant contains the following: alkaloid achyranthine, arginine, histidine, lysine, cystine, amino acids, threonine, lucine, isoleucine, methionine, phenylalanine, tryptophan and carbohydrate, large amount of potash, valine, α-rhamnopyranosyl, ß-D galactopyranosyl, galactose, xylose, ß-D glucopyranosyl, rhamnose and glucose, hormones, ecdysterones and inocoterone. The mode of action is to promote the death of the adipocyte, to reduce insulin resistance and protect against damage to other bodily structures, including the feet. Only small amounts are needed; amaranth seeds can be fed at a daily dose of 20 g. Exercise caution and avoid red pigweed (USA), as it can be high in nitrite and nitrate, if previously sprayed with herbicides or pesticides or in times of drought. Organic is best.

Anorexia

Elderly horses, and horses given a restrictive diet, are specifically prone to becoming anorexic. In older horses their chewing mechanism is not functioning as well as before and their teeth have worn, and these factors combined with a lessening appetite contribute to weight loss. Furthermore, the functionality of the elderly gut has an effect on how well nutrients are absorbed. It is therefore vital that the elderly horse gets a diet high in protein and plant matter, and is provided with other health-enhancing natural phytosupplements. The gut flora needs to be kept at an optimum to prevent anorexia.

Anorexia can also be brought on by stress, anxiety and pain. Horses who have, for whatever reason, 'shut down', will often have lost their appetite and this is followed by alarming weight loss.

A horse may enter into a high-stress cortisol episode when he is being prepped for a race, or big show, and when the performance needs to be absolutely on point, his feed schedules are often kept to a strict formula. More often than not the sports horse's rations are starch/protein/carbohydrate loaded, to be eaten within a set timeframe. As the cortisol increases, so the gastric environment becomes acidic. If, because of his scheduled restrictions, the horse does not get free access to hay or water, this starts a vicious cycle of acidity being churned throughout the gastro-intestinal system, which is upsetting to both the foregut and hindgut and damaging to their linings and tissue.

Thirty-four-year-old American Quarter Horse.
Geertje French

Leaky gut

Causes of this condition include long-term medication, restricted diet, stabling for long periods, intense exercise and heat.

There are many symptoms: irritability, dislike of grooming, girthing and being ridden, loss of appetite, poor and tucked up body condition, teeth grinding, crib-biting, acute and chronic diarrhoea, faecal water syndrome, pot-bellied appearance and poor performance.

Aetiology (manner of causation of disease) may identify changes in the microbial community, mycotoxins, bile acid, frank pathogens and pathobionts.[25]

Therapies can be applied via the diet, making use of alternative therapies including short chain fatty acids, amino acids, nutrients, and probiotics/prebiotics.

Five ways of avoiding leaky gut

1. Allow nature to 'balance' the diet by growing more herbs (forbs) in the pasture, this increases crucial micro- and macro-mineral content. (Be aware that not all supplements contain a full range.) The effect on the horse will be to increase the thickness and structure of the mucosal gel.
2. Antioxidants in the form of herbs, legumes and woody hedgerow bushes act as prebiotics, creating a balance between the secretion and the normal digestion processes. You can prevent or buffer damage to the tight junctions (through increased inflammation) by feeding a wide variety of different fresh green plants.
3. Feed little and often. The 'tight junctions' or 'control gateways' are fully dynamic and can change size according to what is going on in the body. If the horse eats a big meal or gorges his food then the gateways become bigger and laxer, bending themselves under the osmotic pressure of the food/ingested mass. The horse is a trickle feeder, so large and infrequent meals increase the chance of toxins passing through the tight junctions.
4. Check dietary omega-3 levels. Toxins interact with the security gate system creating an opportunity for damage to occur. The chances of damage occurring at this place are higher in horses with low levels of omega-3 as the 'tight junction' part of the security gate system is almost totally reliant on its ability to source and renew itself using omega-3.
5. As far as possible, limit the use of drugs, particularly NSAIDs. The long-term prevalence of ulcers causes an imbalance in the rate of renewal of the pillars or walls (epithelial cells) of the security gate (tight junctions). Also, although the gut is willing and able to repair itself quickly against damage by using prostaglandin, horses given NSAIDs (including all COX-1 and COX-2 inhibitors) will not be able to produce this substance, leaving the security gate system down and open for invasion, which we need to avoid.

How plant chemicals manage inflammation

Inflammation is an immune response to cellular/tissue injury or infection by pathogens and pain. Systemic low-grade inflammation is recognised in an increasing number of chronic diseases such as arthritis. These diseases use the host's own cell signalling pathways to increase inflammation, pain and degeneration, involving a specific immune response including Tumour Necrosis Factor alpha (TNF-a), interleukin-6 and other neutrophil responses that may be controllable by functional or medicinal food. Plant chemicals can use the same pathways to protect, restore and reverse the damage done. Some plant chemicals have one role to play, but some exceptional ones are multi-functional and are called adaptogens.

The best plants are early gentian, dandelion, wild mustard, yarrow, thyme, borage, witch hazel and nettles. Not much grows in the winter and, if you can't find them fresh, feed dried at a dose of 25–60 g daily.

Leaky gut in older horses

A state of low-grade inflammation is a component of obesity and EMS, thought to affect over 50% of horses and linked to multiple diseases in horses, the two most common being laminitis and osteoarthritis. Low-grade inflammation is defined by an increase in tumour necrosis factor (TNF). In the gut an increase in TNF causes a chronic type of dysbiosis of the gut bacteria, the outcome of which is a leaky gut. Older animals age poorly if a state of low-grade inflammation exists, magnified by the use of long-term medications (antibiotics), poor diet, lack of exercise and/or obesity.

One of the best dietary additions for this type of gut condition, especially supportive of older horses, is skull cap (Scutellaria). This plant contains a potent chemical called wogonin, able to significantly reduce TNF production in the gut and elsewhere in the body. It can be given as a supplement or foraged. There is a variety that grows wild in the UK called Scutellaria galericulata, commonly found around any wetland, rivers, canals, marshes, and fens. It is a member of the mint family (Lamiaceae) and all varieties within this family contain low levels of wogonin. Most are well tolerated but it might be best to avoid penny royal (Mentha pulegium).

Feeding a *Lactobacillus* and *Bifidobacteria* probiotic together is an absolute must for horses suffering with leaky gut. The beneficial *Lactobacillus* plays an important role in immune function (protection against viruses) and healthy metabolism. Many equine probiotic supplements combine *Lactobacillus* with *Bifidobacteria*. However, the EquiBiome Test (which gives a real-time snapshot of the microbial community of the equine hindgut) showed that whilst over 90% of horses had low levels of *Bifidobacteria*, indicating the importance of a *Bifidobacteria* probiotic, the levels of *Lactobacillus* were either very high or very low (leaky gut) in two-thirds of all horses. *Lactobacillus* converts sugars to lactic acid. Horses within the high-level group had a history of ulcers, poor performance and hindgut discomfort. Feeding a probiotic containing *Lactobacillus* to horses in this group would be contraindicative. Those horses having *Lactobacillus* within the recommended levels, including the wild Carneddau and Pottakas ponies will be better defended against inflammation (laminitis) and metabolic syndromes. A third of all horses tested had extremely low levels of *Lactobacillus*; horses in this group included those being fed soya and soya hulls as the main ingredients of the hard feed.

Degenerative diseases

Degenerative diseases in horses are common, with multiple dietary interventions and supplements on the market to support optimum health. Human clinical nutritional experts have concluded that the onset of many chronic degenerative diseases can be prevented or slowed down by consuming a widely varied diet of fresh food, and we may be able to transfer that requirement for fresh food to the horse.

Many horses today are fed bagged food and monoculture-type hay/haylage and grazing, providing relatively little variety and diversity. We know that biodiverse meadows have massively declined in favour of 'improved' monoculture grassland and that the previous use of fertilisers has reduced the ability of the soil to produce plants other than grass.

To do a quick comparison, the total energy intake from protein intake was likely to have been higher a hundred years ago, provided by grains such as oats, and horses having access to a wider variety of higher protein forage with a protein content of over 20% and a high vitamin and mineral content.

Both native ponies and working horses would have had access to a variety of wild green leafy plants such as cow parsley, lamb's quarter, wild mustard and sorrels. Those types of green leafy plants contain over 23% protein, chopped gorse (fed as forage) contains 25% protein, willow branches, bark and leaves are 20% protein while marsh grass contains 20% protein and includes significant levels of lysine, methionine and threonine. Compare this to the low protein values of bagged food which struggle to provide 12% – even racehorses are only provided around 12–14%.

Protein is the building block of bone, muscle, tendons and it also provides regeneration for damaged tissue, and renews the immune system. Perhaps horses are potentially eating only half the protein they used to have.

Scent and gastric diseases

Mammals with gastric diseases of cancer, ulcers and irritable bowel syndrome emit a chemical called isoprene on their breath. Plants respond to this 'breathing signal' by producing a monoterpene chemical called perillyl alcohol (POH). This naturally occurring chemical has numerous patents for the treatment of the diseases mentioned, but you can access it free by taking a walk or going for a hack. Pharmaceutical companies tried to make a drug from this volatile chemical, but it proved to be indigestible as nature designed it to be breathed in, rather than swallowed.

Isoprene promotes the production of many other different monoterpenes that are beneficial to health. Insects stimulate and maintain the production through a symbiotic cross relationship with the plant.

Some plants that were once high in monoterpenes are under threat owing to the overuse of insecticides, without which production of these beneficial monoterpenes falls dramatically, making the plant less effective. Thankfully some plants contain more of this chemical than others, the top ten are:

1. Gum rockrose (Cistus ladanifer). This plant has over ten times the chemical production of any other plant. It is a common garden plant in the UK, but only grows wild in southern Europe.
2. Spanish chestnut or sweet chestnut (Castanea sativa) has over four times the chemical production of other plants, except for gum rockrose.
3. Holm oak, holly oak (Quercus ilex) has four times the amount of most others, rising to six times in October.
4. Brittle brush (Encelia farinose) is a common desert shrub of Mexico and California, with 1.5 times the average content.
5. Eucalyptus gunni (which can grow in the UK) has 1.5 times the average content.
6. Scarlet oak has 1.5 times the average content.
7. Chaparral whitethorn (Ceanothus leucodermis), a species of shrub in the buckthorn family Rhamnacea, has 1.3 times the average content.
8. Heather (Calluna vulgaris) has 1.3 times the average content.
9. Sweet acacia.
10. Cootamundra wattle (Acacia baileyana).

Big head

When a horse is being fed on a diet based on poor-quality compound cereal-based feeds, poor-quality hay or bran, he will not get an adequate balance of vital vitamins and minerals and this can then manifest itself in deformities in the bone structure of the upper jaw owing to the normal mineralised bone structures being replaced by fibrous connective tissue. This will be become evident in the enlargement of the upper jaw and face, which may go on to make chewing more difficult as the alignment of the upper and lower jaws becomes distorted.

Aspergillus-associated asthma

This is on the increase and may be underdiagnosed; it is especially common in horses with Cushing's.

The fungus *Aspergillus* produces a range of different metabolites, and some species are pathogenic – i.e. linked to diseases in humans, animals and plants. Recent research suggests that the effect of these is likely to be underestimated. Although the soil is the primary habitat the fungus has been detected in all major biomes, including the gut and lungs.

Filamentous fungi of the *Aspergillus* genus are opportunistic phytopathogens, of which there are between 300 and 400 different species. Five within the family Aspergillaceae (Fumigati, Flavi, Nigri, Terre, and Nid ulante) are reported to cause the disease *Aspergillus*, producing mycotoxins that contaminate agricultural products and cause illness in humans, horses and other animals.

Aspergillus in the microbiome and its role in health

Immune system homeostasis helps the host remove invasive and opportunistic fungi such as *Aspergillus*. However, fungal infections can colonise the lining of the ileum of the gut inducing an intestinal immune response by disturbing homeostasis and at the same time causing lung autoimmunity (whereby the immune system attacks its own cells) through the gut-lung axis. Thus, whereas a healthy gut response equals a healthy gut-lung response, once a fungal infection takes hold in the lung or gut there is a reduction in the alpha diversity score; this causes a change in the intestine's immune tolerance, predisposing both lung and gut to inflammation.

An overgrowth of bacteria and a rise in fungi increases plasma concentrations of Prostaglandin E2 (PGE2) and induces this inflammation in the lungs, promoting pathogenic airway inflammation.

Interestingly most allergic reactions in the airways only occur if the gut microbiome is damaged by antibiotics, as *Candida albicans* fungi play a role in maintaining host immunity and resistance to the pathogenic species of *Aspergillus*.

Aspergillus in soil

Aspergillus is common in soils around the globe; it produces spores that can be breathed in, but that can also be ingested from the soil or plants on contaminated land.

The overuse of agrichemicals in the form of fungicides has created resistant species of *Aspergillus*; a recent study found 4.7% are resistant to the agricultural fungicide tebuconazole, and have a high resistance to azoles used for treating clinical infections, including itraconazole (86%), voriconazole (64%) and isavuconazole (83%). In addition, 51% of the *A. fumigatus* isolates were resistant to three medical azoles, and 14% were resistant to all tested medical azoles.

Aspergillus in food

Another area under observation is the mycotoxin content of distiller's or brewer's grains, which have quickly become a global commodity and, although nutritionally these grains vary hugely in quality and content, unless tested constantly they can contain an unacceptable level of mycotoxins.

The fermentation process triples the content of mycotoxins already naturally present in the grain. It has been estimated that over 25% of the world's grain is contaminated (Seventh Symposium of Veterinary Immunology).

The role of probiotics

Cross-protection immunity (lung and gut) against *Aspergillus* infection comes from the microbial bacteria population. As mentioned above, *antibiotic* treatment and chronic disease alter the composition of the gut microbiome, causing overgrowth of certain intestinal bacteria and *Candida albicans* (thrush), which creates an opportunity for opportunistic *Aspergillus*.

However, *probiotics* are promising new targets for antifungal treatments as they alter the members of the gut microbiome by directly stimulating immune cells and releasing health-promoting metabolites, which, in turn, improves systemic immunity.

Lactobacillus and *Bifidobacteria*, which also act as probiotics, both reduce allergic airway response by increasing the number of Tregs (regulatory T cells) in the lungs. Tregs are a specialised subpopulation of T cells that act to suppress the immune response, thereby maintaining homeostasis and self-tolerance. It has been shown that Tregs can inhibit T cell proliferation and cytokine production and play a critical role in preventing autoimmunity. There are links between high levels of *Lactobacillus* and laminitis so checking the biome of your horse may be a very useful test to have done.

Symptoms of *Aspergillus* infection

- Asthma.
- Lethargy.
- Poor performance.
- Loss of appetite.
- Diarrhoea or free faecal water syndrome (FFWS).
- Frequent illness (always sick and sorry).
- Altered cycles in mares.
- Joint swelling.

Dietary interventions (antifungal foods)

- Apple cider vinegar. The acid and enzymes in apple cider vinegar have been shown to help to kill and get rid of excess yeast in the body.
- Pasture turn out
- Coconut oil.
- Stevia, a naturally very sweet green leafy plant, especially cultivated as an alternative to sugar

beet or cane sugar.
- Garlic.
- Ground flaxseeds and chia seeds and kefir (fermented yoghurt).

How the EquiBiome Test can help[26]

1. Although the gut and lungs share a mucous membrane, identifying a fungal infection in the gut is easier and less invasive. Using population data from affected horses it has been possible to identify a benchmark for horses with *Aspergillus*-associated asthma, and percentages within the gut mycobiome and microbiome.
2. The EquiBiome test accurately identifies the five different species of pathogens, this may help the horse owner to identify the source of contamination – i.e. bedding, food, soil or pasture.
3. Resolution of the infection is possible through restoration of the balance within the microbiome; this improves the immune system response whilst reducing the *Aspergillus* overgrowth.

Diet and feed-related behaviour

A horse who is in both good physical and mental health, meaning that he has no stress or anxiety, is a happy horse. Such horses do not usually exhibit any kind of stereotypical behaviour or other types of behaviour such as depression, aggression, 'shut down' or wanting to resist any kind of handling. This includes grooming and riding.

Nonetheless, there are many types of unnatural behaviours that can be directly linked to the type of diet horses are fed, whether the triggers are a diet with a high starch and carbohydrate content, or a deficiency in vital minerals and vitamins. As explained earlier, inappropriate feed can become a precursor for ulceration and other diseases. In this section we will discuss different kinds of feed-related behaviours, most of which can be rectified through a healthy plant-based diet and ensuring that the horse suffers as little training, travel or competition stress as possible.

Pain-related behaviour

A horse in pain can behave in different ways, depending on the type of pain from which he is suffering. Some horses in pain become aggressive and difficult to catch or handle, others may 'shut down' and become depressed, whereas some may not actually show any kind of unusual behaviour because of their stoical character. However, horses who show an outward tolerance of pain (from human observation) might show it more in their interaction with other horses.

Aggressive behaviour in the paddock.
Geertje French

Ulcers

Horses suffering with stomach ulcers are in constant pain and discomfort. They may become girth-sensitive, which means that when the saddle is put on and the girth tightened, they may suddenly want to kick out, run away or try to bite you. If you find your horse has become girth-sensitive it might be prudent to have him scoped for ulcers. Using antacids and painkillers will only ever really mask the problem. Your horse may also become riding or handling aversive. Contact your vet if you suspect ulcers are making your horse behave in a way not seen before; look to plants to help with ulcers as described in this book.

Colic

Horses who come down with colic will suffer excruciating pain in the gut. The stomach may appear bloated and hard to the touch. The horse may nose his abdomen and start rolling on the ground making grunting noises, lie down and get up constantly, or become erratic and aggressive in his movements. Other symptoms to look out for are weaving, 'shutting down' and box-walking. From the first moment you suspect colic you need to contact your vet immediately. In the meantime, keeping the horse moving and warm may help move the obstruction. Keeping him moving means walking him on a halter – this may take hours, so you may want to use several people to keep up the momentum. Handlers should be aware that the horse may suddenly show aggression or react in other ways because of the physical discomfort. He may also want to lie down – and whatever happens, do not allow this, as he will not want to get up again. If a horse has colic, never hesitate in getting help.

Other types of unnatural behaviour

An issue with calmness in horses

Some horses have a real problem remaining calm and easy to handle; they might become anxious or over-excited for no apparent reason. Here we will explain why diet could be one of the reasons why this might occur.

There are trillions of gut bacteria living within the gut of our horses, communicating through the gut-brain axis. Too many of the wrong species of bacteria increase levels of stress and anxiety through the production of neuroactive peptides, which disrupt the communication between gut and brain.

Healthy gut function is linked to central nervous system health. Hormones, neurotransmitters and immunological factors released from the gut are known to send signals to the brain directly or through autonomic neurons.

If the key to anxiety/overexcitement is diet-related, changing the diet can make all the difference, but first you need to identify the bacteria that are contributing to the disharmony. Autumn is a great time to start the rebalancing process as seeds and seed heads are full of antioxidants that help reduce the bad bacteria whilst feeding the good.

Guarding food resources

Guarding sources of food is a behaviour that can be seen in both wild-roaming horses and in domestic herds. In the wild-roaming herd, guarding food is a natural behaviour when it is scarce and the more dominant horses will try to get the better part. It is different for the horse in a domestic situation, as this horse is much more prone to developing behavioural problems because of an unsettled lifestyle.

There are many horses who suffer with 'environmental disassociation' especially when they have been moved from yard to yard over their lifetime, and they are constantly having to adjust to new dynamics and new 'herds'. These horses are often bullied by other horses who are themselves 'source-guarders'. There are also situations where 'altruistic' horses threaten other horses when they dare come near the hay of a third horse, perhaps the 'altruistic' one's friend. This is not only a matter of inadequate human management (i.e not picking up on the blatant signals from horses who are anxious or in distress when it comes to their feed); it is also a sign that horses are over-anxious because of this 'environmental disassociation', having lost the friends they made over and over again.

There can also be other underlying causes, such as a horse being really hungry all the time because his diet is out of balance, and thus becoming more assertive when it comes to taking the larger share at feeding time.

A good way to negate issues when you have a source-guarding horse who is aggressive and won't submit to the other horses is to move this horse to a quiet corner where he can eat in peace, and so can the other horses.

Feed time behaviour

Some horses become over-excited when they know feeding time is approaching. This may especially become a problem when the horse is not given a continuous ration of hay to feed on in between meals, or when the stomach is allowed to become empty, as can occur when the horse is only fed a few meals per day. As mentioned previously, a horse feels calmer when there is a small amount of feed in the stomach at all times – hence the need for hay to nibble on, or even a straw bed the horse can chew on.

Feed time behaviour can be mild (the horse may just start to pace the stable when he knows food is coming), or it may become more extreme (he might try to bite anyone passing the stable door or start to kick against the door, which could lead to serious injury). The more extreme the behaviour, the more anxious and stressed the horse will become. This might sound 'back to front', but it's something of a vicious circle. The behaviour itself will cause 'stress' acid to form in the stomach, making the horse all the more agitated, especially if the stomach is empty, thus exacerbating the situation and heightening the horse's anxiety. Ensuring that the horse has continual feed in the form of hay, and is fed small meals throughout the day, there should be no reason for him to become over-reactive. (This behaviour may also be seen in horses who are food-guarders.)

Depression and 'shut down'

It is unfortunate, but depression and 'shut down' in horses is not uncommon. There are many reasons why the horse gets into this state of mind. The first one to take into consideration is the health of the gut biome. If the horse is not fed a good source of phytochemicals from, preferably organically grown materials, he will end up with a stomach that is out of kilter. We have already seen the many problems caused by an inadequate diet. And as the stomach has an effect on the brain, it will in turn affect the mood of the horse. We can compare this to the human state of mind when we don't get the right kind of nutrients to keep the mind healthy.

Other causes for depression and 'shut down' can be to do with the fact that the horse is not being offered the opportunity to socialise with other horses. For instance, if you have a stable block where the horses in the first and last stable have no or little interaction with the other horses on the block, these horses will feel lonely and out of the loop. It is easy to remedy this by placing a mirror opposite the stables, so that the horse can see the others and feel less left out.

Horses who have lost their favourite friend may also become depressed, as such a horse has lost a valuable connection. Horses who are being pushed out of the herd or bullied will also experience a sense of being unwanted, and you will see such a horse in the corner of the field with his head down and his facial expression showing sadness.

The horse who is being trained in an aversive manner will either fight, take flight or freeze. When a horse freezes he shuts down completely, as fear holds him down. Boredom may also lead to depression, as the horse has nothing to stimulate his mind. Enrichment, in the form of toys and games, will alleviate boredom and get the mind working.

Stereotypical behaviours

A stereotypical behaviour is one whereby the horse repeats a particular behaviour again and again. Stereotypical behaviours such as weaving, cribbing, and box-walking occur commonly in high-performance horses and also many companion horses. In addition to being unsightly, potentially damaging to the stables and raising general welfare concerns, stereotypical behaviours also result in important health issues such as dental disorders, temporohyoid joint damage, poor performance, weight loss, colic and over-production of stomach acid.

Possible link between selenium and cribbing in horses

New research has found a possible link between selenium and stereotypical behaviour. The equine nutritionist Dr Kathleen Crandell, Ph.D. from Kentucky Equine Research Institute observed the following:

> Cribbing is the most troublesome of these compulsive behaviours. It involves grasping a fixed object with the incisor teeth and aspirating air with an audible grunt. The exact reason horses crib remains unknown. Some suggest that cribbing horses have unmet dietary or management needs. Others believe that altered biological functions are the culprits, such as decreased antioxidant levels or increased oxidative stress. Because trace elements such as selenium, zinc, manganese and copper protect the body from oxidative stress, one research group recently explored the hypothesis that oxidation status may contribute to cribbing. To test this theory, researchers collected blood samples from horses during or immediately after an episode of cribbing and when cribbers were resting. Control horses with no known history of cribbing were also tested. The scientists then analysed the samples for various markers of oxidation. The most important finding in this study was that serum selenium concentration was significantly lower

> in cribbing horses than in controls, with the lowest levels measured while horses were actually cribbing. Based on these data, the researchers concluded: that alterations in serum selenium, an important component of the antioxidant system, may play a role in the pathophysiology of cribbing behaviour in horses, adding further evidence to the theory that cribbing may be related to increased oxidative stress and alterations in essential trace elements. Management also plays an important part in minimising stereotypic behaviours. Strategies such as providing environmental enrichment tools, offering free-choice hay or prolonged grazing, and allowing direct visual contact or prolonged turnout time in groups are thought to improve the welfare of affected horses.[27]

These are certainly interesting findings.

Cribbing can also be mirrored by other horses, as it is not unusual for horses to do as others do. For example, a foal can take over the habit from a cribbing mother, as he is with her all the time and will take his cue from her behaviour.

Some people use cribbing straps to prevent the horse from cribbing and wind-sucking, these straps are put just underneath the jaw and prohibit the horse from fastening his teeth on an object or tensing up to suck wind, as it becomes uncomfortable to do so. This is not a recommended way to stop your horse from this stereotypical behaviour, as it is very uncomfortable and may induce the horse to find something else to concentrate on, such as box- or fence-walking or weaving.

Wind-sucking is done without setting the teeth on an object, but involves the horse tensing his neck and sucking in gulps of air with a grunting noise. One of the things that happens when horses crib or wind-suck is that there is a release of morphine-like proteins in the brain, called endogenous opioids; these include enkephalins and endorphins. They are activated in the pleasure centre of the brain and therefore induce a state of bliss and supress pain, and this can then lead to addiction, which means there is little incentive for the horse to stop the behaviour. There is currently much research being done on how we can help horses who are addicted to their stereotypical behaviours. Keep an eye on the progress these studies are developing.

The need for awareness and understanding

Horses can start to behave in ways not immediately evident as 'problem behaviours', that are put down to stubbornness: 'a breed characteristic', 'they have always done that' and a plethora of other excuses. Behaviours are sometimes seen as the horse just 'being plain nasty'. We need to be aware that any kind of behaviour that is not a distinctively instinctive behaviour must be investigated and never ignored. The horse is not at fault here. More often than not the behaviour has a link to what the horse is being fed and the environment lived in, which can all greatly determine the horse's physical or mental state.

1. Obesity crest scores
   - Carter, R. A., Geor, R J., Staniar, W. B., Cubitt, T. A., & Harris, P. A. (2009). 'Apparent adiposity assessed by standardised scoring systems and morphometric measurements in horses and ponies', *Equine Veterinary Journal* 179(2), 204–10.
2. Equine Henneke Body Condition Score
   - Biddle, A. (2021), 'Evaluation of the microbiome effects of easy and hard keeper horses with the application of the Equine Keeper Status Scale', *Journal of Equine Veterinary Science*, 100, 103465.
3. Insulin-resistant 2
   - Gou, W., Ling, C. W., He, Y., Jiang, Z., Fu, Y., Xu, F., Yang & Zheng, J. S. (2021). 'Interpretable machine learning framework reveals robust gut microbiome features associated with type 2 diabetes', *Diabetes Care*, 44(2), 358–66.
   - Zhang, F., Wang, M., Yang, J., Xu, Q., Liang, C., Chen, B., Zhang, L. (2019). 'Response of gut microbiota in type 2 diabetes to hypoglycaemic agents', *Endocrine*, 66(3), 485–93.
   - Graessler, J., Qin, Y., Zhong, H., Zhang, J., Licinio, J., Wong, M. L., & Bornstein, S. R. (2013). 'Metagenomic sequencing of the human gut microbiome before and after bariatric surgery in obese patients with type 2 diabetes: correlation with inflammatory and metabolic parameters', *The Pharmacogenomics Journal*, 13(6), 514–22.
   - Al-Ishaq, R. K., Abotaleb, M., Kubatka, P., Kajo, K., & Büsselberg, D. (2019). 'Flavonoids and their anti-diabetic effects: cellular mechanisms and effects to improve blood sugar levels', *Biomolecules*, open access journal ISSN 2218–273X), 9(9), 430.
4. Polyphenols and endocrinopathic laminitis
   - de Laat M. A., Pollitt C. C., Kyaw-Tanner M. T., McGowan, C.M., Sillence, M. N. (2013). 'A potential role for lamellar insulin-like growth factor-1 receptor in the pathogenesis of hyperinsulinaemic laminitis', *Veterinary Journal*, 197:302–06.
5. Changes in the nerves of laminitic horses
   - Jones, E., Viñuela-Fernandez, I., Eager, R. A., Delaney, A., Anderson, H., Patel, A., & Fleetwood-Walker, S. M. (2007). 'Neuropathic changes in equine laminitis pain', *Pain*, 132(3), 321–31.
6. Recent discoveries
   - *EquiNews* (2025). 'Barnyard Chemistry: pH and the Equine Digestive Tract', Kentucky Equine Research.
7. Head-shaking
   - Aleman et. al., 'Disruption of gut bacteria in horses' (2022).
8. Uzal, F. A., & Diab, S. S. (2015). 'Gastritis, enteritis, and colitis in horses', *Veterinary Clinics: Equine Practice*, 31(2), 337–58.
9. Båverud, V. (2004). 'Clostridium difficile diarrhea: infection control in horses', *Veterinary Clinics: Equine Practice*, 20(3), 615–630.
10. Navarro, M. A., & Uzal, F. A. (2020). 'Pathobiology and diagnosis of clostridial hepatitis in animals', *Journal of Veterinary Diagnostic Investigation*, 32(2), 192–202.
11. Dean, J. (2017). 'Species at risk: C. Tetani, the horse, and the human', *Animal metropolis: Histories of human-animal relations in urban Canada*, 155–88.
12. Swink, J. M., & Gilsenan, W. F. (2022). 'Clostridial diseases (botulism and tetanus)', *Veterinary Clinics: Equine Practice*, 38(2), 269–82.
13. Garrett, L. A., Brown, R., & Poxton, I. R. (2002). 'A comparative study of the intestinal microbiota of healthy horses and those suffering from equine grass sickness', *Veterinary Microbiology*, 87(1), 81–8.
14. Myofascial and fibromyalgia pain in horses
    - Macgregor, J., & von Schweinitz, D. G. (2006). 'Needle electromyographic activity of myofascial trigger points and control sites in equine cleidoic-brachialis muscle – an observational study', *Acupuncture in Medicine*, 24(2), 61–70.

- Ridgway, K. (1999). 'Acupuncture as a treatment modality for back problems', *Veterinary Clinics of North America: Equine Practice*, 15(1), 211–21.
- Gomez Alvarez, C. B. (2007). 'The biomechanical interaction between vertebral column and limbs in the horse: a kinematical study', Utrecht University.
- Malatji, B. G., Meyer, H., Mason, S., Engelke, U. F., Wevers, R. A., Van Reenen, M., & Reinecke, C. J. (2017). 'A diagnostic biomarker profile for fibromyalgia syndrome based on an NMR metabolomics study of selected patients and controls', *BMC Neurology*, 17, 1–15.

15. Cushing's disease
    - Ireland, J. L. & McGowan, C. M. (2018). 'Epidemiology of pituitary pars intermedia dysfunction: a systematic literature review of clinical presentation, disease prevalence and risk factors', *The Veterinary Journal*, 235, 22–33.
16. van der Kolk, J. H., Heinrichs, M., van Amerongen, J. D., Stooker, R. C., in de Wal, L. J., van den Ingh, T.S., (2004). 'Evaluation of pituitary gland anatomy and histopathologic findings in clinically normal horses and horses and ponies with pituitary pars intermedia adenoma', *Am. J. Vet. Res.* 65, 1701–1707.
    Frank, N., Andrews, F.M., Sommardahl, C.S., Eiler, H., Rohrbach, B.W., Donnell, R.L., (2006.) Evaluation of the combined dexamethasone suppression/thyrotropin-releasing hormone stimulation test for detection of pars intermedia pituitary adenomas in horses. J. Vet. Intern. Med. 20, 987–993.
17. Schott, H. C., (2002). 'Pituitary pars intermedia dysfunction: equine Cushing's disease', *Vet. Clin. N. Am. Equine Pract.*, 18, 237–270.
    McFarlane, D. (2007). 'Advantages and limitations of the equine disease, pituitary pars intermedia dysfunction as a model of spontaneous dopaminergic neurodegenerative disease', *Ageing Research Reviews*, 6(1), 54–63.
18. van Maele-Fabry, G., Hoet, P., Vilain, F. & Lison, D. (2012). 'Occupational exposure to pesticides and Parkinson's disease: a systematic review and meta-analysis of cohort studies', *Environment international*, 46, 30–43.
19. Colic symptoms
    - Welsh, C. E., Duz, M., Parkin, T. D., & Marshall, J. F. (2016). 'Prevalence, survival analysis and multimorbidity of chronic diseases in the general veterinarian-attended horse population of the UK', *Preventive Veterinary Medicine*, 131, 137–45.
20. The ACTH test
    - Kirkwood, N. C., Hughes, K. J. & Stewart, A. J. (2022). 'Prospective case series of clinical signs and adrenocorticotrophin (ACTH) concentrations in seven horses transitioning to pituitary pars intermedia dysfunction (PPID)',. *Veterinary Sciences*, 9(10), 572.
21. Donaldson, M. T., McDonnell, S. M., Schanbacher, B. J., Lamb, S. V., McFarlane, D. & Beech, J. (2005). 'Variation in plasma adrenocorticotropic hormone concentration and dexamethasone suppression test results with season, age, and sex in healthy ponies and horses', *Journal of Veterinary Internal Medicine*, 19(2), 217–22.
22. Copas, V. E. N. & Durham, A. E. (2012). 'Circannual variation in plasma adrenocorticotropic hormone concentrations in the UK in normal horses and ponies, and those with pituitary pars intermedia dysfunction', *Equine Veterinary Journal*, 44(4), 440–3.
23. Place, N. J., McGowan, C. M., Lamb, S. V., Schanbacher, B. J., McGowan, T. and Walsh, D.M. (2010). 'Seasonal variation in serum concentrations of selected metabolic hormones in horses'. Journal of *Veterinary Internal Medicine*, 24: 650–654. https://doi.org/10.1111/j.1939-1676.2010.0500.x
24. Insulin dysregulation test
    - Horn, R. & Bertin, F. R. (2019). 'Evaluation of combined testing to simultaneously diagnose pituitary pars intermedia dysfunction and insulin dysregulation in horses', *Journal of Veterinary Internal Medicine*, 33(5), 2249–56.

25. Leaky gut
   - Stewart, A. S., Pratt-Phillips, S., & Gonzalez, L. M. (2017). 'Alterations in intestinal permeability: the role of the "leaky gut" in health and disease', *Journal of Equine Veterinary Science*, 52, 10–22.
26. *Aspergillus*-associated asthma
   - Cai, L., Gao P., Wang Z., Dai C., Ning Y., Ilkit M., Xue X., Xiao J., Chen C. 'Lung and gut microbiomes in pulmonary aspergillosis: Exploring adjunctive therapies to combat the disease,' Front Immunol. 2022 Aug 12:13:988708. doi: 10.3389/fimmu.2022.988708. PMID: 36032147: PMCID: PMC9411651.
   - Cheng C., Sun J., Zheng F., Wu K., Rui Y. 'Molecular identification of clinical "difficult-to-identify" microbes from sequencing 16S ribosomal DNA and internal transcribed spacer 2', *Annals Clinical Microbiol Antimicrobe*, 2014 Jan 3:13:1. doi: 10.1186/1476-0711-13-1. PMID: 24383440: PMCID: PMC3905965.
   - Dall, C. (2023) 'Exposure to resistant aspergillus is widespread across UK, study finds', *News brief* July 21, 2023 https://www.cidrap.umn.edu/antimicrobial-stewardship/exposure-resistant-aspergillus-widespread-across-uk-study-finds
   - Dobiáš R., Jahn P., Tóthová K., Dobešová O., Višňovská D., Patil R., Škríba A., Jaworská P., Škorič M., Podojil L., Kantorová M., Mrázek J., Krejčí E., Stevens D.A., Havlíček V. 'Diagnosis of aspergillosis in Horses', J. Fungi (Basel). 2023 Jan 25:9(2):161. Doi: 10.3390/jof9020161. PMID: 36836276: PMCID: PMC9966232.
   - Nji Q.N., Babalola O.O., Mwanza M., 'Soil *aspergillus* Species, Pathogenicity and Control Perspectives. J Fungi (Basel). 2023 Jul 20:9(7):766. Doi: 10.3390/jof9070766. PMID: 37504754: PMCID: PMC10381279.
   - Sang Kyu Lee, Hyun-Gu Kang, Ki-Jeong Na, Jae-Ik Han, 'Fungal Dermatitis Caused by Aspergillus sydowii in a Thoroughbred Horse', *Journal of Equine Veterinary Science*, Vol. 32, Issue 12, 2012, Pages 835–39, ISSN 0737-0806.
27. Possible link between selenium and cribbing in horses
   - Omidi, A., Jafari, R., Saeed, N., et al. (2018). 'Potential role for selenium in the pathophysiology of crib-biting behaviour in horses', *Journal of Veterinary Behaviour* 23:10.

11.
Climate Change, Pollution and Their Effect on Horses and Their Environment

We are living in a world where climate change and pollution have become the biggest problems of our time. Our horses are also becoming victims of these problems as they, too, are having to survive in unpredictable times of climate change and an ever-increasingly polluted and toxic environment. Facing up to these challenges needs to be part and parcel of how we tackle our horses' welfare, even though the environment is becoming so problematic that it is impossible to predict the future. It has certainly been proven that it is to the detriment of health and well-being, especially of the microbiome, which has far-reaching consequences and profoundly damaging repercussions for the horse. As disussed earlier, polluted water and toxic soils are one problem and fields that have grasses heavy with herbicides, pesticides, fungicides and fertilisers another. And then there are pollutants nearer to home, in stables, feed rooms and arenas. We also need to take into account the pollution caused by horses themselves.

Climate change

We humans are in control of most things where our horses are concerned, but there is one thing over which we seem to have lost complete control, and that is the weather. The seasons are all mixed up and the changes are not only visible (such as extreme hot or wet weather), but they are also becoming dangerous to the health and well-being of humans and animals alike.

    A lot of research is being done on how we can ensure that what our horses eat is sustainable without compromising on the nutrient levels. We need to look at types of plant that can stand up to both extreme heat and flooding. A great many horses who used to live outside all year round are having to be sheltered in open barns, so they don't suffer in temperatures with which they cannot cope. On the other hand, there is so much flooding of pastures and meadows that horses are often to be seen walking around in just mud, which in itself can cause damage not only to their feet, but their overall health. What had been seen as varied and healthy vegetation is becoming so waterlogged that it is being ruled out as suitable forage and, with this in mind, more work needs to be done on land where horses graze, to improve on drainage and soil quality.

    Another problem with flooding is that the land becomes polluted because drains spill over and contaminate the land not only with effluent, but also other types of bacterial toxins. Rain damage on land can also be seen in the soil losing minerals and other vital compounds.

    The danger of fires in natural environments has increased exponentially world-wide, and there have been many incidents where horses have had to be evacuated from raging wild fires.

(Apart from those clearly the result of natural combustion from high temperatures, we should be aware of those resulting from human behaviour – broken glass magnifying the sun's rays, dropped cigarette butts, barbeques in fields or camp fires not put out properly and even fires started deliberately.)

Everyone realises that climate change is already having a huge impact on the way we live and where we live and horse owners need to take stock of their crisis management. To say that people are struggling to keep their horses safe in the face of climate change is an understatement, and one that is not going to be solved overnight. And with this in mind we need to look at how we can make changes to the environment of horses, such as being prepared to move them to higher ground, and avoid stabling them in places where wild fires are a recurring issue.

Another problem is that there is already a shortage of good-quality hay and a shortage of cereals, as rain ruins crops, which will mean that the cost of feed will go up. As horses are consumers of vast amounts of foodstuffs this should alert our UK farmers to look at more prolific and better solutions for when times complicate the production of feed for horses (and, of course, for other livestock). We already see people no longer able to keep their horses not only because of rising costs of feed, but also because their land is no longer suitable for horses to live on.

Waterlogged meadow.
Geertje French

Clean stream water source.
Geertje French

Considerations on climate change

Every yard and private stable should make a plan of action for when things get dangerous for life and limb including that of the horses, whether that is through flooding, extreme heat or other weather-related calamities.

Water is, of course, an absolute essential for life, and the provision of clean water (and potential drawbacks of pollution and flooding) have been discussed in detail in Chapter 9 and reiterated above. On a local level, catching rainwater and using this to irrigate your fields or pasture is one way to ensure that you have access to water when it is scarce (or when there is a hosepipe ban). Another idea that is a really good investment for those who have their own water supply for horses via a stream, is to install a water filtering system, so the horses are assured of clean, unpolluted water. (In contrast, if natural water on your land is badly polluted you will need to fence the water's edges and verges off so that the horses can't get to it.) If your own supply is compromised, water might need to be bought in.

Another problem with which we may need to cope is that of power failures. It would be prudent to prepare your environment for this eventuality by making sure there are plenty of full-battery loaded torches and LED lights/lanterns about. A big yard usually has a back-up generator and a good supply of fuel. Much can also be achieved by investing in solar panels if there is a suitable place to fit them, as there are now batteries available in which a certain amount of this free energy can be stored in case of emergencies. However, this technology is currently at an early stage and rather expensive, so these scenarios may still feel some way off – but the reality is that they are not and we are forewarned time and again to take precautions.

Industry-produced pollutants

Heavy industry

Heavy industry can encompass many things: tyre disposal, large mechanical plants, garages, the steel industry, stone and gravel quarries and places where wood, textiles or leather are being processed into goods. All of these industries make use of chemical pollutants in their processes, such as solvents, petrol, diesel, gasses, metals and other toxic chemicals, which can become airborne and affect the waterways and surrounding countryside. Many waste materials end up in landfill where they will poison the soil and water over time. In the case of quarries and coal mining there is no way of stopping the dust created from entering waterways, the air and land on surrounding fields.

Heavy road traffic and airports

Where there is heavy traffic or an airport there are also many fuel pollutants that are airborne and will also end up on soil and in water sources. The pollution from these sources can have damaging effects on the horse's pulmonary and respiratory functions. The microbiome can also be badly affected by fuel pollutants.

Industrial farming

Large industrial farms are one of the biggest polluters. Their use of herbicides, pesticides, fungicides and fertilisers is of great concern to the surrounding areas, as they drift and end up in the air, the water sources and on fields. And although much work has been done to curb the use of heavily toxic chemicals, there has also been a return of toxins that were previously banned.

Pharmaceutical and chemical plants and factories

Although all chemical plants and factories have rules and regulations on how they dispose of their waste materials, we need to realise that they don't all follow those rules. There have been many incidents where waste materials have ended up in rivers and in landfill – and the gasses that are released into the air are very difficult to identify. These pollutants can end up in fields and water sources.

Micro-plastics

The plastics we use in everyday life have now turned against us in the form of 'micro-plastics', which are plastic pollutants found in almost every household item and in industrial products and waste. They are tiny particles of plastic that can't even be seen with the naked eye, yet they are used in microfibre fabrics, wet wipes and even in shampoos and other cosmetic products.

The breakdown of plastics is extremely difficult and can take hundreds of years when they are put into landfill, where, because of their chemical make-up, they also release noxious gasses that can build up underground and affect everything, from soil quality to water sources. There are now many companies that will recycle plastics, but the road to actually using recycled plastics has not been easy and is still in a development stage.

The biggest worry about micro-plastics is the fact that they can be absorbed into a human's or animal's system – some fish now have a very high micro-plastic score found in their organs and blood. So, it is not surprising that each and every one of us is unwittingly becoming a victim of these micro-plastics as we ingest them without realising it is happening. Horses are therefore also victims of this pollution and it is impossible to find out where exactly they might be ingesting them. Although there is, in fact, very little we can do about this particularly nasty pollution, we do need to be aware of its impact on our natural world and how it affects everything in our environment.

Noise pollution

It may not be immediately obvious, but noise pollution is something that, despite the name, people often do not percieve as a pollutant. In most cases it is, in fact, an industrial pollutant. Think of roads carrying heavy traffic – they cause a continuous 'rushing' sound – and the area in the vicinity of an airport where the decibels of arriving or ascending air traffic far exceed the normal levels (not forgetting the air pollution they cause). Heavy plant industry and quarry mining also cause noise pollution. Imagine living in a field where you are constantly having to cope with dynamite booms and heavy lorry traffic. Horses are extremely noise-sensitive and this can cause all kinds of problems, such as anxiety and unnaturally high stress levels. The stress caused by noise pollution can have a detrimental effect on the microbiome as excess acid may be produced as a result of the stress, which in turn can exacerbate ulceration. A lot of noise can also make horses hyper-sensitive, as they think they are being attacked by an unseen predator.

Effects of environmental pollutants on horses' health

To let our horses live in any of the environments mentioned above will have a detrimental effect on their health, both physical and mental. Respiratory diseases, unexplained cancers, nervous disorders and infertility in areas where there is heavy pollution are all of great concern. If we consider that the average horse has lungs weighing up to 7 kg and a lung volume capacity of some 50 litres, we can get an idea as to how much polluted air he will take in. Although horses, like humans, have nasal filters, they do not stop toxins from entering the system. As the toxins are breathed in, ingested, or absorbed through the skin, they ultimately end up in the bloodstream and affect every part of the horse, from vital organs, to muscles, bones and – even more problematicly – the nervous system.

Toxic materials in arenas and the stable environment

One of the major problems facing horses is the use of highly toxic arena materials. It used to be that arenas were made up of clean sand. These days, however, one of the most toxic materials used is a mixture of rubber, plastics and old carpet, which gets chopped up and used as a thick layer of arena material. This material is spongy and soft underfoot, and although this may be a good way of ensuring 'under hoof' comfort, it is probably one of the most poisonous materials currently advertised as a great arena surface material.

The British Horse Society (BHS) has already brought out a damning article on the use of this material. If you take into account the fact that rubber, plastic and carpets have a high degree of toxic, chemically manipulated ingredients you may question why this is being advertised as such a wonderful arena surface material. Chopping up these materials not only releases the toxins but also puts horses and people at risk of ingesting the resultant fine dust and the gasses constantly released as the material gets pulverised further by the constant friction of the horses being ridden on its surface.

Another problem arises when the horses bring this material into their stables or fields via their hooves and tiny particles that cling to their skin. These toxins can get inhaled and ingested, causing all kinds of problems in the digestive tract of the horses and their organs, including the fragile tissue of the lungs. There is also a potential problem with hormonal imbalance.

Another material of concern is the rubber matting on which many horses are stabled. As these mats start to break down, which they do when they get a lot of use and when they come in contact with urine and faeces, they also give off toxic gasses and tiny particles that pollute the stable environment, and these too get ingested and breathed in. The particles can also attach themselves to the horses' coats and be absorbed into the skin.

We need to do everything we can to keep these materials away from our horses as they are a real hazard and threat to a healthy and clean environment. Also, we need to look beyond the arena and stable surfaces and to consider the whole yard environment. Metals that are left to rust, such as old cars, machinery or rusting barrels have no place in a stableyard as rust gives off a noxious gas and the fine dust from rusting materials is also extremely damaging for horses and humans. Piles of assorted rubbish may or may not be toxic, but they might well include material on which horses could hurt themselves.

Wood shavings

Using wood shavings for stable bedding can seem to be a good alternative to straw bedding but, although it can be a good substitute, we need to bear in mind that a lot of wood shavings contain wood preservatives and other materials that are not stated on the bales. By using shavings, you may be creating another toxic environment for the horse. Once wood shavings are broken down by the horse's feet, they will produce dust particles that are then ingested and breathed in by the horse. An oat straw bedding is preferable, as the horse will munch on the good fibre along with ad lib hay.

Deep oat straw bedding.
Geertje French

Taking into account that the majority of domestically kept horses get very little turnout time, either because there is no adequate grazing pasture available or because they live in an exclusively urban environment, an oat straw bed is not only comfortable to lie on and provides an extra snack to stave off boredom, it is also less dusty than shavings and, as long as you can trace its source, much more sustainable.

Feed storage

Horse feed needs to be kept dry and free from insects and other undesirable elements. Avoid leaving feed bags standing around; they need to be kept in airtight tubs and checked for rodent and insect/mite invasion on a regular basis. The feed room needs to be well aired and kept at a fairly constant temperature so feed does not get moist and start to grow fungal or mould spores, which are poisonous to the horse. Clean feed buckets and tubs regularly and never put new food on top of old food, as this can also cause mould and fungi spore problems.

Haylage bales need to be consumed within four days, as the moment the haylage is exposed to air it will start to deteriorate and mould and fungus will start to grow quickly. Hay needs to be stored in a clean and dry environment. Old hay can get very dusty, and such dust inhaled by horses can carry harmful spores into the lungs and bloodstream. When hay gets damp, it will also be a great place for mould and fungal spores to develop. The nutrient content is often destroyed if hay is kept for too long. Soaking old hay will reduce some of the dust content, but the negative side is that you might also be leaching out any nutrients that are still present.

Enrichment tools and toys

Improving enrichment for horses is a brilliant way of keeping them occupied, away from boredom and engaged. But here, too, there is a pollution trap. Make sure you only buy toys that have been certified for use by animals. A lot of toys, like balls and so-called puzzle toys come from countries such as China, where they may have been made using uncertified plastic or rubber materials high in toxins, or where dyes are used containing lead or other toxic products. Check your source. When using any toy, whether purchased or home-made, be sure to take them away when they start to break down or deteriorate. Dispose of any toys responsibly.

Textiles and other materials

Old rugs, bandages, fly hoods and old grooming equipment are all products that need to be disposed of in a responsible manner. If at all possible, look for a recycling company that will accept horse-related textiles and other fibrous products.

Another consideration regarding textiles and materials comes in the form of children's horse parties, where horses and ponies are put into 'fun' costumes – these seem to be all the rage. Many of these so-called 'costumes' are made of highly flammable rayon/plastic-based materials. Another thing people use is glitter, for manes and tails, just to give that extra bit of glamour. Please resist using these materials, as glitter is one of the most noxious and polluting materials on earth. These materials are not biodegradable, even when labelling claims that they are; they are made up from all different kinds of plastics and metals. Glitter can also be inhaled, because the particles are often tiny. Again, this material does not break down in your horse's system and can find its way into organs and get stuck in the lungs, which can cause all kinds of serious problems.

Horse cleaning products

The market for horse shampoo, conditioners, coat oils, hoof preparations and other equine beauty products is enormous. It is another area where caution needs to be your mantra. Many of these products also contain toxins and chemicals that may not be necessarily healthy for your horse. Try to source your products from responsible manufacturers and preferably only use organically certified products. Dispose of containers in a recycling bin.

Yard management summary

The yard where horses are stabled must be kept hygienic and clear of rubbish.

- Broken fencing needs repairing as soon as possible, to avoid damage to horses and, similarly, stables need to be kept free from broken materials such as wooden structures.
- Keep stables free from dust build-up and cobwebs, as they can be damaging to the horse's respiratory system and microbiome.
- Stable water sources, such as buckets and mechanical water bowls, also need regular cleaning to ensure there is no bacterial build up.
- When cutting bale ties, make sure that you dispose of the ties responsibly as they can be left in the bale material and be accidently ingested by horses, and this can cause choking or damage in the gut. Horses can also get entangled in bits of tie and rope material.

Field management

When you or your yard manager want to use weedkillers, make absolutely sure that horses are not back in those fields for a minimum of two weeks. Even weedkillers claimed to be no problem for animals need to be handled with great care.

With any spraying of weedkillers, but also with the use of fungicides or fertilisers, it is imperative that these products are handled with caution and all precautions are taken so that horses and their humans are kept away from any kind of direct or, indeed, indirect contact with these products. Only use them when there is no possibility of these toxic chemicals ending up in stables/yards/water sources, and check that the wind direction does not carry these materials toward the horses' environment. Ask your yard manager what exactly they use for weed control.

Fields and meadows are also a breeding ground for bacteria and undesirable worm infestation when there is no harrowing or clean-up of faeces, so make it a routine to keep your meadows and fields clean. Rotating grazing fields and meadows gives the soil time to recover from over-grazing.

Medication waste

This is a difficult issue, as most horses will at some stage in their lives be given medication for a variety of illnesses, or preventative products such as wormers. We need to be aware that the waste products of these medications/drugs will end up in the horses' urine or faecal matter, both in the stable and the field. Of course, it is not easy to isolate these waste products, but the problem should be taken into account especially in the case of faecal matter, which all gets thrown on to the same muck heap so that, in effect, you are polluting the muck heap. The problem goes further, as muck heaps are often turned into a component for home garden compost and can therefore end up on people's allotments and gardens where foodstuffs are grown. If your horse is on medication for a long period, it might be necessary to collect the faecal matter and dispose of this separately and responsibly to keep your general muck heap free from medication waste.

All waste material from medication should be disposed of in a responsible manner. Old medication needs to be returned to the veterinary clinic and not thrown into the general waste.

Horses in the wild/free-roaming

You would think that horses living in the wild, or horses free-roaming but monitored by humans, are living a perfect life. However, there are now so many places that have become dumping grounds for plastics, chemicals and other suspect waste materials that it is hardly the equine paradise one might imagine. There are now a number of places where horses roam freely on what are essentially toxic waste heaps, unchecked by landowners or council departments. Fly-tipping is also a big problem. Horses have been found walking through household waste materials and waste building materials, which may contain among other materials, paint containers and paint associated products, nails stuck in old wood, broken metal frames, electric flexes, batteries and a myriad of other highly toxic materials. These horses usually get their water from natural sources and often these, too, are heavily polluted. If you have a free-roaming herd ensure that you check their area frequently to keep them free from polluting materials.

12.
End of Life Care for Your Horse

This is a very difficult time for any horse owner to have to consider and it is a subject that is not often discussed. However, being able to face the unthinkable is an important part of reality for anyone working with horses because very few horses die from natural causes. Becoming old and arriving at the end of their time is, of course, one of the reasons why some do, but this still requires us to assist them in making the transition in comfort, without stress or pain. We have the responsibility to ensure that our horses receive the very best of care and welfare throughout their life and this does not stop when our horses come to the end of their life. If anything, we need to consider that the end-of-life journey is the most intensive and emotionally demanding of any period they are in our care. And it is at this time that we need to help our horse to transition with dignity. It requires courage and your unconditional love to show your horse the compassion and grace that he deserves.

The main reasons for end-of-life in horses is that they become so ill, either physically or mentally, or so badly injured in an accident, that there is no other way but to show them the respect and love they deserve and decide to opt for end-of-life care in the form of euthanasia. In the end this will be something your vet will indicate as the kindest course of action to take. Of course, in case of an accident there may be no time to discuss or give end-of-life care, but it will still require you to follow the rules and regulations that are attached to the aftermath of a horse's death.

Circumstances when euthanasia needs to be considered

- Chronic pain from a condition that is no longer curable, such as advanced or uncurable laminitis or colic.
- Extreme sudden weight loss and/or complete loss of appetite, including no drinking. (There are a number of extreme weight loss or loss of appetite causes, some of these may not be discovered unless an autopsy has been performed.)
- When your horse needs to undergo a surgical/medical procedure and it becomes clear that the prognosis shows that there will be a non-reversible great loss of quality of life.
- If your horse has to be stabled for the rest of his life and the suffering can only be managed through lifelong use of continuous analgesic intervention, so that there is no quality of life for him.
- Depression is something that is a difficult condition to come to terms with, because we are often convinced that, with our patience and help and the administration of antidepressants

(which can have severe side-affects), we will be able to help our horse to overcome this extremely debilitating condition. However, once the depression is so deep-seated that the horse has completely shut down there is no way back. Depression has its root in many causes. It may occur because the horse is required to work beyond his capabilities and therefore 'shuts down'. Or the horse may feel the loss of a stable or field friend, either because his companion has moved on or died. Isolation from other horses, whatever the reason, and the consequent loneliness induces depression. Horses suffering with physical illness, such as ulcers or Cushing's disease, may also become depressed as a result of changes in the brain. Severe nutritional deficiency may be another cause.
- Unmanageable behaviour or medical issues that become dangerous for the horse and/or handlers.

Other than the above, there are a number of other circumstances which may lead to a vet advising immediate euthanasia. Never hesitate to contact your vet when the above or other seemingly insurmountable issues present themselves. Your vet will, together with you, decide when the moment for euthanasia has arrived. Although it may be tempting, don't be persuaded by others, like some unqualified practitioners of alternative medicine, that they have the answer and that their particular treatment will cure your horse or restore quality of life. Although professional equine alternative medicine practitioners can be of great benefit when used in the right circumstances, be aware that there are also practitioners who will not shy away from persuading you that they can bring your horse back to a healthy life with their 'special' brand of medicine, even when a vet has already concluded that it would be cruel to continue treatment and thus unnecessary suffering. Of course, seeking a second opinion from another vet or your alternative medicine practitioner may be worth a try, but a good practitioner would never go against the final and reasonably evidential advice and recommendations put forward by an experienced equine vet.

Protocol – process – application of euthanasia

Every country and local authority has their own rules and laws when it comes to the application of euthanasia. Please be advised always to seek their guidance. In the UK the following rules apply:
- Euthanasia may only be administered when the effect is guaranteed.
- Euthanasia may only be administered by a highly qualified and experienced vet.
- The vet will ask for identification of the horse, to verify that there is no foul play.
- The owner or yard manager or designated person has to sign a consent form.
- In cases of an equine needing to be immediately euthanased, such as after a yard, field or traffic accident, a vet is authorised to go ahead to prevent prolonged suffering. In such instances, the two previous points are not mandatory as it is a case of acute action.
- There are a number of procedures that may be used for euthanasia. Your vet will discuss these options with you.
- In normal circumstances the environment where the euthanasia is going to take place should be made very comfortable for the horse and must be large enough for the horse to lie down

stretched out and there needs to be enough room for the vet and handlers. Overall, the environment should be assessed for safety, as euthanasia can be unpredictable as to how the horse is going to react. It needs to be safe for the horse and everyone involved.
- In the case of immediate euthanasia there will be little time to do any kind of preparation, and people need to ensure as much space and safety as is possible at that moment.
- It is highly recommended that whenever possible the horse is sedated before the application of the euthanasia method.
- Loss of consciousness needs to be achieved as quickly as possible so that the horse is not being subjected to cardiac arrest or respiratory failure, both of which can be extremely painful and very stressful for the horse. The whole aim of euthanasia is to prevent any more suffering; not sedating the horse beforehand may incur greater suffering, something to be avoided at all cost.
- Death will be confirmed by heartbeat cessation, ceasing of respiratory function i.e. no movement in nostrils, lungs or thorax, no corneal eye reflex.

Another thing to consider is to ensure that the actual process is not being carried out in the hearing or smell of other horses. (In the case of an extreme emergency this may not be possible, but should still be considered.) As horses are extremely sensitive to external stimuli, it will greatly upset and stress them if they become aware of something happening that brings them to a state of panic of an unknown quantity. However, if at all possible, bring the horses' equine companions near to say goodbye before the procedure is carried out.

Also, consider the horse's human carers and friends; speak to them about what is going to happen. In all eventualities it is important that every single process and procedure is carried out with dignity, grace and respect – not only for the horse, but for all who are concerned with him.

Unavoidable practicalities of end-of-life issues for you and your horse

Insurance

When you are looking at insurance for your horse it is of great importance to both of you to consider the following points.
- What is covered in the policy when it comes to end-of-life proceedings and after your horse has died?
- Does it include end-of-life vet fees, including emergency coverage in case of acute attention, for instance when your horse is involved in a traffic accident, a fatal accident in the yard or considered plans for euthanasia?
- Does it make provision for heavy plant hire, such as diggers or other machinery in the event that you want a home burial (the rules of which are discussed later in this chapter), or the collection and disposal of your equine after death?
- Does it cover cremation costs?

You will need to get in touch with your insurance as soon as possible after your horse has died. (It should not normally be necessary to contact your insurance company prior to euthanasia when the procedure is on the instigation of a vet.)

Livery yard policy and protocol

- When stabling your horse with a commercial or privately owned livery yard it is important to find out what their policies and protocol consists of in the event of your horse needing immediate veterinary attention in case of an accident or when end-of-life proceedings are necessary.
- Make sure the yard is insured for all eventualities and has the right protocols in place in case of euthanasia so that, if they have to take charge of the whole process, they employ an experienced and qualified equine vet to apply the procedure.
- The yard needs to show that they have all health and safety regulations in place in case of end-of-life procedures. They have to be able to show you definitively that these regulations are adhered to. They also need to have the contact details of the relevant local authority to ensure correct and dignified removal of the body.
- Have the discussion about what they are willing to undertake in case you, for whatever reason, cannot be present during your horse's end-of-life stage and subsequent euthanasia. You may have to sign an agreement that you agree with the yard manager that, in the event the worst needs to happen, you allow them to follow all legal proceedings. Also that they inform you immediately when it is necessary to undertake any of the above proceedings.

Home burial

If you have the facilities to opt for the home burial of your horse, you need to consider the following points.

Every country will have its own rules and regulations. It is therefore advisable that you find out about these before you are faced with unforeseen events. In the UK you will need to inform your local authority of your intentions. Most will only consider a licence for home burial when you have kept your horse as a 'pet'. Your local authority will make the decision based on whether they consider him to have been a pet or a working horse. The latter category covers horses working for commercial purposes, such as in timber-felling practices or transport, including horse and carriage transport for funerals or entertainment. Racehorses and sports horses used for commercial gain come under working horses. You may consider the horse you owned to have been both a workhorse and a pet, but always check with your council.

If you have your heart set on a home burial this may require a discussion with your local authority, and your application may be granted provided that all guidelines are followed. Some local authorities may show leniency when you can show that, although your horse was a working animal you are emotionally attached to him and had a close human to animal relationship.

Assuming that you have obtained basic permission for a home burial, it will still be the case that the plot you are designating for this purpose will have to adhere to very specific guidelines, about which each local authority may have their own rules. If you carry out a home burial without local authority permission and without adhering to the legal guidelines, you may incur a heavy fine.

Your burial arrangements and/or collection of your horse from the premises where he is being kept need to be in order before euthanasia is carried out. If possible, it would be prudent to have everything in place before any end-of-life situation presents itself, whether you are dealing with an elderly, ailing horse or even in case of a fatal accident. For example, knowing who to contact for big plant/machinery hire is essential if you plan a home burial, or which company to use for collection of the body.

A home burial may be conducted along the same ritualistic ceremonies as a human burial. You may want your religious advisor to be present to conduct prayers. Flowers may be laid on the grave and a headstone erected. Invite those people close to you to be present to lend support. There may be people who have known the horse and who would want to be present and they might like to do a reading.

Cremation

There are specialised companies that deal with equine cremations. It would be advisable to know who you can contact before the necessity to use them arises. If you would like to receive a part of your horse's ashes to be kept in an urn or to bury on a home plot, or you want to distribute some of the ashes in a special place, such a company will be able to advise you on all these issues. There may also be an opportunity to be present at the cremation, in which case it may be conducted on the same lines as a human cremation.

Often people have a plaque made up in remembrance of their horse, which can be placed somewhere suitable, perhaps alongside a photograph.

Further considerations

- The first thing to do is to inform your insurance company.
- Inform your farrier.
- Inform your hay and food delivery contractors.
- Inform the breeder where necessary.
- You may want to put a notice in your preferred horse magazine.

Coming to terms with loss

The hardest part of losing our horse is the feelings we are left with afterwards. Mourning is a journey that we need to accept as something that evolves in stages. We may be left with a feeling of guilt, convincing ourselves that we could have done more for our horse.

These feelings are perfectly normal and will fade when you come to realise that, unless there has been avoidable negligence on your part, you should not add to your anguish by apportioning blame. You will feel that there is a huge hole left in your life, and it is heart-breaking to no longer have the daily responsibility of caring for your horse. To see the empty barn or stable, or the field where his friends may be roaming around not understanding what has happened to their companion. Seek solace by spending a bit more time with the ones left behind; reassure them and yourself that their friend is no longer suffering. Talk to your friends and loved ones about the happy times. You may even want to set up a small memorial where you can place some photographs and light a candle. Walking the favourite route you used to take with your horse is also a way of remembering and relishing the joy you experienced with your horse on those rides. Take your time in disposing of your horse's tack, rugs, toys or other items. Even though you may feel that you do not want to be reminded of your loss by seeing these things around you, to get rid of them immediately may, at a later point, feel like a mistake. You may like to mark the anniversary of their passing with a special ritual or ceremony. As time goes by, the feeling of acute pain and loss will lead to healing.

List of Abbreviations

Within this text, a number of abbreviations are used, most of which represent the names of diseases or substances related to their treatment. Although these abbreviations are explained at first use, the following is a list provided for easy reference.

ACP	acepromazine
ACTH	adrenocorticotropic
AMR	antimicrobial resistant/ce
AI	artificial intelligence
BMI	body mass index
COPD	chronic obstructive pulmonary disease
EGUS	equine gastric ulcer syndrome
EMS	equine metabolic syndrome
FFWS	free faecal water syndrome
GLA	gamma-linolenic acid
GC	glucose consumption
IR	insulin resistant/ce
IRMS	insulin-resistant metabolic syndrome
MSH	melanocyte stimulating hormone
MLN	mesenteric lymph nodes
NGS	next generation sequencing
NIS	nutritionally improved straw
NO	nitric oxide
NSAID(s)	non-steroidal anti-inflammatory drug(s)
POH	perillyl alcohol
PPID	pituitary pars intermedia dysfunction/Cushing's (disease).
PSSM	polysaccharide storage myopathy
SCFAs	short chain fatty acids
SEGUS	squamous equine ulcer syndrome
SSSI	site of special scientific interest
VAC	Vitex agnus-castus (also known as chaste tree)
VOCs	volatile organic compounds
WSCs	water-soluble carbohydrates

About the Authors

Carol Hughes is an equine physiotherapist, phyto nutritionist and microbiologist and has spent more than 30 years in equine health care. She has collaborated in research projects with leading vets and universities. Projects include the exploration of anti-obesity, anti-inflammatory and anti-ulcerogenic plant secondary compounds on horses. She has also studied the use of genomic sequencing and the microbiome of horses used in competition and leisure.

Geertje French is a qualified equine behaviourist and nutritionist. Much of her research has focused on the correlation between gut maladies and feed-related behaviours. Geertje has more than 50 years' experience with horses both as an eventer and an active advocate for natural horsemanship.

Acknowledgement

The authors would like to thank Martin Diggle for his unfailing dedication during the editing of this book.